The New Entrepreneurs

# The New Entrepreneurs

*How Race, Class, and Gender*
*Shape American Enterprise*

Zulema Valdez

Stanford University Press
Stanford, California

Stanford University Press
Stanford, California

Printed in the United States of America on acid-free, archival-quality paper

Library of Congress Cataloging-in-Publication Data

Valdez, Zulema.
    The new entrepreneurs : how race, class, and gender shape American enterprise / Zulema Valdez.
        p. cm.
    Includes bibliographical references and index.
    ISBN 978-0-8047-7320-1 (cloth : alk. paper)—ISBN 978-0-8047-7321-8 (pbk. : alk. paper)
    1. Hispanic American businesspeople—Texas—Houston.  2. Hispanic American business enterprises—Texas—Houston.  3. Hispanic Americans—Texas—Houston—Social conditions.  4. Hispanic Americans—Texas—Houston—Economic conditions.
I. Title.
    HD2358.5.U62V35  2011
    338'.040896807641411—dc22        2010037530

Typeset by Westchester Book Group in 10/14 Minion

*This book is dedicated with love to my parents,*
*Joel G. Valdez and Margarita Zavala Valdez.*

# Contents

# Illustrations

## Tables

## Figure

# Acknowledgments

THIS BOOK WAS MADE POSSIBLE with research support from several sources. The NSF/ASA Fund for the Advancement of the Discipline and the Mexican American and Latina/o Studies Center at Texas A&M University provided research money that allowed me to hire San Juanita Garcia, Leslie Meyer, and Charity Clay to conduct many of the interviews, and Jennifer Guillen to type, translate, and transcribe them. Receiving a Ford Foundation Minority Postdoctoral Fellowship was crucially important in giving me the time to write.

I thank many friends and colleagues for formal and informal discussions and written comments that helped me to develop my ideas and make the book stronger. I especially thank Rebecca Emigh, Vilma Ortiz, Ivan Szelenyi, Yen Le Espiritu, and Ivan Light, mentors who served on my graduate committees while I was at UCLA. I am grateful to you for helping me to complete my first project on ethnic entrepreneurs, which left unanswered questions that sparked my interest in this second project. M. Bianet Castellanos, Nitasha Tamar Sharma, Dylan Riley, and Rachel Lara Cohen provided invaluable support and comments throughout the development and writing of this book, as well as much needed coffee breaks and cocktails in equal measure. I also thank several people and resources that helped me with the process of writing, including Kerry Ann Rockquemore's "Monday Motivator," Tanya Golash-Boza's "Daily Writing Updates," Robert Courtney Smith's suggestion to start a daily writing journal, and my write-on-site partner, Shona Jackson. I also thank my partner, Andrew Yinger, for his careful editing of select passages and for taking care of our home and pets during crunch-time moments of extreme teaching and writing. I love you.

For guidance in the book-publishing process, I thank Vilna Bashi, Angie Y. Chung, Catherine Y. Lee and Nadia Y. Kim. I acknowledge that some of the ideas in this book were first published in Valdez (2008a, 2008b). I thank Taylor and Francis (www.informaworld.com) and The University of New Orleans for permission to use this material. The editorial staff at Stanford University Press, especially Kate Wahl, has been supportive, positive, and helpful throughout, for which I am very grateful.

I would like to thank my colleagues in the Department of Sociology at Texas A&M University for their support and advice, with a special thanks to Joe Feagin, Mark Fossett, Rogelio Saenz, Nadia Flores, Joseph Jewell, Sarah Gatson, Nancy Plankey Videla, Rob Mackin, Wendy Leo Moore, Ed Murguia, Paul Almeida and Ruben May.

Finally, I would like to thank the entrepreneurs who shared their stories for this book, without which it could not have been written.

The New Entrepreneurs

# 1 Introduction

**FOLLOWING THE PASSAGE** of the 1986 Immigration Reform and Control Act, which made it illegal for employers to knowingly hire unauthorized workers, Doña Toña's husband lost his job.[1] The next day, she sent him to the grocery store and with their last $10 instructed him to buy a bag of flour, sugar, lard, and two packets of yeast. Although Doña Toña's husband resisted, arguing that he needed the money to buy gas and find a new job, she convinced him after a few tears to do what she asked. She used the ingredients to bake her mother's *conchas*, *empanadas*, and *cuernos* in her kitchen from memory. Like the fragrance of a freshly baked apple pie on the windowsill, the smell of *pan mexicano* wafted through the Mexican neighborhood, and the people came. "Out of those ten dollars I made eighty at the end of the day." Doña Toña made sweet breads the next day and the day after that, until she earned enough to file her husband's legal papers and then her own. During those desperate months, she kept her job of two years at the Port of Houston, where she washed Toyotas as they were being unloaded from Japanese ships. Her combined income from bread making and car washing was just enough to cover their expenses. After her husband returned to work, Doña Toña found a better-paying job as a janitor at Exxon, and she continued to bake and sell sweet bread and tacos to fellow employees. It was there that she got the idea to open a restaurant:

> The [White] American[2] who owned half of the business started talking about wanting some Mexican food and asked me to make him some. . . . I told him I could make them some chicken mole. After that I started making more and more meals, including tamales. The owner of the company said that I could

1

really cook just about anything and that I should open up my own business. I told him I didn't have the cash for it. He told me I was in a country where I could do anything. . . . I decided that when I finished paying off my house I would [start] a restaurant.

In the late 1980s Doña Toña, then a thirty-six-year-old Mexican immigrant with a fourth-grade education, used the equity in her house to secure a bank loan. With that $62,000 and her children's unpaid labor she opened her restaurant, El Pambazo. El Pambazo is located in her neighborhood, Little Mexico, a historic Mexican enclave in eastern Houston. The restaurant is one of several businesses on Main Street, a four-lane, pot-hole-riddled road that is flanked by parking lots, liquor stores, car repair shops, taco trucks, and other restaurants. El Pambazo's large glass windows are painted to advertise *aguas frescas* and homemade tortillas. Inside there are posters of Emiliano Zapata, La Virgen de Guadalupe, and other Mexican iconography taped to yellow walls. Two televisions tuned to Spanish-language channels and a jukebox entertain the customers. On any given day the breakfast and lunch crowd is generally made up of dusty, paint-splattered Mexican men who work in the construction or service industry. At dinnertime, the restaurant caters to Mexican families from the neighborhood. A young Mexican waitress, two if it's busy, takes orders in Spanish. Today as in the past, Doña Toña does all the cooking and works twelve hours a day, every day. She earns $30,000 a year, or just over $7 an hour. She considers herself to be a success, which she attributes to her drive, ambition, hard work, and positive attitude. "I always had an idea that I was going to be someone when I grew up."

ROB ALFARO IS a thirty-seven-year-old naturalized U.S. citizen from El Salvador who self-identifies as Hispanic Italian (he was born in El Salvador, his mother is Salvadoran and his father is Italian). He speaks fluent English, Spanish, and Italian and holds an associate's degree in business. Rob[3] comes from an upper-middle-class family of business owners. His dream of owning a restaurant started when he was just nine years old, after spending the first of many summers working in his grandparents' restaurant. With ample sources of economic and social support, Rob left his job as a manager of his brother's successful restaurant in Boston to start his own business two years ago. He financed A Taste of Venice with resources from several different sources. He used his personal savings first ($250,000), noting that his financial status was strong enough that he "didn't need to borrow from a bank." Nevertheless, he accepted additional investment capital from his brother and sister-in-law ($215,000). Finally, he applied and qualified for a credit line of $100,000 from a national bank. A Taste of Venice, an elegantly styled Italian restaurant in an upscale business district located in Greater Houston, broke even the first year and generated $90,000 in profit the next year. Rob attributes his financial success to his experience in and knowledge of running a business from the ground up, as well as patience, faith, timing, and "having the guts" to work hard and fight.

DOÑA TOÑA AND MR. ALFARO share a common group identity as Latino/a immigrants and a common occupation as self-employed restaurateurs. The similarities between them end there, however. Doña Toña is a lower-class Mexican immigrant woman who lives and works in a poor Mexican enclave. Rob is a middle-class, self-identified Hispanic Italian man whose upscale restaurant and home are located in a predominately White planned community in Greater Houston. Doña Toña has been in business for more than twenty years, a phenomenal achievement in an industry in which 90 percent of businesses fail within the first six months of opening. Yet, Doña Toña earns only $7 an hour, or just below minimum wage; she earned more when she was employed as a janitor for Exxon. In contrast, Rob's brief but impressive stint as a business owner has garnered him substantial profits.

The objective of this book is to explain the collective experience and divergent life chances of Latino/a immigrant entrepreneurs, like Doña Toña and Rob, in America. Against the classic theory of "ethnic entrepreneurship," which emphasizes the essential role of ethnicity in facilitating immigrant business ownership through social capital, or economic and social resources generated by co-ethnic social networks (Light 1972; Portes and Rumbaut 2001, 2006; Waldinger et al. 1990), the book considers how multiple dimensions of identity and belonging affect the entrepreneurial outcomes of a diverse group of Latino/a immigrant men and women from different class backgrounds.

The intersection of class, gender, race, and (not *only*) ethnicity conditions the unequal starting position of Latinos/as within the highly stratified American society, a society that is comprised of three interlocking systems of power and oppression: capitalism, patriarchy, and White supremacy (Browne and Misra 2003; Collins 2000). In this unequal structural context, Latinos/as are differently positioned within hierarchically organized class, gender, racial, and ethnic group classifications.[4] These distinct yet intersecting classifications combine to determine the social location of groups of individual Latinos/as that share similar positions within the American social structure. By *social location*, I refer to Patricia Zavella's (1991:75) conception of the ways in which socially constructed categories such as race, class, and gender reflect structures of oppression (and privilege) that combine to produce a diversity of Latino/a identities and experiences.[5]

While structure may condition the social location of Latinos/as, it alone does not determine their life chances; Latinos'/as' life chances are shaped by the integration of structure and agency.[6] In other words, those same multiple dimensions of intersectionality that indicate Latinos'/as' social location also provide the basis for agency among group members in the form of *social capital*: the capacity to mobilize resources based on the recognition of shared group affiliations (Coleman 1988; Portes and Sensenbrenner 1993). The accumulation of social capital by affiliated members of a given group generates economic and noneconomic resources and support that may compensate for structural inequality. In this way, social capital may facilitate Latinos'/as' social and economic incorporation, or socioeconomic assimilation, thereby advancing the group as a whole. Accordingly, the intersection of class, gender, race, and ethnicity conditions the unequal starting position *and* the compensatory social capital that groups of individual Latinos/as bring to the market. Thus, it is through the integration of structure and agency that Latino/a life chances are realized. In the *embedded market*,[7] a term I use to capture the integration of structure and agency within the American economy, structural inequality and group-based resource-mobilization strategies converge to shape the entrepreneurial life chances of Latinos/as. Importantly, whether the social capital that is generated is ultimately sufficient to offset or overcome structural inequality is influenced primarily by Latinos'/as' stratified position within the social structure.

The aim of this book is to demonstrate that through the integration of structure and agency, class, gender, race, and ethnicity intersect to create, maintain, transform, and reproduce the work lives of Latino/a immigrant entrepreneurs in America. For a more complete picture of their socioeconomic incorporation, the entrepreneurial outcomes of Latino/a business owners are compared to those of U.S.-born, non-Hispanic White and Black entrepreneurs.[8] The first half of the book investigates the relationship between structural inequality and agency, in terms of Latinos'/as' individual and collective resource-mobilization strategies, in the context of a highly stratified American social structure. This analysis is guided by two central questions. First, how does structural inequality rooted in the intersection of class, gender, race, and ethnicity shape Latino/a entrepreneurs' capacity to mobilize group-based resources and support? Second, what is the relationship between Latino/a entrepreneurs' access to and use of such resources, which may help or hinder enterprise, and their consequent entrepreneurial success?

The dominant approach to "ethnic entrepreneurship" employs a monolithic, homogenous treatment of ethnicity and underscores its primacy in explaining the entrepreneurial activity of different ethnic groups. In particular, it presumes that members of the same ethnic group possess the same ethnic-based resources and support, or social capital, and consequently share the same entrepreneurial outcomes. Yet, a closer look at individual ethnic group members exposes differences across class, gender, and race, which may lead to a variety of entrepreneurial experiences and outcomes among a diverse group of co-ethnics. For example, middle-class Latinos/as are more likely to possess resources that are highly valued in the modern market economy, such as substantial schooling and skills, and economic resources such as personal savings, inheritance, or the creditworthiness needed to access financial capital through market-based institutions, such as a national bank or investment firm (Valdez 2008b). Since a strong class position is generally equated with a strong market position, it stands to reason that middle-class Latinos/as are favorably predisposed to successful business ownership, when compared to working-class or poor Latinos/as.

Moreover, *social capital* may provide additional economic and noneconomic resources and support that, though not always essential, may improve Latino/as' market position even further. Middle-class Latinos, for example, benefit disproportionately from social relationships rooted in their racial, ethnic, and gender group affiliations, which create the conditions for social capital resources to emerge, such as co-ethnic, co-racial, or male-dominated business information networks, or some combination of the three, or opportunities for informal or semiformal lending. In Rob's case, a strong class position and family history of business ownership provided him with ample resources in the form of education, skills, work experience, business networks, financial resources, and support to start a successful and lucrative business. Middle-class Latinas also benefit from greater access and use of market capital and social capital than their lower-class counterparts, although gender inequality is observed when middle-class Latinas' resources are compared to those of middle-class Latinos.

In contrast, lower-class Latinos/as are likely to possess fewer resources that are valued in the market economy, and thus confront greater market uncertainty. Although disadvantaged Latinos'/as' gender, racial, and ethnic ties generate social capital, its compensatory effect is constrained by their social location, as their position within the unequal social structure circumscribes the social capital that is ultimately produced. Because they have fewer market and social capital resources from which to draw, the path to economic integration through business ownership is far from easy. Disadvantaged Latinos/as frequently engage in business ownership with insufficient resources and support. Often the impetus for this activity is rooted in a vulnerable labor market situation (for example, job dissatisfaction, unemployment or underemployment, blocked mobility based on ethnic, racial, or gender discrimination, or a combination thereof). Moreover, there is no guarantee that, once established, the business will prosper. Although Doña Toña's modest bank loan and family support were sufficient to start and maintain her business, her stagnant, below-minimum-wage income is less than desirable and, frankly, less than she expected.

What is clear from an intersectional approach to enterprise is that although Doña Toña and Rob can both be characterized as Latino/a immigrant entrepreneurs, their common Latino/a identity and entrepreneurial activity do not explain their divergent life chances. Against the traditional approach to "ethnic entrepreneurship," Latinos'/as' combined race, class, gender, and ethnic identities influence their ability to access and use market and social capital differently; these multiple dimensions shape the entrepreneurial outcomes of Latino/a entrepreneurs because they matter in a society that is stratified not only by ethnicity, but by the complex intersection of race, class, and gender as well. Ultimately, Latino/a business ownership is conditioned and inequality reproduced by the integration of structure and agency in the embedded American economy.

The second half of the book investigates the social aspect of Latino/a entrepreneurs' socioeconomic incorporation. After all, Latino/a entrepreneurs do not only work in the American economy; they live in American society as individuals and as collective members of distinct groups. How they identify themselves and others—ethnically, racially, or both—represents the recognition of membership in privileged or oppressed groups, or both. These multiple and simultaneous memberships influence Latinos'/as' social location as well as their social capital resources and, ultimately, their entrepreneurial outcomes.

Counter to the assumptions of the ethnic entrepreneurship approach, which characterizes specific ethnic groups as fostering strong communities that engender social capital and thus entrepreneurialism, all Latino/a ethnic group members, regardless of ethnicity (Salvadoran, Mexican American, Cuban, and so on), report the use of ethnic-based social capital, such as co-ethnic moneylending or co-ethnic business networks. Moreover, White and Black entrepreneurs who self-identify ethnically (for example, as Greek American or Caribbean, respectively) *also* report the use of ethnic-based social capital. The ubiquity of ethnic-based social capital regardless of a specific ethnic group classification or rate of entrepreneurial participation suggests that it is not relegated to distinct, entrepreneurially oriented ethnic groups only; rather, ethnicity is always associated with the mobilization of social capital resources among co-ethnics. At the same time, ethnicity is one of multiple dimensions of intersectionality that combine to affect the accumulation of resources in positive, neutral, and sometimes negative ways.

For example, Latinos/as may self-identify racially as Latino/a or Hispanic in an effort to mobilize social capital rooted in racial group affiliation. At other times, ethnic-identified Latinos/as may invoke a racial classification to label non-co-ethnic Latinos/as; in this process of racialization, racial identity may be imposed to stereotype or express prejudice or bias against other (non-co-ethnic) Latinos/as. This race-making process is endemic to racially structured societies and effectively decreases resource mobilization between self-identified ethnic group members and their non-co-ethnic Latino/a counterparts. Overall, the contingent use of ethnic and racial identities among Latinos/as reinforces existing ethnic and racial hierarchies that are externally imposed from *within*, that is, by the members themselves. This process of racialization, in turn, reproduces ethnic and racial inequality in American enterprise. In contrast, Black and White business owners are more likely to self-identify racially than ethnically and are more likely to use these terms interchangeably. The emphasis on racial group membership underscores the salience of race among these U.S.-born groups. These observations pose a challenge to the assumptions and predictions of the ethnic entrepreneurship approach, calling into question the presumed essential role of ethnicity in facilitating business ownership, as gender and race combine with ethnicity to condition the social capital that is generated, and its capacity to offset structural inequality.

Finally, Latino/a entrepreneurs, like Whites and Blacks, characterize themselves as "rugged individualists" who are striving for the American dream. Regardless of class, gender, race, or ethnicity, the American creed ideology that hard work, dedication, a positive outlook, and courage are all one needs to succeed is fully adopted by American entrepreneurs. Even among those who experience structural inequality or recognize its impact on others, entrepreneurs do not generally link their fate to the unequal American social structure. Their contradictory location, as self-made, rugged individualists on the one hand and as members of unequal collectivities on the other, alters their understanding of the salience of social location in shaping and reproducing business ownership. The ideology of rugged individualism dampens the extent to which Latino/a entrepreneurs identify group-based structural inequality, or understand its marked effects on their life chances. By identifying as rugged individualists, Latino/a, White, and Black entrepreneurs are actively engaged in reproducing the highly stratified American society and its ideology, which celebrates individualism and meritocracy while downplaying classism, racism, and sexism.

## The Case of Latino/a Entrepreneurs in Houston

This book applies the embedded market approach to the case of Latino/a immigrant entrepreneurs in Houston, Texas. There are structural-contextual factors that are unique to Houston, such as its distinctive history of tripartite race relations (White, Black, and Mexican and Latino/a), rather than the White/Black binary that characterizes race relations across most of the United States. Sociospatial relationships between and across Latinos/as, Blacks, and Whites from different class backgrounds reflect this history and persist to this day, as observed in the intense racial and class segregation that characterizes many of Houston's communities and neighborhoods (Clark and Blue 2004; Sui and Wu 2006), including those in which this study took place.

Moreover, Houston's long history of Mexican-origin settlement, combined with the more recent influx of substantial numbers of Central and South American immigrants, is unprecedented outside of the Southwest. New Latino/a immigrants arrive daily and settle in immigrant barrios riddled with high poverty, crime, and joblessness on the one hand, and strong ethnic communities with thriving ethnic enclave economies on the other (Rodriguez 1993). At the same time, multiple generations of predominately poor Mexican-origin people live and work in ethnically concentrated communities, while middle-class Mexican Americans and Latinos/as reside in neighboring communities or suburbs that are often more ethnically or racially diverse (Valdez 1993). Taken together, the intergenerational settlement patterns of the Mexican-origin population in Houston, its proximity to the U.S.-Mexico border (which ensures continuing waves of new arrivals), and its large and growing Latin American population ensure that Latino/a Houstonians will follow multiple pathways and trajectories of socioeconomic assimilation that may not reflect those outside of the city, the state of Texas, or the Southwest more generally. Houston's sociohistorical context certainly shapes Latinos'/as' entrepreneurial outcomes; the book's central findings and conclusions are moored to this specific setting.

That said, Houston represents a microcosm of larger economic and demographic processes that are taking place in traditional "immigrant gateway cities" across the United States, such as Chicago, New York, and Los Angeles, as well as "new destination" cities, such as Columbus, Ohio, and Hazelton, Pennsylvania. As in many of the metropolitan areas in the United States, Houston has undergone a restructuring of its economy in the last forty years in response to global capitalism. As more progressive immigration policies have taken hold during this same period, Houston has experienced a marked increase in non-White immigration from Asian, Latin American, African, and Caribbean countries. These twin structural forces have led to an observed increase in business ownership across Houston and the United States, especially among the foreign-born (Light 1972). From the perspective of this larger context, it is reasonable to conclude that many of Houston's Latino/a immigrant entrepreneurs share the same structural conditions and thus experience similar patterns of socioeconomic assimilation as those outside of Houston.

## Houston Race Relations in Historical Context

Mexicans occupied Texas before it gained its independence from Mexico and was established as a republic in 1836, and before it was annexed to the United States in 1845. Prior to joining the Union, Mexican Texas sought to increase its population by enacting a liberal immigration policy that recruited White settlers from the United States with the promise of a free parcel of land. Slave-owning southern Whites heeded the Mexican government's call and migrated to Mexican Texas in large numbers, surpassing the state's own Mexican population by the 1830s. After annexation to the United States, and following the Mexican Revolution of 1910, migration along the Mexico-Texas border intensified but this time in reverse, as Mexicans fled their war-torn country in search of plentiful work and good wages in the Texas agriculture and cattle-ranching industries (Foley 1999:41). Thus, well before (and after) joining the Union, Texas race relations extended beyond the conventional White/Black binary. In Texas, Mexicans represented "a second color menace" to a majority of its White inhabitants, even as they continued to hire and recruit Mexican workers for their cheap and plentiful labor (Foley 1999:41; Perea 1997).

Like Blacks, Mexicans confronted de facto and de jure racism and discrimination aimed at securing White racial privilege, power, and domination. Whites' antipathy toward Blacks and Mexicans, their fear of the "browning," or "mongrelization," of America, fomented racial violence and terrorism against Black and Mexican men and women. Following Reconstruction (1865–77), Jim Crow policies effectively disenfranchised Blacks and Mexicans from voting by removing them from voter registration rolls and enacting literacy tests and a poll tax, and legally segregated them from Whites in schools, parks, and churches (Perea 1997). Miscegenation laws prevented intermarriage between Whites and Blacks or Mexicans until 1967, when such laws were overturned by the Supreme Court in the case *Loving v. Virginia*.

Although Blacks and Mexicans shared similar conditions of racial oppression, they also experienced and continue to experience distinct forms of it. The reasons for this are rooted in the long history of slavery and exploitation of Blacks at the hands of White southerners, which preceded their settlement in Texas and established the White/Black racial hierarchy *before* the introduction of Mexicans and Latinos/as to the racial landscape. Mexicans were thus given the opportunity to define their position within the preexisting structure of a bifurcated racial hierarchy. For the most part, Mexican racial projects (Omi and Winant 1994) attempted to construct a meaning of *Mexicanness* or of "being Mexican" that was equated with *Whiteness* or "being White," or, at the very least, sought to position Mexicans as somewhere in between Whites and Blacks. Although most Whites in Texas "were descended from transplanted Southerners who had fought hard to maintain the 'color line' in Texas and to extend its barriers to Mexicans," the successful construction of Mexicans as being *closer* to Whites than Blacks and in some cases, "usually light-skinned, middle class Mexicans," equated with Whites (Foley 1999:5), distinguishes their racial oppression when compared to that of Blacks. Texas's legacy of Jim Crow and the early establishment of tripartite race relations, which positioned Whites at the top of the racial hierarchy, Blacks at the bottom, and Mexicans in between, are arguably still in place today. At the same time, Mexicans continue to be characterized as "racial foreigners" and "aliens," labels that are not ascribed to Blacks or Whites and that prevent the Mexican-origin population from truly "becoming American" in the eyes of many Whites (and Blacks). While Mexicans achieve a degree of relative flexibility when compared to Blacks along the racial hierarchy, their eventual "assimilation into the [White] American mainstream" is unlikely, especially in the context of growing anti-immigrant sentiment, large-scale demographic changes in Houston that reflect a persistent and growing population of Mexican and Latin American immigrants and their descendants, and a restructuring economy that negatively affects ethnic and racial minorities disproportionately.

## Free Enterprise City

Houston's economy expanded beyond cotton and cattle after the Civil War and at the start of the Industrial Revolution, with the development of shipping and rail transportation systems. The discovery of oil in 1901 spurred its economic growth even further, increasing its commerce, real estate development, and labor market. To encourage investment, politicians and policy makers eschewed regulations and restrictions on businesses, taxes, and zoning. As the quintessential "free enterprise city" (Feagin 1988), Houston strived for a business-friendly climate that included "weak unions, cheap labor, low taxes, deliberately ineffective land-use controls, and minimal municipal services" (Klineberg 2002:4). In the 1980s, however, due to global competition and a nationwide economic downturn, Houston's oil and real estate boom went bust.

The local and national recession coupled with progressive immigration policies ushered in a period of restructuring for the U.S. economy. Economic restructuring produced an "hourglass economy," characterized by a growing low-skilled service sector, a shrinking blue-collar, durable goods manufacturing sector, and a competitive white-collar, high-tech, and professional service sector. Although jobs at the bottom and at the top remain plentiful, the "narrowing middle" forces occupational segregation and constrains intergenerational mobility, especially among non-White racial and ethnic minorities (Portes and Rumbaut 2001).

Houston's economic transition resulted in an increase in White unemployment, which forced those workers' exodus from the city, as blue-collar Whites searched for good-paying jobs and new housing, preferably in White suburbs. In this economic context, Blacks and Latinos/as were hit particularly hard. Many lacked the skills and resources to compete successfully in the knowledge-based, high-tech sector of the economy, while those in search of the few good jobs that were left confronted discriminatory and racist practices by White employers. At the same time, documented and undocumented immigrants, mostly from Mexico and other Latin American countries, took advantage of the increase in low-skilled, low-wage service sector employment. They moved into readily available low-income housing, helped along by desperate landlords who sought to fill their large, vacant, and increasingly dilapidated complexes (Shah 2005). These economic conditions combined to hinder the social and economic integration of ethnic and racial minorities (Harrison and Bluestone 1988; Quillian 2003; Waldinger and Feliciano 2004). Not surprisingly, self-employment and small-business ownership increased during this same period. As a large and growing segment of the U.S. economy, entrepreneurship offers an avenue of economic absorption, especially among foreign-born men and women (Borjas 1986; Valdez 2009; Yuengert 1995).

Latinos/as represent a large, growing, and emergent American racial group. Recent census figures indicate that this population, which reflects 12.5 percent of the U.S. total, increased from 22.4 million in 1990 to 35.3 million in 2000 (a 58 percent increase; Saenz 2004). Not surprisingly, the rise in the Latino/a population has contributed to an unprecedented growth in Latino/a businesses. From 1997 to 2000, Latino/a businesses increased by 31 percent (compared to 6 percent for non-Latino/a businesses). In 2002, Latinos/as owned 1.6 million businesses and employed 1.5 million persons. Although this group maintains a considerable presence in American enterprise, its economic returns have not kept pace with those of other groups.

The demographic profile of Latino/a, White, and Black Houstonian entrepreneurs reflects that of the Southwest and the United States more generally (see Table 1.1). U.S.-born non-Hispanic Whites are more likely to be self-employed than U.S.-born Blacks or foreign-born Latinos/as.[9] White men report the highest rate of entrepreneurship (11 percent), followed by "Other Latinos/as," which include South and Central American immigrants, at fewer than 10 percent.[10] In contrast, U.S.-born Black women fall behind all other groups (3 percent). Interestingly, while Mexican immigrant women make up just 5 percent of the Mexican-origin entrepreneurs, they are disproportionately concentrated in the restaurant business. Fully 20 percent are restaurateurs, compared to 7.5 percent of Mexican men, the group with the highest percentage of restaurateurs among men. U.S.-born Black and White women trail behind Mexicans, at 2.3 percent and 2 percent, respectively. Notably, women in each respective group are more likely to own restaurants than their male counterparts, with the exception of "Other Latinos/as."

In previous research, I have shown that influential background characteristics, such as age, education, and married status, contribute to the divergent entrepreneurial participation rates of these groups, although differences persist after controlling for these and other factors, such as social capital (Valdez 2006, 2008b). Entrepreneurial participation generally increases with age. Foreign-born Mexican men and women, at forty-one years old and thirty-eight years old, respectively, are much younger than the other groups, whose age is forty-six, on average. This age difference may explain, in part, Mexican immigrants' lower self-employment participation rates overall.

The Mexican-origin population is less educated than Whites, "Other Latinos/as," and Blacks. Since an increase in education is associated with an increase in self-employment participation, their self-employment participation is negatively affected by their lower educational attainment when compared to other groups. Fully 54.4 percent of foreign-born Mexican men and 56.5 percent of foreign-born Mexican women report earning an eighth-grade education or less, but only around 8 percent report earning a bachelor's degree or better (see Table 1.1). In comparison, 46 percent of White men, 37 percent of White women, 29 percent of "Other Latino/a" men, and 28 percent of Black men earn a bachelor's degree or better. Like Mexicans, only 8.5 percent of "Other Latino/a" women earn a bachelor's degree or better, which suggests that the lower educational attainment of Latinas, more generally, hinders their self-employment outcomes disproportionately.

Not surprisingly, speaking English is associated with an increase in self-employment participation, and most U.S.-born, non-Hispanic Whites and Blacks are fluent in English; fewer Latinos/as report speaking English "well" or "very well" (between 50 and 80 percent). Regarding married status, which is associated with an increase in self-employment, particularly among men, around 70 percent of this entrepreneurial population is married. Foreign-born Mexican men are more likely to be married than any other group (84 percent), followed by U.S.-born White men (80 percent). In contrast, the group least likely to be married is self-employed Black women (47 percent). Generally, foreign-born Mexicans are younger and less educated than the other groups, Whites are better educated, and Black women are least likely to

**Table 1.1** Descriptive Characteristics of Latino/a, White, and Black Entrepreneurs in Houston, 2000

| | Foreign-born Mexican | | Foreign-born Other Latino/a* | | U.S.-born White | | U.S.-born Black | |
|---|---|---|---|---|---|---|---|---|
| | Men | Women | Men | Women | Men | Women | Men | Women |
| Self-Employed | 6.2% | 5.1% | 9.7% | 4.8% | 10.9% | 6.1% | 6.1% | 3.1% |
| Restaurateurs | 7.5% | 19.9% | 2.1% | 0% | 1.5% | 2.0% | 1.6% | 2.3% |
| Education | | | | | | | | |
| Eighth grade or less | 54.4% | 56.5% | 30.9% | 30.5% | 6.7% | 4.6% | 11.3% | 7.1% |
| High school | 20.7% | 20.8% | 34.3% | 18.4% | 20.1% | 24.3% | 29.7% | 38.0% |
| Some college | 17.3% | 14.5% | 6.4% | 42.6% | 26.9% | 34.3% | 30.8% | 38.1% |
| BA or graduate/professional | 7.6% | 8.2% | 28.9% | 8.5% | 46.3% | 36.8% | 28.1% | 16.8% |
| Married | 83.6% | 63.2% | 71.3% | 66.7% | 79.4% | 72.7% | 72.8% | 46.5% |
| Mean Age | 40.73 | 38.38 | 46.00 | 51.45 | 46.85 | 46.65 | 46.34 | 46.34 |
| Mean English | 0.73 | 0.52 | 0.74 | 0.8 | n/a† | n/a | n/a | n/a |
| Population | 54,740 | 28,857 | 10,169 | 8,808 | 545,369 | 442,145 | 110,959 | 131,550 |

U.S.: Bureau of the Census 2000, 5% Integrated Public Use Microdata Series (Ruggles, Sobek, Alexander et al. 2009).

* Due to small sample size, non-Mexican Latinos/as are collapsed into one category, "Other Latino/a," which includes Caribbean (Puerto Rican and Cuban), Central American (Salvadoran, Guatemalan, Costa Rican, Honduran, and Nicaraguan), and South American (Argentinean, Bolivian, Chilean, Colombian, Ecuadorian, Peruvian, and Venezuelan) immigrants.

† Not applicable.

be married. It is important to consider how these influential background characteristics affect the individual and collective self-employment outcomes of Latinos/as, Whites, and Blacks in the stratified American social structure.

## Overview of Study and Methods

In 1960, prior to Houston's economic restructuring, Whites made up the vast majority of Houstonians (70 percent), followed by Blacks (22.9 percent), and then Latinos/as (7 percent), mostly of Mexican origin. Today a diverse group of Latinos/as from Mexico, the Caribbean, and Central and South America comprise 37.4 percent of Houston's 2 million residents, followed by Whites (30.8 percent), Blacks (25.0 percent), and Asians (6.8 percent) (U.S. Bureau of the Census, 2000). Latinos/as, the largest and fastest-growing minority population in the United States, and the group with the largest increase in business ownership since 1996, are generally overlooked in studies of ethnic entrepreneurship (with the exception of Cubans; see Portes 1987; Portes and Bach 1985; Portes and Stepick 1993). At the same time, ethnic entrepreneurship has been studied extensively in the West, East, and Midwest but is rarely studied in the South. My study of Latino/a entrepreneurs in Houston, the fourth-largest city and the second-largest home of Latinos/as in the United States, with an additional consideration of White and Black entrepreneurs, examines an understudied group in an understudied region in comparative perspective.

I focus on the restaurant industry for its relative ease of entry (for would-be entrepreneurs) and to hold the job content constant. I sample a variety of restaurants from smaller, family-style eateries to larger, more formal establishments. That restaurants differ to such an extent makes this industry ideal for examining a diverse sample of American entrepreneurs. This research design allows me to compare entrepreneurial outcomes within and across groups that differ by class, gender, race, and ethnicity.

My study took place over four years (2005–9) of ethnographic observation and included fifty-four face-to-face interviews with Latino/a, White, and Black entrepreneurs who live and work in Houston, Texas (thirty-four Latinos/as and ten White and Black entrepreneurs each). In addition to interviewing entrepreneurs, I visited or ate lunch or dinner at the restaurants of my respondents more than once, and at other restaurants not included in the study, to observe the day-to-day restaurant experience—the role and duties of the owner, relationships and interactions among the owner, customers, and employees, the changing customer base during lunch, during dinner, or on the weekends, and so on. I also met with and interviewed several community organizers, business leaders, and business consultants about the Houston restaurant industry.

Participants were sampled in a variety of ways, which included targeted sampling (Verdaguer 2009), dispersed referral snowball sampling (Mahler 1995), and organization-based network sampling (Bernard 1988). First, I used a well-known and exhaustive Houston online restaurant guide searchable by zip code to locate restaurants in specific areas of ethnic and racial concentration and increase the chances of finding my target population of Latino/a, Black, and White men and women entrepreneurs from different class backgrounds.[11] Because it was sometimes difficult to find Latino/a and especially Black restaurateurs using this online source only, I also employed snowball sampling, asking restaurateurs (previously unknown to me) with whom I had completed interviews for referrals. I also interviewed restaurateurs whom I met or was introduced to through contacts with community business leaders or organizers, and through business fairs and expos, such as the Houston Hispanic Chamber of Commerce Annual Business Expo. The names of the participants, restaurants, and communities in this study have been changed to protect their confidentiality.

The average length of an interview was approximately ninety minutes. The shortest interview ran forty minutes; longer interviews lasted more than three hours. Monetary compensation in the amount of $20–$50 was provided to each restaurateur who completed an interview (the higher compensation was offered when the respondent was hesitant or when he or she rescheduled the interview more than once). From the start of this project, I realized that my own social location, as a professional, second-generation Mexican American woman from California with, at best, an intermediate-level command of Spanish, might influence my ability to successfully secure or conduct interviews with non-English-speaking entrepreneurs. To address this concern, I hired San Juanita Garcia, a Mexican-origin naturalized U.S. citizen raised in Houston, to conduct most of the interviews with Spanish-only speakers. She also conducted additional interviews and observations with English- and Spanish-speaking Latino/a entrepreneurs in the Greater Houston area. To minimize the potential for bias due to different racial backgrounds, I hired Lesley Meyer, a White graduate student born and raised in Texas, and Charity

Clay, a Black graduate student familiar with Houston, to conduct the inter-views with White and Black entrepreneurs, respectively.

To make certain that I interviewed a diverse population of Latino/a entrepreneurs that varied by class and ethnicity, I sampled from three different communities: Little Mexico, a predominately Mexican enclave; Little Latin America, a community that is best described as a Latino/a enclave, with residents originating from North, South, and Central America and the Caribbean; and the Greater Houston area, where I also sought out White and Black entrepreneurs. Black entrepreneurs were located in racially segregated areas of Black concentration in Little Mexico, and also in the South Ward, a historic, predominately Black enclave. In addition to the Greater Houston area, White entrepreneurs were sampled in Houston Heights, a predominately White upper-class community. In what follows I include a brief description of the ethnically and racially concentrated areas in which this study was conducted, using information provided by the U.S. Census Bureau (U.S. Bureau of the Census 2000).

The area of Little Latin America (population 49,691) is approximately three square miles; it is located in southwestern Houston, Texas. Formerly known (somewhat infamously) as a haven for white middle-class singles, Little Latin America changed dramatically in the wake of the oil bust of the 1970s. Today, Little Latin America is overwhelmingly Latino/a (71 percent). Of this population, 41 percent are of Mexican descent and 29 percent are Central and South American immigrants and their descendants. More than half of the Little Latin America community is foreign-born, of which 86 percent originate from Mexico or other Latin American countries.

Houston Heights (population 15,642) covers three and a half square miles and is located in southwest Houston, adjacent to Little Latin America. With a median household income of almost $88,000 and Whites making up around 89 percent of the total population, Houston Heights is one of the most exclusive, predominately White, middle- and upper-class areas of Houston. It can be characterized as a largely upscale residential community, noted for its numerous churches (and single synagogue), parks, and charter schools. Its commercial district is concentrated along three multilane streets and is comprised of retail and grocery stores, upscale restaurants and fast-food chains, and smaller, family-owned businesses. More than 9 percent of the Houston Heights community is self-employed, the largest percentage of self-employed workers of all the research sites (at less than 5 percent, the South Ward records the lowest percentage of self-employed workers). Not surprisingly, it is also the community with the highest labor force participation (70 percent), home ownership (81 percent), and residents with college degrees (70 percent).

Little Mexico (population 28,679) is a historic Mexican enclave in eastern Houston that covers just over six square miles. Settled by Mexican laborers and professionals fleeing the 1910 Mexican civil war, Little Mexico is the home of multiple generations of U.S.-born Mexican Americans and some newly arriving Mexican immigrants. The majority of the population is Latino/a (65 percent), and at 55 percent, predominately of Mexican origin; a significant portion of the population, however, is Black (31 percent). Predictably, Mexican and Black residents are concentrated in different, segregated areas of Little Mexico. Little Mexico is the poorest of the research sites included in this study. It has the lowest labor force participation (44 percent), and the smallest percentage of college-educated residents (5 percent) and is the only research site with a majority of residents who are unemployed or not in the labor force (56 percent). Additionally, more than 30 percent of the households in Little Mexico fall below the poverty line, a threshold that denotes it as a likely "underclass" community (Wilson 1987).

The South Ward (population 29,753) is a historically Black community located to the east of downtown Houston that was originally settled by freedmen after the Civil War. Although the residents of the South Ward are predominately Black Americans who were born and raised in Houston, a modest number migrated from Louisiana (in the early 1920s and following the devastating aftermath of Hurricane Katrina). The South Ward is a poverty-stricken area with few businesses, often owned by Korean or Chinese immigrant, "middleman minority" entrepreneurs (Bonacich 1973), and fewer customers. This area is known as Houston's "toughest, proudest, and baddest ghetto."[12] I originally selected the South Ward for my study because of its high Black concentration and its historic ties to the Black community, which I thought would increase the likelihood of locating Black-owned restaurants. Unfortunately, the limited number of Black-owned businesses, or any businesses, in this economically disadvantaged area led me to widen my search for Black entrepreneurs. I subsequently located additional Black entrepreneurs in Greater Houston and in Little Mexico. Table 1.2 lists additional characteristics of the research sites.

**Table 1.2** Characteristics of the Research Sites

|  | Little Mexico | Little Latin America | South Ward | Houston Heights | Greater Houston |
|---|---|---|---|---|---|
| Median Household Income ($) | 21,864 | 26,026 | 23,835 | 87,985 | 36,616 |
| Households Below Poverty Line (%) | 31.3 | 29.2 | 25.8 | 2.0 | 16.0 |
| Race (%) |  |  |  |  |  |
|   Black | 30.7 | 9.0 | 79.5 | 1.0 | 25.3 |
|   White | 41.9 | 48.4 | 10.1 | 88.8 | 49.3 |
|   Other | 24.1 | 37.2 | 9.3 | 8.7 | 22.3 |
|   Two or more races | 3.3 | 5.4 | 1.1 | 1.5 | 3.1 |
| Latino/a (%) |  |  |  |  |  |
|   Mexican | 54.7 | 41.1 | 14.1 | 4.8 | 27.0 |
|   Puerto Rican | .1 | .3 | .0 | .3 | .4 |
|   Cuban | .0 | .8 | .1 | .5 | .3 |
|   Other Latino/a | 10.4 | 29.1 | 2.9 | 2.3 | 9.7 |
|   Not Latino/a | 34.8 | 28.7 | 82.9 | 92.1 | 62.6 |
| Nativity (%) |  |  |  |  |  |
|   Native-born | 71.7 | 41.2 | 91.4 | 89.2 | 73.6 |
|   Foreign-born | 28.3 | 58.8 | 8.6 | 10.8 | 26.4 |
| Gender (%) |  |  |  |  |  |
|   Male | 50.8 | 54.4 | 47.3 | 48.0 | 49.9 |
|   Female | 49.2 | 45.6 | 52.7 | 52.0 | 50.1 |
| Labor Force Participation (%) | 44.3 | 63.3 | 50.7 | 70.1 | 63.2 |
|   Employed | 38.5 | 58.3 | 44.2 | 68.6 | 58.4 |
|   Unemployed | 5.8 | 4.9 | 6.5 | 1.5 | 4.8 |
|   Not in labor force | 55.7 | 36.7 | 49.3 | 29.9 | 36.8 |
| Self-employed | 5.8 | 6.2 | 4.7 | 9.4 | 6.2 |
| Education (age 25 and older) |  |  |  |  |  |
|   Less than ninth grade | 33.9 | 33.8 | 14.4 | 1.4 | 14.8 |
|   Ninth to twelfth grade (no degree) | 28.7 | 18.1 | 24.8 | 3.2 | 14.8 |
|   High school graduate | 22.2 | 15.4 | 32.5 | 9.0 | 20.4 |
|   Some college | 10.3 | 10.9 | 18.4 | 16.6 | 19.1 |
| BA/graduate/professional | 4.9 | 21.7 | 9.8 | 69.7 | 30.9 |
| Homeowner (%) | 47.2 | 6.1 | 68.9 | 81.4 | 45.8 |
| Renter (%) | 52.8 | 93.9 | 31.1 | 18.6 | 54.2 |
| Median Age | 28.3 | 26.6 | 34.2 | 39.9 | 30.9 |
| Population | 28,679 | 49,691 | 29,753 | 15,964 | 1,953,631 |

U.S. Bureau of the Census 2000.

## The Plan of the Book

Chapter 2 introduces my theoretical approach, the embedded market. This approach connects two separate threads of sociological knowledge: a macro-level theory of intersectionality advanced by Black feminist scholars, which explains structural oppression and privilege as stemming from the intersection of class, gender, and race; and the traditional ethnic entrepreneurship paradigm, which emerged in concert with theories of minority incorporation. That approach highlights the role of ethnicity in fostering business ownership through ethnic-based social capital, capturing a process of "delayed assimilation" (Portes and Rumbaut 2001; Zhou 1997:84). The embedded market approach maintains that the American social structure is comprised of class, gender, racial, and ethnic group hierarchies, which intersect to create structural inequality. In this context, social capital stemming from these multiple dimensions may offset structural disadvantage; however, its effect is both compensatory and contingent. Accordingly, the intersection of class, gender, race, and ethnicity may *help or hinder* the life chances of Latino/a entrepreneurs through the integration of structure and agency.

Chapters 3 through 5 consider how the intersection of class, gender, race, and ethnicity affect Latino/a entrepreneurs' economic outcomes differently, and compare Latino/a entrepreneurs to their White and Black counterparts. Specifically, Chapter 3 investigates how such intersections shape Latinos'/as' entrepreneurial dreams—their motivations for and expectations of business ownership—and identifies similarities and differences across racial groups. This chapter exposes the intersection of class, gender, race, and ethnicity in creating and reproducing unequal entrepreneurial motivations, to offer a more complete picture of the heterogeneity of Latinos'/as' work and social lives, and the variety of conditions that propel them toward enterprise. Chapter 4 examines how structural inequality mediates Latino/a entrepreneurs' resource-mobilization strategies and their capacity to generate both social and economic resources. This chapter reveals that Latinos/as, Whites, and Blacks may employ similar resource-mobilization strategies, regardless of class, gender, ethnicity, or race; however, their ability to produce assets is determined largely by their intersectional location, which ultimately affects their ability to start and maintain businesses. In Chapter 5, I investigate Latinos'/as' entrepreneurial "success" in terms of their economic and social objectives. This chapter also explores the dynamic and contingent meaning of success, which changes based on the intersections of class, gender, race, and ethnicity.

Whereas Chapters 3 through 5 focus on Latino/a entrepreneurs' economic outcomes, Chapters 6 through 8 examine Latino/a entrepreneurs' social integration, specifically, how class, gender, race, and ethnicity create, transform, and reproduce Latino/a entrepreneurs' identity, as members of privileged and oppressed groups on the one hand, and as "rugged individualists" on the other. Chapter 6 focuses on the distinct yet interdependent roles of ethnicity and race in shaping and reproducing ethnic and racial identity formation, and how these different identities affect Latino/a, White, and Black entrepreneurs' life chances. Chapter 7 reveals that Latino/a, White, and Black entrepreneurs, as actors within the highly stratified American social structure, engage in its reproduction through their belief and conviction in the American creed and "rugged individualism" ideologies.

Although the book's central findings reveal that Latino/a entrepreneurs can (and do) achieve some measure of socioeconomic integration, the American dream remains partially fulfilled. Unequal outcomes between the middle and lower classes, between men and women, and among Whites, Latinos/as, and Blacks substantiate the constraints of individual agency within the American social structure. The intersection of class, gender, race, and ethnicity reproduces structural inequality in America through systems of oppression rooted in capitalism, patriarchy, and White supremacy, even as they provide the basis for individual and collective agency. It is this interdependence of structure and agency that shapes and reproduces the entrepreneurial life chances of Latinos/as. Ultimately the embedded market approach decenters the role of ethnicity and ethnic group membership in explanations of "ethnic entrepreneurship" in favor of an intersectionality approach that considers seriously the unequal structural context in which Latinos/as from different social locations are embedded, for a more comprehensive and systematic approach to American enterprise.

# 2 The Embedded Market
Race, Class, and Gender in American Enterprise

## Theorizing Ethnic Entrepreneurship

Since Ivan Light's *Ethnic Enterprise in America* (1972), social scientists concerned with immigrant adaptation and incorporation recognize ethnic entrepreneurship, defined simply as business ownership among immigrant ethnic minorities, as a distinct form (Light 1972; Light and Bonacich 1988; Portes and Bach 1985; Portes and Rumbaut 2001, 2006; Waldinger et al. 1990). The interest in ethnic enterprise reflects an observed increase in self-employment that started in the 1970s and that reversed a previous trend toward its decline. This reversal was due, in part, to the dual structural forces of economic restructuring, a consequence of globalization, and large-scale, non-White immigration from African, Caribbean, Asian, and Latin American sending countries, following more progressive immigration policies such as the Hart Cellar Act (1965), which abolished national origins quotas. These twin shifts in the American economy and society set the stage for immigrant minorities to pursue business ownership in an attempt to improve their economic integration in the face of increased labor market competition and market uncertainty (Light and Roach 1986).

Early studies of ethnic entrepreneurship, like much of the previous work on the socioeconomic incorporation or assimilation processes of immigrants in America, focused almost exclusively on the cultural endowments of distinct groups to explain entrepreneurial activity. An entrepreneurial "orientation" was ascribed to those immigrant groups whose rates of self-employment or business ownership far exceeded that of the U.S.-born, native (White) population. Entrepreneurialism was often credited to specific ethnic group characteristics and features, such as the Anglo-Saxon Protestant ethic (Weber 1930), the German-Jewish "rich cultural heritage" of "distinct religious and cultural traditions" (Portes and Sensenbrenner 1993:1330), the Chinese "clan" values of "shared collective responsibility and mutual loyalty" (Nee and Nee 1973:64), and the "Orientals' . . . strong ethnic network of collective, ethnically based morality" (Lovell-Troy 1980:85). In contrast, the negligible rates of business ownership among other ethnic (and racial) groups, such as U.S.- and foreign-born Mexicans or Blacks, were attributed, in part, to a lack of such key cultural features and attributes and close-knit ties. After all, if these groups possessed the entrepreneurial spirit and ethnic solidarity that other groups displayed, their rates of business ownership would presumably be closer to those of entrepreneurial ethnic groups—but that was not the case. Thus, Black and Mexican entrepreneurs, albeit a small and select subgroup, were largely overlooked or characterized typically by their individual motivations and achievements rather than defined as the product of collective action and mutual aid (Butler 2005; see Light 1972:21). Unfortunately, this "common sense" understanding of Mexican and Black business ownership in America failed to account for the long history of collective capital accumulation and mutual aid among Black entrepreneurs that dates back to before the Civil War (Butler 2005:40) and among the Mexican-origin population in the Southwest (De León 2001; Foley 1999).

Contemporary approaches to ethnic entrepreneurship retain a cultural component but are more complex. The "modes of incorporation" framework developed by Portes and Rumbaut (2001, 2006) offers the prevailing view. This approach combines individual-, group-, and structural-level processes to explain ethnic enterprise. These include individual-level human capital attainment (in other words, education and work experience), the strength and viability of the ethnic community—in terms of its ability to generate economic resources and social support based on group members' ethnic cohesiveness—and finally, the structural context that immigrant groups experience in the host society, in particular, the "context of reception" (Portes and Rumbaut 2001, 2006) or "opportunity structure of the economy" (Waldinger et al. 1990).

Portes and Rumbaut (2001, 2006) argue that individual motivation and human capital attainment, social processes rooted in the ethnic community, and the structural conditions, or "context of reception," that ethnic groups confront after arrival and settlement constitute the "modes of incorporation" that interact to shape their socioeconomic incorporation and, in particular, their entrepreneurial outcomes. As they succinctly state, "The basic idea is simple: Individuals with similar background skills may be channeled toward very different positions in the stratification system, depending on the type of community and labor market in which they become incorporated" (Portes and Rumbaut 2006:83). For Portes and Rumbaut (2001, 2006), individual-level characteristics or attributes, such as possessing an entrepreneurial motivation, work experience, and schooling, comprise a partial and perhaps secondary explanation for business ownership among immigrant group members. First and foremost is the reception context that an immigrant group confronts upon arrival, specifically, the particularistic government policies that determine the size of and economic support for the group, such as the composition of the ethnic community and opportunities for government-subsidized loans for refugees, and the group's position within the labor market, which is determined partially by the overlapping properties of aggregate human capital and community dynamics.

In the stratified American labor market, human capital skills constrain the occupational opportunities of workers within the restructured, hourglass economy, which is characterized by a growing low- or no-skilled sector, a highly skilled managerial, professional, and technical sector, and a shrinking "middle" sector (for example, good-paying, low-skilled jobs in durable goods manufacturing) (Portes and Rumbaut 2001). Additionally, non-White immigrant groups are likely to confront a negative societal reception context, such as an anti-immigrant sentiment, which may further hinder their labor market integration. These groups may experience statistical or institutional discrimination, or "common sense" assumptions made by employers about immigrant, racial, and ethnic minority groups that may bias them against hiring disadvantaged groups (Kirschenmen and Neckerman 1991; Wilson 1997). Such negative structural forces hinder the economic incorporation of immigrant and ethnic minority group members, thereby preventing socioeconomic parity with "mainstream" (White middle-class) America (Alba and Nee 2003).

In the face of a negative reception context, the composition of the co-ethnic community becomes crucially important for new arrivals. For example, a professional or entrepreneurial co-ethnic community offers resourceful and supportive networks that may ease an otherwise disadvantaged context. Rather than going it alone, ethnic group members are "introduced from the start to the whole range of opportunities available in the host labor market," including enterprise (Portes and Rumbaut 2006:87, 92). To illustrate, from the early 1960s to the late 1970s, a managerial and professional class of Cuban refugees fled the Castro regime and sought shelter in the United States. Their settlement was made easier with U.S. government support for refugees in the form of financial aid, health care, scholarships, and business loans (Portes and Stepick 1993). Their geographic concentration in Miami facilitated and consolidated further the emergence of ethnic solidarity, which provided the basis for the development of ethnic-based social capital: the mobilization of economic and social resources and support based on group affiliation. Cuban immigrant networks shared information on housing, job opportunities, and mutual aid societies among co-ethnic members (Portes and Bach 1985; Sanders and Nee 1996; Wilson and Martin 1982; Wilson and Portes 1980). For example, mutual aid associations often provided start-up capital to would-be Cuban entrepreneurs in the form of "character loans"—low-interest loans granted to co-ethnics based solely on their family reputation in Cuba (Portes and Stepick 1993). In this way, the combination of individual, group, and structural forces promoted and facilitated Cuban immigrant enterprise (Light and Bonacich 1988; Portes and Rumbaut 2001; Waldinger et al. 1990).

Moreover, the dominant "modes of incorporation" framework explains the near absence of enterprise among disadvantaged ethnic and racial minority groups as the result of insufficient human capital combined with a decidedly adverse labor market and co-ethnic community context (Borjas and Bronars 1989; Logan, Alba, and McNulty 1994; Portes and Bach 1985). For example, Blacks are characterized, on average, as possessing limited education and skills and residing in poor, segregated, urban communities. Such communities are thought to reinforce and reproduce members' socioeconomic stagnation and possible decline, as "there is often a kind of collective expectation that new arrivals should not be 'uppity' and should not try to surpass, at least at the start, the collective status of their elders" (Portes and Rumbaut 2006:87). In this negative reception context, opportunities and support for enterprise are constrained; the few Black-owned businesses that do emerge are described as "undercapitalized" (Silverman 2000:83), with merchants that "have historically experienced and continue to experience co-ethnic disadvantages in serving their own" (Lee 2002:21). Likewise, Portes and Bach (1985) contrast the entrepreneurial success of Cubans with the lack of success among the Mexican-origin population. They suggest that Mexicans are hindered by limited human capital, a history of low-wage labor recruitment, and "weak communities that have emerged under their precarious conditions of arrival and settlement" (Portes and Bach 1985:245; Portes and Rumbaut 2001:278). Without the aid of a strong ethnic community, would-be Mexican entrepreneurs face significant hurdles, such as the "dispersal of their ethnic enterprises" (Light and Bonacich 1988), "consumer discrimination" on the open market (Borjas and Bronars 1989), and fewer "multiplier effects for the community" (Wilson and Martin 1982:150). In this context, the Mexican-origin population is perceived largely as relegated to the low-wage sector of the general labor market (Portes and Bach 1985:245).

In sum, the prevailing approach to ethnic entrepreneurship identifies the different "modes of incorporation" (Portes and Rumbaut 2006) that influence a variety of entrepreneurial outcomes across diverse ethnic groups in the United States. Human capital and entrepreneurial motivations, labor market opportunities, and the composition of the co-ethnic community combine to determine an immigrant's entrepreneurial fate, which effectively reproduces the entrepreneurial character of the ethnic group as a whole. Accordingly, the disproportionately high entrepreneurial activity among Cuban, Chinese, Greek, and Korean entrepreneurs can be explained by the different combinations of these determinants, whereas negligible entrepreneurial activity among non-Cuban Latinos/as and Blacks is explained in the same way; that is, with different combinations or the absence of these same determinants (Portes and Rumbaut 2006).

Although this model can explain any given ethnic group's success or failure in enterprise as the combination of individual-, group-, and structural-level effects, it is largely descriptive, imprecise, and post-factum with respect to how these factors coalesce and why they matter for particular groups in specific contexts (Portes and Rumbaut 2006:75; Rath 2002; Valdez 2008a; Waldinger et al. 1990). Additionally, there are some neglected factors and weaknesses in the framework: (1) It conflates the distinct concepts of class and ethnicity; (2) it dismisses "nonentrepreneurial" ethnic groups from serious consideration; and (3) it fails to account for or confront the additional, distinct, and intersecting roles of race, class, and gender.

### The Conflation of Class with Ethnicity

Although the context of reception is not defined in a comprehensive or explicit manner, the "relevant" contexts for immigrant groups include "the policies of the receiving government, the conditions of the host labor market and the characteristics of their own ethnic communities" (Portes and Rumbaut 2006:84). In two of these contexts, the labor market and the ethnic community, an immigrant's individual and collective class position is overlooked, reduced to individual-level human capital skills or conflated with ethnicity. In contrast, the role of ethnicity is emphasized. For example, Portes and Rumbaut (2006:85) note that an individual immigrant's skills and resources interact with group-level "statistical discrimination" in the labor market, which may "contribute to the confinement of the group to the low-wage segment of the labor market." From their perspective, occupational segregation is conditioned on a combination of individual-level skills and group-based discrimination, which relegates certain ethnic groups to work that is associated with their particular group (for example, "Mexican work"). This "ethnicized" conception of labor market dynamics explicitly acknowledges the role of ethnicity (in generating group-based discrimination and constraining opportunities in the labor market) but neglects to fully appreciate that an individual's "skills and resources" may also represent the characteristics of a collective group of individuals that share the same class position. Accordingly, the class situation of a given group of individuals interacts with their respective ethnic group affiliations; it is this interaction that shapes the labor market position of individuals that are affiliated with different ethnic groups *and* social classes within the stratified American economy.

The conflation of class with ethnicity is also observed in the description of the characteristics that are ascribed to the ethnic community itself, a second context of reception. Simply put, this perspective argues that upon arrival, immigrants are dependent upon their ethnic communities for resources and support to facilitate their economic incorporation. Consequently, "the characteristics of the ethnic community acquire decisive importance in molding their entry into the labor market and hence their prospects for future mobility" (Portes and Rumbaut 2006:87). By virtue of their ethnic group affiliation, then, low-skilled immigrant workers are "trapped in positions held to be 'appropriate' for their group," while "professional and business people can escape discrimination" (2006:86). Here again, the centrality of ethnicity in shaping immigrants' labor market outcomes is clearly emphasized, while the role of class is conflated with ethnicity, or at best, acknowledged implicitly as a "characteristic" of the ethnic community only. The assumption that is built into this conception of an ethnic group is that individual members share the same class position and consequently share the same labor market outcomes. Furthermore, once established, the implicit class situation that is ascribed to the entire ethnic community is reproduced since the character of the ethnic network, whether working-class or entrepreneurial, is self-perpetuating (2006:87). This reasoning, however, fails to appreciate that the capacity or ability to surmount the "ethnicized" secondary labor market to become a professional, manager, or entrepreneur in the American economy rests largely on an individual immigrant's social-class position, *regardless of ethnicity*. Yet, if class, a capitalist social group formation, is reduced to individual "skills and resources," or conflated with ethnicity, the class position of individuals and collectivities is ignored and its contribution erased. Its distinct role in shaping economic action is not, however, solely conditioned on or influenced by ethnicity. Thus, it is imperative to account for the separate effects of class to limit the extent to which it becomes "culturalized" into ethnic terms (for example, the ethnicization of the labor market or the idea that entrepreneurship is primarily rooted in or distinguished by ethnicity). As Gimenez (2007:111) cautions, the salience of ethnic or racial identity is often privileged in contemporary studies of stratification; however, "when class divisions are taken into consideration, it becomes clear that many of the problems afflicting [ethnic group members] are not due entirely to their 'identity' but to their class position." The embedded market approach takes this concern seriously, as it attempts to distinguish between these distinct yet intersecting social group formations and their effect on entrepreneurship within the stratified American economy.

### The Absence of Research on Entrepreneurship Among Nonentrepreneurial Ethnic Groups

The disproportionate focus on specific entrepreneurial ethnic groups, such as Cubans or Koreans, whose self-employment participation rates far exceed those of the American mainstream (Light and Bonacich 1988; Portes and Bach 1985; Portes and Rumbaut 2006), coincides with a dearth of research on those ethnic and racial groups with low rates or negligible entrepreneurial activity, such as Mexicans or Blacks. In the rare case when proponents of the ethnic entrepreneurship paradigm investigate a nonentrepreneurial group, it is often in comparison to one that is deemed to be highly entrepreneurial, to highlight the latter group's marked entrepreneurial participation and success (see Lee 2002; Light 1972; Portes and Bach 1985; Portes and Rumbaut 2006; Waldinger et al. 1990). In this type of comparative research design, the determinants of entrepreneurship identified by the "modes of incorporation" framework, namely, individual skills and resources, a supportive co-ethnic community, and structural opportunity, are assessed for each ethnic group to explain their observed high or low participation rates. These studies generally conclude that the ethnic group with high rates possesses those essential characteristics and features that facilitate business ownership, while the ethnic group with low rates does not; the nonentrepreneurial group is thus characterized as working-class, or relegated to low-wage work in the secondary sector of the labor market (Portes and Bach 1985). Notably, those members of nonentrepreneurial ethnic groups that do engage in entrepreneurial activity are overlooked in this analytic strategy, rarely if ever studied *as* ethnic entrepreneurs. This common practice of dismissing the entrepreneurial activity of nonentrepreneurial ethnic group members ultimately limits our understanding of ethnic enterprise and confines our discussion and conception of ethnic entrepreneurs to those groups with markedly high rates of participation and economic success only.

In those rare instances where nonentrepreneurial ethnic groups are investigated independently—and there is a growing research interest in this area—researchers may sometimes refer to them as "ethnic entrepreneurs," in keeping with the terminology of the ethnic entrepreneurship paradigm. Nevertheless, most of these studies concede that the group in question is not entrepreneurial in the traditional sense, that is, as an ethnic group with an above-average rate of business ownership associated with economic mobility. Mexican immigrant day laborers, gardeners, and *domésticas*, for example, are often characterized as survival-strategy entrepreneurs whose economic activity is understood as a hybrid form of self-employment. Their entrepreneurial activity is described as highly self-exploitative, glorified wage work that is performed by formerly unemployed or underemployed low-skilled wage workers (Light 2002; Marger 1990; Portes and Bach 1985; Ramirez and Hondagneu-Sotelo 2009; Valenzuela 2003).

The tendency to examine entrepreneurial ethnic groups in comparative perspective using a bifurcating framework that separates ethnic groups by participation rates or that accepts the premise that entrepreneurs affiliated with nonentrepreneurial groups are not entrepreneurial, per se, but instead are engaged in an activity that is entrepreneurial-like-but-not-quite, limits a comprehensive understanding of American enterprise. Important questions are left unanswered, such as, What, if anything, do entrepreneurs that are members of nonentrepreneurial groups share with those who are affiliated with entrepreneurially oriented groups? How do entrepreneurs in nonentrepreneurial groups engage in and perform this activity in the presumed absence of the traditional determinants that entrepreneurial ethnic groups require? Are there unidentified characteristics that facilitate entrepreneurship among non-entrepreneurially oriented groups, in particular?

### The Failure to Account for or Confront the Intersection of Race, Class, and Gender

The monolithic focus on and primacy of ethnicity forwarded by the ethnic entrepreneurship paradigm contributes to the neglect or conflation, or both, of ethnicity with other social group formations, such as class, and rejects the possibility that other *nonethnic* groups, distinct from ethnicity, such as those rooted in gender or race, might also influence the entrepreneurial outcomes of affiliated members in significant and unique ways. For example, the ethnic entrepreneurship paradigm is careful in its consideration of the entrepreneurial activity that is performed by racial groups, such as Blacks. Although this perspective does not dismiss the possibility of racial group entrepreneurship from consideration altogether, it does not readily embrace race as an organizing principle for this economic activity either. While Black entrepreneurs, like Mexicans, may be included in comparative studies of ethnic entrepreneurship, they are also commonly regarded as the nonentrepreneurial case. The failure of the ethnic entrepreneurship approach to characterize Blacks as full-fledged entrepreneurs in their own right, however, is not due solely to their disproportionately low rates of participation, as in the case of Mexicans. It is instead related to the canon's emphasis on *ethnic* group membership at the expense or exclusion of all other possible group affiliations. Thus, when Black entrepreneurs are considered in the comparative framework, their racial group affiliation is generally de-emphasized, while their ethnic identity as African Americans is emphasized. To make the argument that Blacks constitute an ethnic group, proponents of this approach call attention to the 4.1 million African Americans that migrated from the South to the industrializing North between 1910 and 1930 in search of racial equality and increased labor market opportunities. They maintain that this African American migration parallels the migration experience of foreign-born immigrants, thus allowing for a comparison of entrepreneurship across these *ethnic* groups (see Waldinger et al. 1990).

The contemporary characterization of Black entrepreneurs as nonentrepreneurial African American ethnic group members, however, ignores the well-documented, fairly widespread, and long history of entrepreneurship among Blacks following Reconstruction and prior to the Great Migration (Boyd 1998; Butler 2005; Drake and Cayton 1962; Massey and Denton [1993] 1998). As early as 1900, Booker T. Washington founded the National Negro Business League, and a "Buy Black" political movement was well under way. Both were instrumental in growing Black-owned businesses to such a degree that they doubled from just under ten thousand businesses in 1900 to almost twenty thousand by 1910 (Levenstein 2004:1–3). John Sibley Butler (2005) takes issue with scholars of ethnic enterprise for neglecting this history of Black business ownership, stating, "In reality, some Afro Americans exhibited the same type of entrepreneurial spirit as other groups who immigrated to this country, but, in a curious kind of way, scholars have reacted [to Black enterprise] differently. When the Afro-American tradition has been recognized, it has been misinterpreted and scandalized" (Butler 2005:36). He argues further that many of the characteristics of Black business owners identified by scholars working in the area of Black racial entrepreneurship, notably in Booker T. Washington's *The Negro in Business* (1907), Henry M. Minton's *Early History of Negroes in Business in Philadelphia* (1901), and Abram L. Harris's *The Negro as Capitalist* (1936), are similar to those used to describe ethnic entrepreneurs, but this research has been largely ignored by scholars of ethnic enterprise.

Moreover, the attempt to reconceptualize a racial classification as an ethnic classification to somehow "equalize" the assessment of entrepreneurship across African Americans and other ethnic groups, fails to appreciate the unique historical and contemporary conditions of systemic racism and structural exclusion experienced by non-White racial groups in America. Although the "modes of incorporation" framework acknowledges that non-White groups may face a negative societal reception based on phenotype, it generally concludes that such discrimination tends to increase entrepreneurial activity, as a form of reactive solidarity. This is not the case, however, for African Americans, which leaves this group vulnerable to other interpretations, such as cultural racism, a component of color-blind racism (Bonilla-Silva 2006) that relies on cultural rather than structural factors to explain persistent racial disparities in socioeconomic outcomes.

Taken as a whole, the ethnic entrepreneurship paradigm consistently underscores the cultural basis of entrepreneurship by attributing this activity to certain primordial features presumably rooted in the home country or by characterizing specific ethnic groups as possessing certain attributes that encourage co-ethnic solidarity and facilitate enterprise. The emphasis on and primacy of ethnicity, however, overlook the extent to which other nonethnic group affiliations may affect business ownership, and effectively limit the study of American entrepreneurship to those predominately male and middle-class members of ethnic groups with high rates of business ownership that are commonly associated with economic mobility, such as Koreans, Chinese, and Cubans (see Light and Bonacich 1988; Portes and Bach 1985; Portes and Rumbaut 2006). As a consequence, ethnic or racial groups with below-average participation rates are easily dismissed from consideration or characterized as survival-strategy self-employed workers only (see Light 2002; Marger 1990; Ramirez and Hondagneu-Sotelo 2009). In a similar fashion, gender is largely overlooked in studies of ethnic entrepreneurship, or men and women are investigated separately. Little is known about the growing population of immigrant women entrepreneurs from Mexico, El Salvador, and Cuba, or why Latinas comprise the fastest-growing segment of ethnic entrepreneurs in the United States (Pearce 2005). Ultimately, the ethnic entrepreneurship approach lacks a systematic explanation for why and how ethnic group affiliations affect business ownership in a given reception context, constrains the study of American enterprise to a select group of successful ethnic entrepreneurs, and overlooks the extent to which nonethnic group affiliations such as those rooted in race, class, and gender affect entrepreneurial activity.

## Beyond Ethnic Entrepreneurship

The embedded market approach moves away from the traditional framework's emphasis on the centrality and primacy of ethnicity at the individual, group, and structural levels and the interaction of these effects. It begins with the premise that the relationship between group affiliation, ethnic or otherwise, and economic action originates in and is maintained and reproduced by the social structure in which it is embedded. In other words, it situates the role of group affiliation *within* the context of the American social structure.

The American social structure is comprised of three interlocking systems of power and oppression: capitalism, patriarchy, and White supremacy.[1] Each system is organized hierarchically along the categories of class, gender, and race or ethnicity, respectively (Collins 2000; Crenshaw 1991). Accordingly, the intersection of class, gender, race, and (not *only*) ethnicity conditions the hierarchical position of individuals and groups within the highly stratified American social structure. In this context, a given ethnic or racial group is not monolithic, as individual members are differently positioned within intersecting class, gender, racial, and ethnic hierarchies. Thus, the social location of a diverse group of individual members of a given group, such as Latinos/as from different class backgrounds, shapes an unequal starting position within this structural context (Browne and Misra 2003; Collins 2000).

Structure alone, however, does not dictate the life chances of Latinos/as, because agency rooted in and circumscribed by their individual and collective social locations may serve to offset structural inequality. That is, Latinos'/as' multiple dimensions of intersectionality provide the basis for the emergence of compensatory support, stemming from, for example, ethnic- or gender-based networks. Resources that stem from such reciprocal ties, such as co-ethnic lending or gender-based business information channels, may help to counteract a disadvantaged social location. In this way, the *integration of structure and agency* (Giddens 1973) conditions the entrepreneurial outcomes of Latinos/as in America.

## Capitalism, Patriarchy, and White Supremacy

Capitalism is an economic system characterized by the private ownership of property and capital, where goods and services are produced and sold on the free market for a profit that is determined by the law of supply and demand. The dynamics of capitalism produce inequality that is based on a class hierarchy of privilege and oppression. Classes are comprised of groups of individuals who share a similar relationship to capital and the free market. Positioned at the top of the class hierarchy are those who own property, such as capitalists or small-business owners, and those who possess marketable skills, education, and credentials, such as professionals and managers. Those members of the upper and middle classes garner greater socioeconomic rewards and status (for example, wealth, income, employment security), are better positioned as sellers or buyers within the market economy, and exert power and control over the subordinate classes, those smaller or self-employed business owners, wage earners, and unemployed and underemployed workers who lack property or possess limited skills. Such class positions are hierarchically situated within the American economy and society.

The advent of global capitalism ushered in a restructuring of the U.S. economy as corporations sought to maximize profits by moving the manufacturing sector and associated labor force overseas. Today, the structure of the American economy resembles an hourglass. At the top of the hourglass are high-tech, high-skilled businesses and jobs, where capitalists and wage workers in managerial and professional occupations enjoy greater income returns, business longevity, and job security. At the bottom of the hourglass, low- or no-skilled service jobs are plentiful and survival-strategy self-employment is on the rise, although these business owners earn substantially less than their middle- and upper-class counterparts. In the narrowing middle, blue-collar jobs in goods-producing industries are on the decline, forcing occupational segregation and constraining intergenerational mobility (Portes and Rumbaut 2001; Portes and Zhou 1993:82-85). Wage and wealth disparities are felt acutely in the hourglass economy, as inequality between the upper classes at the top and lower classes at the bottom persists and grows larger.

Although patriarchy predates capitalism, it works "in articulation" with it (Walby 1989:215). In a socially constructed patriarchal system of oppression and privilege, men are ascribed the primary authority and responsibility over family and community. As the principal owners of property and skills, men import the preexisting patriarchal hierarchy into the capitalist system "to maintain their power [by] segmenting the labor market [by gender] and playing workers off each other" (Hartmann 1976:138). Patriarchy justifies the maintenance and reproduction of men's power and control over women's labor in the domestic and public spheres, as observed in the devaluation of household work and the "persistent fact" of gender stratification and discrimination in occupations, promotions, and wage inequality in the American labor market (Browne and Misra 2003). Gender differences are also observed in small-business ownership and self-employment. Although women entrepreneurs, and Latinas in particular, constitute the fastest-growing segment of small-business owners (Pearce 2005), they continue to lag behind men in self-employment participation and economic returns due to lower levels of human capital, including managerial experience, and fewer networks from which to mobilize resources (Boden and Nucci 2000; Minniti and Nardone 2007:223). Ultimately, men's domination over women's work in the home and on the job ensures women's continuing subordination, oppression, and exploitation (Walby 1989), as well as their economic dependence on men (Hartmann 1976) and, among entrepreneurs, their lower rates of business ownership and economic mobility (Valdez 2006).

Similarly, White supremacy is a hegemonic, hierarchical system of racial stratification (Bonilla-Silva 2006; Feagin 2006; Omi and Winant 1994). White racial group members maintain the top position within the racial hierarchy, which guarantees their superiority, domination, and control over non-White groups. Historically, the emergence of White supremacy in America justified non-White racial exploitation and secured "red land and black labor," which contributed to and safeguarded the wealth of White Americans (Mills 2003:43). Scientific racism, or the racial project that asserts non-White genetic or biological inferiority, provided the "objective" criteria necessary to continue racial exploitation and inequality during the preindustrial and industrial eras (Wilson 1987). Following World War II and a changing economy, the meaning of race as fixed, primordial, and rooted in biology gave way to today's social constructivist approach, which emphasizes ethnicity and culture to explain differences between groups. The changing meaning of race set the stage for the 1960s civil rights movement, a political, legal, and social struggle for racial equality that sought to dismantle legal racism in America by targeting its racist and discriminatory laws and practices, including restrictive immigration policies, racial segregation in public places, and antimiscegenation laws (Omi and Winant 1994).

The 1960s sociohistorical moment of progressive race politics is reflected today in greater intergroup racial tolerance and equality than in the past. Nevertheless, the eruption of a neoconservative backlash in the 1980s (Omi and Winant 1994) saw the erosion of race equity programs (such as affirmative action) and the emergence of a new racial ideology, that of color-blind racism, which maintains that the contemporary United States is a racial democracy and, as a result, any and all observable racial group disparities or perceived racial group inequities are attributable to "anything but" racism (Bonilla-Silva 2006). This mainstream and hegemonic racial ideology ensures that White supremacy will persist as an independent, racially hierarchical system in the American social structure for at least the foreseeable future, thereby guaranteeing that the "actual social values and enduring politico-economic structures . . . continue to reflect the history of White domination" (Crenshaw 1988:1336; Mills 2003:36–37). Accordingly, Whites will continue to remain more likely to garner greater socioeconomic rewards than non-Whites in America (Bonilla-Silva 2006).

In sum, the American social structure is constituted by the interlocking systems of capitalism, patriarchy, and White supremacy. Each of these three systems requires the hierarchical ordering of unequal power relations along the dynamic classifications of class, gender, and race or ethnicity, respectively (Omi and Winant 1994). The interdependence of these systems poses a necessary challenge to the preexisting hierarchical ordering of each, requiring a new sorting that captures these intersecting power relations in a "matrix of domination," or the way in which intersecting oppressions are organized within the social structure (Collins 1997:18).

In this context, then, it is insufficient to conclude that the position of Latinos/as along one structural dimension (that is, ethnicity) can reasonably predict their socioeconomic opportunities and outcomes, because those who identify as such are likely to vary across other salient dimensions as well (for instance, class, gender). Regarding ethnic entrepreneurship, the suggestion that ethnicity (in terms of a specific group's aggregate human capital, resources and support, and "reception context") can explain Latino/a enterprise neglects a serious consideration of class, gender, and race, and how these intersecting and interdependent positions also affect Latinos'/as' entrepreneurial outcomes. In a similar fashion, Marxist scholars' emphasis on social class only, as defined by property ownership, skills, power and authority, is insufficient to predict the emergence, maintenance and reproduction of entrepreneurialism. Neither ethnicity nor class, in isolation, can fully account for the life chances of Latino/a entrepreneurs, because each represents one dimension only of the interlocking systems of capitalism, patriarchy, and White supremacy. A comprehensive and systematic explanation of Latino/a enterprise requires an understanding of how distinct yet intersecting dimensions of class, gender, race, and ethnicity combine to shape the position of Latinos/as within the unequal American social structure.

Furthermore, Latinos/as who recognize themselves and others as sharing a common intersectional position may comprise a social group based on that shared position. Group affiliation is not trivial in a highly stratified society, as it provides the basis for agency among members in the form of social capital: the capacity to mobilize resources based on group membership (Coleman 1988; Granovetter 1985; Portes and Sensenbrenner 1993). Accordingly, the embedded market approach maintains that the intersection of class, gender, race, and ethnicity shapes the unequal starting position *and* the compensatory social capital that Latinos/as bring to the market, which conditions their ability to engage and succeed in enterprise. It concludes that the integration of structure and agency conditions Latino/a enterprise in America.

## The Embedded Market

The modern American market economy is an instituted process, "embedded and enmeshed in institutions" that are economic and social and that reinforce its stability, structure, and functioning (Polanyi 1957:35–36). This economy is comprised of three forms of economic incorporation: *market exchange*, or the free exchange of goods and services coordinated by price; *reciprocity*, or long-term symmetrical social relationships that elicit trust and obligation; and *redistribution*, or the asymmetrical collection, allocation, and distribution of commodities by a central actor (that is, the state) (Polanyi 1957:35). As these three forms of economic integration typify the American economy, they also constitute social relations within the American social structure. Relationships based on market exchange are of primary importance in the market, as they represent the dominant form of economic integration. Relationships of reciprocity or redistribution coexist alongside relations of market exchange as secondary and subordinate forms that influence the market to a lesser extent than those of market exchange (Polanyi 1957:35–36). Each of these different relationships uniquely contributes to the process of economic incorporation.

The American market economy is embedded within the larger social structure, made up of three interlocking systems of oppression and privilege— capitalism, patriarchy, and White supremacy. The categories of stratification associated with each system, namely, class, gender, and race or ethnicity, intersect to shape the extent to which groups of individuals that are affiliated with each category may engage in relations of market exchange, reciprocity, and redistribution. In the embedded market, such relationships are crucial for economic action, as they circumscribe the overall *market capacity*, or the economic and social resources and support that a given group brings to the market (Giddens 1973). Thus, the intersection of class, gender, race, and ethnicity may facilitate or constrain the life chances of entrepreneurs within this context.

## Market Capacity: Market, Social, and Government Capital

Recognizing that the intersection of distinct and dynamic class, gender, racial, and ethnic classifications combine to determine the position of groups of individuals within an amalgamated matrix of domination, it is still possible to specify the resources and attributes that are generally or primarily associated with each dimension and that directly relate to and shape the forms of exchange (that is, market, reciprocal, redistributive) in which they engage. Although group formations are interdependent and socially constructed, and therefore fluid and contested, an empirical analysis of intersectionality must endeavor to distinguish between them.

Taking each in turn, classes roughly correspond to group differences in key economic indicators. These indicators include the ownership of property and wealth (that is, personal savings, assets, and investments) and human capital (that is, education and work experience). Classes, in turn, simultaneously reproduce these indicators as various forms of *market capital*, or resources that are related to class background. Distinct classes, then, access and use market capital differently, which facilitates or constrains their economic action. Differences in market capital are observed across classes in all aspects of entrepreneurial activity, from the sources of start-up capital used to the potential for economic success. Because market capital is used primarily in relations of market exchange, the dominant form of economic integration in the American economy, it is likely to have a direct and positive influence on entrepreneurial outcomes. Clearly, those would-be entrepreneurs who have access to substantial market capital are likely to be middle-class to begin with; as such, they are already well positioned to participate in the market economy *before* they attempt to start a business.[2]

To illustrate, a would-be Latino/a entrepreneur with access to market capital, such as substantial personal savings or the ability to apply for and receive a bank loan from a national bank, suggests a priori a strong market position. After all, market institutions lend money on the expectation that their investment will generate a profitable return.[3] Because such exchanges are limited to those with sufficient creditworthiness or collateral or to those who can compete openly in the market economy, Latinos/as with access to market capital are more likely to enjoy positive entrepreneurial outcomes. Moreover, the more market capital accumulated to invest in a business, the stronger and more profitable the business and the more powerful and privileged the would-be entrepreneur. The old adage "It takes money to make money" is not lost here.

While market capital is rooted in relations of market exchange, social capital is rooted in relations of reciprocity (Polanyi 1957). In the American economy, reciprocal relationships constitute a secondary form of economic exchange. Reciprocal relationships are based primarily on long-term symmetrical social relationships that develop from the recognition, identification, and investment in a collectivity, such as that rooted in race, ethnicity, or gender. Such relationships create the conditions for the emergence of group-based social capital, such as enforceable trust, reciprocal obligations, and information sharing (Portes and Sensenbrenner 1993). Social capital provides group members with access to economic and social resources. For example, researchers observe that ethnic-based social capital fosters the development of co-ethnic information networks, access to cheap and reliable co-ethnic labor, and the emergence of co-ethnic, semiformal lending organizations, such as the Chinese or Korean rotation credit associations (Light and Bonacich 1988; Portes and Rumbaut 2006; Waldinger et al. 1990). From the perspective of the embedded market, reciprocal relationships in America are not limited to ethnic group membership alone; gender and racial group affiliations and even family membership also provide the basis for long-term symmetrical social relationships that generate social capital.

Family-based social capital stemming from "collective interests and strong personal ties" (Sanders and Nee 1996:231) generates economic and noneconomic resources, such as unpaid family labor, financial capital, business information, intrafamily loans, and the intergenerational transmission of wealth (in other words, inheritance), all of which encourage entrepreneurship (Aldrich and Cliff 2003; Fairlie and Robb 2004; Valdez 2008b). The use of family-based social capital is well established among different ethnic and racial groups, such as White Americans, who are more likely to emphasize nuclear family cohesion (Bonacich 1975), and ethnic minorities, whose use of cohesive kinship networks and extended family ties are characteristic of their cultural traditions (Kim and Hurh 1985; Light et al. 1994; Yoon 1991).

Because group-based social capital is rooted in reciprocity (a secondary form of economic integration), it facilitates enterprise in the market economy to a lesser extent than market capital (which is based largely on the primary market exchange relationship). It is likely, however, that gender, racial, ethnic, or family-based social capital, or some combination of these, generates economic resources and social support that may compensate for market capital disadvantages associated with a weak class position, for example, among the lower or underclasses. Thus, group-based social capital becomes especially relevant in the context of market uncertainty or disadvantage, as it may augment or compensate for a lack of market capital. In this way, access to social capital may influence the life chances of affiliated individuals to advance the group as a whole (Granovetter 1985; Polanyi 1944, 1957; Swedberg and Granovetter 1992:60). From this perspective, entrepreneurial outcomes are positively influenced by whom you know, and who knows you.

Similarly, relationships of redistribution, as an accompanying form of exchange in the market economy, constitute another avenue of economic integration. Redistributive relationships arise from the state, which collects taxes and redistributes it to members of the polity. State-sponsored resources, or *government capital*, may advantage qualified polity members in the market economy. For example, guaranteed, government-backed lending programs provide government loans to targeted individuals and groups. Citizens, refugees, unemployed workers, women, and minorities are some of the groups that have benefited from subsidized business loans, tax relief for new business start-ups, entrepreneurial or occupational training, and low- or no-cost legal services, to name a few. Members of the polity who qualify for government capital will likely enjoy improved entrepreneurial opportunities, when compared to non-polity members who do not qualify for government aid (for example, unauthorized immigrants). The ability to access government capital is particularly salient for those polity members who have limited access to market or social capital, as it may provide the additional resources needed to augment or compensate for their shortage. In this way, "your government works for you" to improve polity members' entrepreneurial outcomes.

Overall, the separate contributions of market capital, social capital, and government capital combine to determine the sum total of resources and attributes, or *market capacity*, that entrepreneurs bring to market. Market capacity in synthesis, then, includes the distinct contribution of market capital, which includes skills, education, and work experience as well as tangible material goods related to class background; social capital, a more intangible resource that fosters group-based solidarity, trust, and reciprocal obligations (see Portes and Sensenbrenner 1993:1322); and finally, government capital, or access to resources based on polity membership, such as a government loan or subsidy. Ultimately, the market capacity of individuals and collectivities reflects the intersection of race, ethnicity, class, and gender within the highly stratified American social structure. As such, it represents the extent to which would-be entrepreneurs are embedded in the market economy and conditions their entrepreneurial outcomes.

## Conclusion

Starting with the premise that the American social structure is characterized by three interlocking systems of oppression, group affiliations rooted in class, gender, race, and ethnicity circumscribe the forms of exchange (market, reciprocal, redistributive) in which groups of individuals engage. The market exchange relationship is the dominant form of economic integration in a market economy, although relationships of reciprocity and redistribution coexist as secondary forms. Given that market exchange is the primary form, would-be entrepreneurs with access to market capital, typically those with a strong class position (for example, the middle class), are likely to succeed in enterprise. In contrast, reciprocal and redistributive relations of exchange are secondary forms of economic integration. Under conditions of market disadvantage, reciprocal or redistributive relationships may act as compensatory mechanisms that serve to augment entrepreneurial outcomes through the use of social and government capital, respectively (Polanyi 1944; Swedberg and Granovetter 1992). Entrepreneurs who rely on social or government capital may improve their chances in the market. Whether the accumulated social or government capital is sufficient to overcome market uncertainty, however, is related to their social location. While compensatory capital may offset disadvantage, its composition and influence are ultimately circumscribed by Latinos'/as' social location within the unequal American social structure.

# 3 Entrepreneurial Dreams in an Intersectional Context

WHAT DRIVES LATINO/A IMMIGRANTS to start their own businesses in America, and what do they expect to achieve? The ethnic entrepreneurship approach suggests that a combination of factors leads specific groups to engage in business ownership, from a cultural disposition toward enterprise to a negative societal reception context, such as "blocked mobility" in the labor market (Light 1972; Portes and Rumbaut 2001, 2006; Waldinger et al. 1990). While these characteristics and dynamics are successfully applied to Korean and Cuban immigrants to explain their entrepreneurial outcomes, they are less convincing in explaining a lack of entrepreneurship among nonentrepreneurial groups, such as Mexicans and Blacks. Yet, these groups are just as easily characterized as demonstrating a cultural proclivity toward enterprise or confronting discrimination in the American labor market that would conceivably push them into starting a business. After all, possessing an entrepreneurial orientation provides an apt description for Mexicans in Mexico, as almost a quarter of that population is self-employed. In the United States, however, only 6 percent of Mexican immigrants are formally self-employed (Fairlie and Woodruff 2006:1–2).[1] Likewise, John Sibley Butler (2005) demonstrates persuasively that Blacks engaged in entrepreneurship both prior to and following the Civil War. In fact, many of the same group-based resources and structural forces that were attributed to facilitating Black enterprise at the turn of the twentieth century—namely, racial residential and occupational segregation and discrimination—are associated with ethnic enterprise today. These factors are still present among Black communities; however, only 5 percent of this population is self-employed.

Furthermore, the ethnic entrepreneurship perspective maintains that business ownership is associated with economic mobility, a way of "making it" in America, of "striving for the American Dream" (Lee 2000; Portes and Rumbaut 2001). Korean entrepreneurs, for example, are characterized as "successful" because researchers observe their above-average rates of business ownership in profitable enterprises (Portes and Rumbaut 2006:23). On balance, ethnic entrepreneurs are generally thought to outperform their co-ethnic wage worker counterparts in earnings and socioeconomic mobility (Portes and Bach 1985).

Still, the economic impetus for business ownership, specifically, the presumed positive relationship between entrepreneurship and economic mobility, is not guaranteed. Previous research shows that some self-employed workers actually earn less and experience lower earnings growth than do similarly skilled workers who are employed in the general labor market (Hamilton 2000:628). In several studies of the earnings of self-employed immigrants, Borjas (1985, 1986, 1987, 1990) concludes that all things being equal, the earnings of self-employed immigrants are at best not markedly different from those of their wage worker counterparts. Mixed findings in the earnings of Korean entrepreneurs and more recent waves of Mariel Cubans[2] challenge the notion that ethnic entrepreneurship is associated with economic mobility (Bates 1997; Portes and Jensen 1989). For example, Light and Bonacich (1988:278) report that some Korean entrepreneurs and their unpaid family members are concentrated in low-skilled, low-wage industries, average eighty hours per work week, and suffer from physical and mental exhaustion. More recently, I have shown that entrepreneurship among nonentrepreneurial Blacks and Mexicans is sometimes but not always associated with economic progress and may actually lower earnings (Valdez 2006, 2008b). Taken as a whole, this research calls into question the presumed relationship between entrepreneurship and economic mobility (Bates 1997; Valdez 2008b).

Notably, the majority of studies regarding "ethnic entrepreneurs," "ethnic enclave economies," or "ethnic entrepreneurship" focus on those (predominately male and middle-class members of) ethnic minority groups with high rates of business ownership that are commonly associated with economic mobility, such as Koreans, Chinese, and Cubans (Light and Bonacich 1988; Portes and Bach 1985; Portes and Rumbaut 2006). Generally, when nonentrepreneurial groups, such as Mexicans and Blacks, are examined they are rarely characterized as ethnic entrepreneurs who are making it in America. Entrepreneurship among these groups is instead thought to be a survival-strategy or hybrid form of self-employment that is performed by formerly unemployed or under-employed low-skilled wage workers only (Light and Roach 1996; Ramirez and Hondagneu-Sotelo 2009; Valenzuela 2003).

The embedded market approach offers an alternative to the either/or classification of ethnic groups as successful entrepreneurs on the one hand and struggling-for-survival self-employed workers on the other. Instead this approach maintains that entrepreneurial outcomes rest on the intersectional position of groups of individuals within the unequal social structure in which they are embedded. To begin to demonstrate how intersectionality shapes entrepreneurship, this chapter investigates the case of Latino/a entrepreneurs; specifically, it explores the reasons why Latinos/as from different class, gender, racial, and ethnic backgrounds engage in business ownership in the first place. An examination of Latinos'/as' motivations for and expectations of business ownership—what they hope to gain or achieve—and the extent to which they differ from one another, as well as from White and Black entrepreneurs, helps to expose patterns of entry that are rooted their social location. It also reveals their belief in and attempt to improve their unequal position within the American economy through enterprise, and demonstrates how the interdependence of agency and structure influences their decision to pursue enterprise and their capacity to improve their socio-economic conditions.

Not surprisingly, most Latinos/as, regardless of their social location, engage in entrepreneurial activity to make more money, in keeping with the predictions of the ethnic entrepreneurship approach. The additional, careful consideration of class, gender, and race, however, uncovers differences in Latinos'/as' economic and noneconomic, or social, motivations, which vary along these multiple dimensions and which include (1) the desire for autonomy, which ranks as high as economic mobility as the main reason for deciding to go into business, and (2) job satisfaction in enterprise or job dissatisfaction in previous employment. Typically, aspects of job satisfaction or dissatisfaction accompany either economic mobility or autonomy, or both, as a secondary reason for business ownership.

Additionally, there are some racial group similarities as well as distinct differences in Latino/a, White, and Black entrepreneurial motivations and expectations. For example, all business owners, regardless of race, indicate that a family history of business ownership, or "entrepreneurial capital" (Aldrich, Renzulli, and Langton 1998), is important in fostering their own entrepreneurial endeavors. White entrepreneurs, however, are more likely to take over an existing family business by inheriting it from the previous generation. Moreover, and unlike the majority of entrepreneurs, heirs to the family restaurant do not generally express a strong desire to own a business. Instead they are more likely to claim that they "just fell into" it. Importantly, White entrepreneurs are disproportionately middle-class and male when compared to their Latino/a and Black counterparts and, in contrast to Latino/a immigrants, are likely to have lived in the United States for multiple generations. Their stronger intersectional position thus increases Whites' opportunity to inherit the family business when compared to Latinos/as and Blacks, even as they reveal ambivalence toward ownership.

Black business owners, in contrast, express a greater desire for autonomy and job satisfaction (in enterprise) than White or Latino/a entrepreneurs. For them, being independent and achieving nonpecuniary goals, such as giving back to the community, trump economic factors. While these observations suggest that Black business owners are truly entrepreneurial in the classical sense of risk-taking, autonomous innovators, this conclusion neglects a consideration of their disadvantaged social location within the larger American social structure. When the structural context is considered, the entrepreneurial spirit that characterizes Black entrepreneurs also reveals the devastating impact of systemic racism in America's social and economic institutions, which pushes more Blacks toward being their own bosses, regardless or perhaps in spite of the prospect for financial gain or loss.

## Entrepreneurship as a Strategy of Economic Mobility and Autonomy

Although Latino/a entrepreneurs from diverse backgrounds offer a variety of reasons for starting their businesses, the two main reasons given are to earn more money and to achieve autonomy, regardless of class, gender, race, or ethnicity. These primary motivations are supported by previous research (Blanchflower 2004; Butler and Greene 1997; Douglas and Shepherd 2000, 2002; Hamilton 2000). For example, Douglas and Shepherd (2000) find that individuals decide to become entrepreneurs if they believe they can increase their earnings or gain greater independence than through wage work. Moreover, Georgellis, Sessions, and Tsitsianis (2007) conclude that these key determinants predict not only entry, but whether business owners stay in business over the long term.

The common themes of earning more money and being one's own boss are often expressed in tandem by Latino/a entrepreneurs. Señor Valenzuela is a middle-class, sixty-one-year-old, first-generation immigrant. After questioning his job prospects in Mexico, he migrated in 1973 just one semester short of earning an engineering degree. He found work as a manager in a Mexican restaurant, where he worked for more than twenty years before opening his own. Today, he owns two full-service restaurants in Greater Houston. His wife works full-time in the restaurant as the corporate secretary in charge of bookkeeping. The restaurant where the interview took place, Rancho Chile, was the first restaurant he opened. Rancho Chile is a large, Spanish-style beige and green restaurant with a terra-cotta roof and an ample parking lot. The restaurant is located just off of the freeway and is close to several large businesses, which include a beer factory and a large national bank. On the day of the interview, the employees from those businesses appeared to make up the majority of the diverse lunch crowd at Rancho Chile.

Señor Valenzuela enjoyed working as a manager. It wasn't until he had children that he decided to strike out on his own.

> *Why did you decide to start a business?*
> Seeking independence and a good future for my children. The first fifteen or sixteen years [in the United States] I had no interest in a business. I just worked. But as time went by, I decided to open up a restaurant. When my family came, I became interested in it.

Likewise, Nando Perez, a thirty-six-year-old naturalized citizen and high school graduate, wanted to be his own boss to make more money than he did as an employee in the low-wage labor market:

> If you work for yourself you make more money, and if you work for someone else you just do your job and you go home. If someone offered me to work for any other people instead [of myself], I wouldn't do it because I know I can still run my business and make more than what they offer me.

In Nando's case, although he went into business to "make more money," he also stated that he "always wanted to work for [himself]." He further added, "I've worked for other people; they never appreciate your work. Sometimes they just have bad days, and . . . when they work they throw everything on you." Today, Nando owns two *taquerías*, one in Little Latin America and one in Greater Houston. Señor Valenzuela and Nando represent the vast majority of Latino/a entrepreneurs that turn to business ownership to improve their economic conditions by making more money, living a little better, and improving their children's economic future. They also express the common desire to be their own boss. This latter sentiment is generally expressed alongside the need to improve one's economic conditions, but not always.

For Señora Abrego, a fifty-year-old Salvadoran naturalized citizen with a grade school education, economic concerns were never mentioned; being her own boss was the sole driving force behind her business:

> It's not the same thing to go work elsewhere [and] having your business. One is better for money [working elsewhere] and the other is better because nobody tells you what to do [owning a business]. . . . What made me open this [business] up was that I wanted to work for myself. I didn't want anyone else bossing me around, or punching a time card, or coming in and out at certain times. With this type of business, it's slave work, but here I still can come and go as I please.

Although Nando expressed a desire to make more money and Señora Abrego did not, in both cases the quest for independence or freedom is juxtaposed with negative statements regarding wage work. For others, such as Señor Valenzuela, being their own boss is more about the benefits of business ownership than the detriments of wage work, which he enjoyed. Thus, economic mobility and autonomy appear to provide the initial incentives to pursue business ownership; however, these distinct goals are often combined with aspects of *job dissatisfaction* in previous employment or the potential for *job satisfaction* that former wage workers will presumably enjoy as entrepreneurs. Notably it is these secondary factors that vary by entrepreneurs' intersectional social location.

## Worker Dissatisfaction and Owner Satisfaction

Largely relegated to lower-class immigrant men and women, dirty, dangerous, or difficult jobs in the U.S. labor market include low-wage, low-skilled jobs such as bricklayer, roofer, doméstica, janitor, and car washer. These gender-specific, low-skilled jobs are disproportionately performed by lower-class Latinos/as, especially those of Mexican origin (Douglas and Saenz 2008; Hondagneu-Sotelo 1994; Smith and Winders 2008; Valenzuela 2003). Many Mexican men and women restaurateurs from disadvantaged-class backgrounds were previously employed in such occupations. They shared the belief that becoming a business owner would improve their working conditions and lead to a better life. So, in addition to making more money or being their own boss, job dissatisfaction in previous employment provides a significant and additional incentive for disadvantaged Mexican immigrants to pursue business ownership.

As an undocumented, Spanish-speaking Mexican immigrant with a grade school education, Don José, then twenty-five (now sixty-six), was relegated to work in the low-skilled, low-wage construction industry for decades. He started his restaurant, Café Taco, located in Little Mexico, in 1977. From the street, the small, flat-roofed, one-story building has the look and feel of a liquor store positioned on the corner of a dilapidated strip mall. Its doors and windows have white, wrought-iron bars for security. The exterior and interior walls are covered in Mexican murals in brightly painted colors to disguise and discourage graffiti. Like most entrepreneurs, Don José went into business to improve his economic condition. He also wanted to escape his physically demanding job:

> I started to see that all the restaurant owners [in Little Mexico] were doing well. Then the work [as a roofer] started getting harder for me. . . . I would see my friends that had businesses were living better than I was. . . . They didn't work like a donkey up on the roofs like I did and they made more money.

Similarly, Doña Toña, a fifty-three-year-old Mexican immigrant from Michoacán with a fourth-grade education, left her job as a janitor at Exxon—which she held for over a decade—to open a Mexican restaurant. She went into business for herself to "live better," by earning more money and getting away from the harsh chemicals at work:

> I used to kill myself working. . . . I was getting really affected by the chemicals that we used . . . cutting my hands with the chemicals to clean. I was getting sick a lot. I was always really tired too.

The adverse physical working conditions associated with dirty, dangerous, or difficult jobs provide the additional incentive for many like José and Toña to seek an alternative livelihood through enterprise. For others, experiences with verbal abuse, anti-immigrant sentiment, or racial or ethnic discrimination at the hands of their employers or customers facilitate their entry. Because Mexican immigrants in America are disproportionately unauthorized, poor, and uneducated when compared to other immigrant minority groups, they are especially likely to experience a negative societal reception context (Portes and Rumbaut 2001) that racializes dirty, dangerous, or difficult work as "Mexican" or "immigrant" work (Douglas and Saenz 2008).

Francisco Pinto is a fifty-eight-year-old, "1.5-generation"[3] Mexican immigrant who grew up in Central Texas and Utah. He went to college in Texas, where he earned a bachelor's degree in geography. To pay the bills while in school, Don Francisco worked as a janitor. After graduating, he landed a job with Texas parks and recreation. In the three months before he started his new job, he moved home to help his parents run their Mexican restaurant, Cocina Pinto, in Little Mexico. That was thirty years ago. Today, he owns the business and runs it with his wife, a first-generation Vietnamese immigrant. He spoke at length of the poor working conditions and racial discrimination he faced in his previous employment:

> They would put all the *mexicanos* in the janitor crew to clean the elementary schools, which were horrible! They'd have parties . . . popcorn [everywhere]. We cleaned the bathrooms. . . . Man, kids would pee on the walls. . . . It'd take you hours to clean one room. And [the management company] only put *mexicanos* there. . . . That school didn't have the minimum wage. That's why all the *mexicanos* were put cleaning the schools. And my Anglo friends would all get the Ford dealership; they'd go clean the telephone company and that kinda job.

Francisco's perception of discrimination was born out about a year later when a successful discrimination lawsuit was brought by the ACLU against the company he worked for. (He and the other Latino/a workers were each awarded $1,500.)

In contrast to disadvantaged Mexican-origin restaurateurs, middle-class Latinos/as rarely mentioned dissatisfaction in previous employment as a reason for starting a business. For these more privileged Latinos/as, the potential for *job satisfaction* through enterprise provided the initial impetus (rather than an escape from *job dissatisfaction*). Rob, the thirty-seven-year-old middle-class entrepreneur introduced at the beginning of this book, highlighted only the positive aspects of business ownership as motivating his entry:

> As a chef [in someone else's restaurant] I found out that I really enjoy that work environment. I had good luck and good people skills, so I was a good manager, and I always got compliments on the way I greeted people. . . . As

soon as I found out I was doing a good job for other people, I said, you know what, if it works for other people it will work for me.

In addition to her desire to achieve autonomy in the workplace, Rita, a forty-seven-year-old middle-class naturalized citizen, spoke of entrepreneurship as a way to challenge herself, to prove that she could achieve her goals:

> To be honest I never though of working for somebody else. . . . I wanted to do this. I don't know how to word it, the will of wanting to . . . *como los ganas.* . . . See, what I'm saying, it's just a, wanting to *do something*, maybe for yourself. I did it for me, really.

Rob's and Rita's reasons for starting a business represent an aspect of entrepreneurship that is absent among lower-class Latinos/as. Specifically, middle-class privilege allows some Latinos/as to perceive enterprise as an opportunity for job satisfaction, rather than an alternative to job dissatisfaction. The focus on the positive aspects of entrepreneurship among middle-class Latinos/as and the focus on the negative aspects of the job left behind among lower-class Mexican immigrants capture two sides of the same coin that differ across ethnic, racial, and class position. Along with these multiple dimensions of intersectionality, gender also plays a distinct role in business entry, especially in business ownership through entrepreneurial succession.

## Entrepreneurial Succession

Just under half of the Latino/a entrepreneurs in this study report a family history of business ownership, and of that half the majority are middle-class and male. This disproportionate distribution is in keeping with previous studies that suggest a propensity for enterprise among the children of business owners, especially among men (Dunn and Holtz-Eakin 1996; Fairlie and Robb 2004; Lentz and Laband 1990, 1993), and in reproducing middle-class entrepreneurialism (Goldthorpe et al. 1969; Western and Wright 1994). Children of entrepreneurs may inherit the family business; however, most family enterprises do not outlast the initial generation (Stavrou 1999:43). My sample of immigrant entrepreneurs includes only one 1.5-generation Mexican male, Francisco Pinto, who took over his family's business. Although many Latino/a restaurateurs expressed a desire for their offspring to do so, the majority of business owners were pessimistic about the possibility of their children taking over the family business one day, especially because many of the children characterized their parents' work as "slavery," "too much work," "working for peanuts," and the like.

Despite the empirical evidence that suggests that businesses are seldom passed on to the next generation, Aldrich, Renzulli, and Langton (1998:291) argue that the presence of a family-owned business alone constitutes entrepreneurial capital, which increases the likelihood of an entrepreneurial occupational inheritance or succession from one generation to the next, whether members of the younger generation take over a family business or start one of their own. Through a process of socialization, children of entrepreneurs may come to recognize "self-employment as a career" and "see self-employment as a realistic alternative to conventional employment" (Carroll and Mosakowski 1987:576, quoted in Aldrich, Renzulli, and Langton 1998:295).

Accordingly, I find that Latino/a entrepreneurs with a family history of business ownership reveal a confidence in pursuing entrepreneurship as an alternative to wage work that is unique when compared to their peers without such experience. Rob, the thirty-seven-year-old economically successful entrepreneur mentioned earlier, dreamed of being a restaurateur at the age of nine, after spending his summer vacation working in his grandparents' restaurant back in El Salvador. As an adult in the United States he worked as a chef for someone else before pursuing entrepreneurship, although he never wavered from his childhood goal, nor did he question his ability to achieve that goal. Similarly, Martín, a middle-class naturalized citizen from El Salvador with a family history of enterprise, did not turn to entrepreneurship initially. Nevertheless, after getting laid off and searching for work for one year, Martín viewed business ownership as his logical next step:

> I started [my business] out of necessity. I have a lot of experience in the medical supply industry. But the company moved to Florida and I got laid off. I looked for work for a year [in this same industry] and couldn't find any work. . . . My family has always been in the food industry. My family has owned Salvadoran restaurants . . . and meat markets. I've always dreamed of owning a business. So I found a partner and opened my first restaurant.

Rob and Martín lend evidence to the concept of entrepreneurial succession. While they did not take over their families' businesses but instead started their own, the knowledge and familiarity gleaned from that family history left them confident that they too could succeed in enterprise.

Notably, and against the traditional and widespread view that would-be entrepreneurs are risk takers, those Latinos/as with a history of family business ownership express a familiarity and security with enterprise. Entrepreneurship is not generally perceived as risky or insecure; instead, children of entrepreneurs regard it as easy, natural, and comfortable. As Miguel, a forty-seven-year-old middle-class Mexican naturalized citizen explains:

> I don't know any other way different. My family, my parents, they were self-employed. They owned restaurants in Mexico. It was natural. . . . It's not genetic, exactly, but it's inherited . . . cultural.

Miguel characterizes his entrepreneurial activity as "natural" and "cultural," in keeping with the assumptions of the ethnic entrepreneurship approach that often ascribe an "entrepreneurial orientation" or "inclination" to specific foreign-born groups, such as Koreans, Chinese, and Cubans (Portes and Zhou 1992). Yet, the intergenerational transmission of entrepreneurial activity, or entrepreneurial capital, was not observed equally among all Latinos/as with a family history of enterprise. The vast majority of Latino/a entrepreneurs who benefited from entrepreneurial capital were middle-class men, like Rob, Martín, and Miguel.

Although a small minority of Latinas are middle-class, they, along with lower-class men and women, sometimes acknowledged a history of family-owned business. For these disadvantaged groups, however, entrepreneurial capital did not translate into business ownership to the same degree or in the same way that it did for middle-class Latinos. Rather, it appears that the intersection of class and gender disproportionately hinders Latinas' ability to start and maintain businesses by limiting their use of entrepreneurial capital, a resource that is accessed almost exclusively by middle-class men.

To illustrate, Doña María and Señora León are lower-class Mexican immigrant women entrepreneurs with a family history of enterprise. Like middle-class men, Doña María spoke of a familiarity with business ownership rooted in her family history:

> My mom had a business [in Mexico]. She used to sell food for cows, oil, everything that you sell on a ranch. We would also kill chickens and we would sell them; I would go on the streets and sell them. My husband's family also had businesses. . . . His mom and brothers have little restaurants and sell fruit.

Similarly, Señora León ascribed her entrepreneurial activity to her family history:

> I came from people, like my mom, who had businesses.... You carry that with you from a young age. When I was a child I saw her and her clothes shop; it is something that you have since that time; you carry that with you throughout life.

María's entrepreneurial capital stems from her experience in helping her mother run an informal business out of her home and watching her grandparents, on her father's side, run more formal establishments. Señora León's entrepreneurial capital consists of her mother's small, formal retail clothing business. For María and Señora León, their entrepreneurial capital appears to facilitate their own entrepreneurial pursuits, and closely mirrors that of middle-class men.

A closer examination of each Latina's process of entrepreneurial succession, however, reveals a pathway to ownership that is not in keeping with that of their middle-class male counterparts and that is unavailable to most lower-class Latinos/as. In particular, María's restaurant was established for her by her husband with help from his ethnic and male networks, whereas Señora León took over her *husband's* family restaurant, which she claimed was the "easiest [work] I could get." So although María and Señora León reveal their family history in enterprise, much like their Latino middle-class counterparts, their actual entrepreneurial succession was realized through their husbands' resources, networks, and support. These findings suggest that "entrepreneurial capital" is not sufficient to foster entrepreneurialism, as class or gender disadvantages may hinder entrepreneurial succession among lower-class Latinos/as with a history of business enterprise. Overall, a history of family enterprise facilitates entrepreneurship among middle-class men, with rare instances of occupational inheritance among middle-class women and the lower classes. Generally, however, disadvantages rooted in class or gender, or both, constrain opportunities for entrepreneurial succession.

Overall, the pecuniary and nonpecuniary motivations for Latino/a enterprise include economic mobility, autonomy, job dissatisfaction in previous employment, perceived job satisfaction in enterprise, and entrepreneurial succession. Economic mobility and autonomy comprise the primary motivations for enterprise among Latinos/as regardless of class or gender. Secondary motivations include job dissatisfaction, which is more prevalent among lower-class Mexican immigrants, and job satisfaction in enterprise, a common motivator among middle-class Latinos/as. Finally, although Latinos/as from diverse backgrounds may report a family history of enterprise, middle-class men are more likely to translate their entrepreneurial capital into business ownership. Taken together, findings suggest that there are similarities in Latinos'/as' primary motivations for and expectations of business ownership associated with economic progress and autonomy, and differences by class and gender in the secondary motivations and expectations of business ownership related to job satisfaction and dissatisfaction. Whereas the similarities align with the common sense notion of American enterprise as an avenue of upward mobility and autonomy, distinct patterns emerge by class and gender, patterns associated with their hierarchical positioning within the stratified social structure.

## Racial Group Differences in Becoming an Entrepreneur

Like Latinos/as, White and Black entrepreneurs are sometimes, but not always, motivated by the prospect of making more money or the potential for independence. Moreover, they sometimes share an expectation of job satisfaction as a business owner, as well as the desire to escape undesirable working conditions associated with wage work. There are, however, some racial group differences in the reasons behind owning a business that correspond to social location. In particular, White business owners are disproportionately male and middle-class; thus, their reasons for starting a business emphasize job satisfaction or other positive motivations associated with their more privileged social location, such as inheriting the family business.

As Oliver and Shapiro (2006) and others have shown (Conley 1999; Feagin 1999), acquiring wealth, such as inheriting a business or property, does not rest simply on individual characteristics or class advantage, such as individual or aggregate human capital attainment. Racial differences in wealth creation and its reproduction are rooted in an unequal American social structure that is organized hierarchically along racial and ethnic classifications. In this context, a history of state policies that enforce racial segregation and destabilize Black communities and other communities of color, along with a legacy of personal and institutional racism and discrimination, have, over time, "cemented" minority groups "to the bottom of society's economic hierarchy" (2006:5). The disenfranchisement of the Black community has negatively affected Blacks' entrepreneurial activity in the extreme and "at every stage of business development" (Fairlie and Robb 2008:2018). Gender also plays a role in conditioning inequality. In the United States, men acquire more wealth and property through inheritance than women (Conley and Ryvicker 2005; Warren, Rowlingson, and Whyley 2001). Taken together, racial, ethnic, and gender disparities in wealth and inheritance set the stage for the unequal distribution of inheritance, as White middle-class men surpass the rate of inheritance among White women, Blacks, and Latinos/as.

White middle-class men possess more entrepreneurial capital and benefit from entrepreneurial succession to a greater extent than White women, Latinos/as, or Blacks; they are also more likely to inherit the family restaurant. Fully four out of the ten Whites interviewed for this study inherited their restaurants, and all were middle-class men. For these four heirs, most if not all of their work history and experience consist solely of working in their parents' restaurants. Because they were the primary beneficiaries of entrepreneurial capital and succession, their expectations of entrepreneurship were generally positive. Yet, their motivations differ from those of the majority of Latinos/as and Blacks. In particular, White middle-class men that inherit a family business often express the strong desire for freedom or economic mobility through enterprise that is similar to non-Whites' motivations; yet, at times, they characterize business ownership as something they just "fell into."

Tony Frank is a fifty-one-year-old White middle-class business owner who inherited his parents' burger joint in Houston Heights. The brightly painted, sit-down eatery is located on the corner of a busy business district, sandwiched between two bustling, four-lane streets. It has a small parking lot that is shared with a barbeque shack next door. These twin family-owned restaurants seem to reinforce or validate each other's presence, even as they look entirely out of place. They are the last standing old-school eateries on the block, dwarfed by larger and more modern corporate and franchise operations nearby, including a Toyota car dealership, a McDonald's, and a Blockbuster. Inside Lonestar Burger, four booths line one side of a wall; the counter and kitchen area are on the opposite side. Ten tables or so fill the open seating area in the center of the restaurant. The ambience is friendly, and there is usually music playing—unexpectedly, not country and western but old standards such as Frank Sinatra's "The Best Is Yet to Come."

When asked why he went into business for himself, Tony replied that he "always knew" that he was going to take over the family business one day. It was either that or he would have to go out and find a job. When his mother died suddenly, he had to make a quick decision:

Well, I started here when I was in high school, so my dad owned it, and [when] he died in eighty-six, my mom became the owner. So, I worked for my dad and my mom. She died in ninety-nine, and that's when I became the owner, if that makes sense. That goes back to when I was seventeen. . . . I didn't really just one day say, "Hey I want to be the owner"; I didn't think, "I want this to be my career." Well—well, after my mom died, that's how it happened, basically . . . basically it was this or go look for a job. I just figured, you know, being the owner of a business would be better than going out there and looking for something. This is all I've known since high school.

Tony apologized after his interview for not having "anything special" to say, or a "long story" about how he came to be a business owner. He seemed to think that his experience of "falling into it" was boring or unusual in its banality, and not at all what I was after. Of course, the frequency and ease with which Tony and other White, middle-class, and male entrepreneurs acquire their lucrative businesses through inheritance is remarkable when compared to the almost negligible opportunities for Latinos/as, Blacks, and White women to inherit similar, financially-rewarding establishments. Among the minorities sampled, only one (lower) middle-class Black man and two Latinos/as— a middle-class man and a married, lower-class couple—inherited the family restaurant.

For Francisco Pinto, the fifty-eight-year-old Mexican immigrant introduced earlier in this chapter, the decision to take over his parents' business was similar to that of Mr. Frank and other White middle-class entrepreneurs—an opportunity arose and he "stepped into it." After graduating from college with a degree in earth science, Francisco had a three-month window before starting a job as a forest ranger. He went to Houston to help out his parents before taking that job, but he never left.

*Why did you decide to go into business for yourself?*
I kinda just stepped into it. My [degree] was in earth science so I got a job as a forest ranger. I was going to work in Mammoth Cave, Kentucky. . . . Well, they [the Department of the Interior] gave me a pamphlet about this big [arms outstretched, laughing]. [It had a list of rules for the job, including:] "No facial hair" (I had a beard at the time you know), no this and no that; you gotta do this and not that [laughing]. Plus the pay wasn't really good. . . . When it was time to go . . . I figured, "I'll spend the summer with my parents here and see how it all works out," and I just stayed here.

Unlike the majority of White, middle-class male heirs, Francisco held down various jobs, earned a college degree, and even landed a job in his chosen career. Still, after working in the restaurant for three months he became enamored with the neighborhood and appreciated the lack of "corporate stress." After his mother died three and a half years ago (his father had died fifteen years before), he simply took over the business. Since then he's done some minor repairs and made a few changes but has vowed never to change his mom's recipes—"We won't change 'em for nothing!"

For Joseph Robinson, a forty-nine-year-old, self-identified African American[4] business owner, the decision to take over the family business had more to do with keeping "the family legacy alive" than anything else. As a full-time firefighter who loved his job, Joseph was not looking for a change. He felt compelled to take over the family business, Southern Soul, a soul food restaurant now in its third generation, because he believes that few African Americans are willing to take such opportunities when and if they arise, and fewer African Americans have that chance. He has managed to keep his job as a firefighter while he runs the restaurant, and he is hopeful that his two boys will take over the business one day (he was explicit about his sons; he did not mention the possibility of his daughter taking over the restaurant). Although Francisco and Joseph represent minority heirs that "fell into" business in much the same way that White middle-class heirs did, they were the only minority entrepreneurs interviewed to do so. Moreover, they both accumulated substantial work experience prior to taking over their family businesses, earned college degrees, landed jobs they trained in, and needed additional financial support in the process. In contrast, the majority of White middle-class heirs took over their profitable family businesses seamlessly, often without additional work experience, education beyond high school, or monetary aid.

A distinctive racial difference in entrepreneurial motivations was also observed among Black entrepreneurs. In particular, Black business owners were more likely to emphasize noneconomic reasons for starting their businesses when compared to Latinos/as and Whites. This group of entrepreneurs often expressed a deep desire to improve or build up the Black community, and emphasized the need for autonomy in their work lives. Mrs. Louise Brown, a thirty-four-year-old Black woman with a bachelor's degree in psychology, was one of many Black entrepreneurs who emphasized a social justice aspect of enterprise. Mrs. Brown has lived in the South Ward for her entire life. This geographically concentrated community is poor (26 percent of households fall below the poverty line) and overwhelmingly Black (80 percent). Businesses that are located in the South Ward are few and far between and often sprinkled around residential areas. Besides a liquor store across the street, Mrs. Brown's restaurant is one of two businesses located in a run-down strip mall (the other is a salon specializing in hair extensions and beauty supplies). This oasis of three businesses is flanked by houses, apartment buildings, and a number of abandoned residential and commercial buildings. With the help of her husband, Mrs. Brown opened the fledgling restaurant four months ago, primarily to "make a change in our community":

> We see that here [in the South Ward] there are not really any nice restaurants in the area . . . and we also want to partner with some colleges. . . . We're going to start incorporating days where the community can come in and learn about educational opportunities, like going back to school and furthering their education to help improve the community.

Related to community building and investment, Stacey Holmes, a thirty-five-year-old self-identified Black woman, sees herself as a role model. She has owned Stacey's Soul Food Kitchen in the South Ward since 2007. The restaurant is located off the main street, but there is precious little pedestrian or car traffic in the area. The building, a white, brick, and wood duplex with peeling paint, a black wrought-iron security door, and a red hand-painted sign hanging over the front door, shares the building with a Black-owned barbershop. On one side of Stacey's Kitchen is an empty dirt lot that serves as the parking lot for both businesses; the other side of the duplex is peppered with older residential homes, some of which are clearly vacant, with boarded up windows, many more empty lots, and a church. The Houston cityscape is clearly visible in the distance. Ms. Holmes is currently working on her culinary arts degree online from a large, private, for-profit university. She suggested that she was motivated to open her business to show minority women what they can accomplish.

> I'm surrounded by professional Black women. My sister is a police officer, my cousin has a medical clinic, my other cousin is an attorney. . . . Being surrounded by professionals makes it important for me to take this [restaurant] and run with it to hold up my end. . . . We black women, minorities, we have it hard, so it's *very* important for me to reach the top.

In addition to Black entrepreneurs' frequently expressed longing to improve the Black community, a second motivation usually trumps economic concerns: the desire to be their own boss. Like lower-class Latinos/as, Black entrepreneurs often seek refuge from the conditions of wage work through enterprise. The jobs they leave are not typically characterized as dirty, dangerous, or difficult jobs, but rather, are one rung up the ladder, although they often report incidents of discrimination, a lack of respect, and little or no flexibility in scheduling. Others emphasize a desire to be independent, especially with respect to their job duties, tasks, and responsibilities. Unlike Latinos/as and Whites, however, being autonomous takes precedence and is more universal among Blacks than their desire to make more money.

In 2007, at the age of forty-six, Andre, an African American business owner, opened Chicago Dogs in the South Ward. He opened the business primarily to avoid taking orders from an employer: "I don't like people telling me what to do." He further stated that while he was a good employee, he wanted to reap the rewards of his own labor.

> I can always bet on me. I know I'm going to do an excellent job, and I'd rather give myself one hundred percent than give it to someone else. Even though I give one hundred percent at all my jobs, why would I give another person the one hundred percent I could give myself? I'd rather just cut out the middle man.

In contrast, Ms. Holmes suggested that she is a better owner than worker. With a sense of humor, she described her employee work ethic as less than desirable:

> I'm not a good employee. Sometimes I might not want to go to work, so I would be like "Forget it," but now [as a business owner] I gotta go to work! [laughing]

Although Ms. Holmes acknowledges that she "ain't made a quarter" in business, she "knows" she is better off working for herself and in an occupation that she enjoys. Like Stacey Holmes, many Black entrepreneurs claim that they are not in it for the money, a statement that is rarely expressed by Latinos/as or Whites. Lending credence to such claims, several Black entrepreneurs hold down additional jobs to make ends meet, again, in contrast to most White or Latino/a entrepreneurs, for whom owning a business is their only job.

## Conclusion

The ethnic entrepreneurship approach suggests that a combination of factors leads specific immigrant groups to engage in business ownership, from a cultural disposition or "orientation" toward enterprise to a negative reception context in the host society (Light 1972; Portes and Rumbaut 2001, 2006; Waldinger et al. 1990). For example, an anti-immigrant sentiment among the American "mainstream," coupled with a lack of good-paying, semiskilled jobs in the hourglass economy, may lead to discriminatory practices in the labor market against immigrant minority groups that overly affect their economic integration. High unemployment or underemployment rates, low or stagnant wages, and blocked opportunities for advancement may push ethnic groups with specific characteristics and features and geographically concentrated, strong, and cohesive communities into business ownership. The traditional approach further argues that participation in ethnic entrepreneurship is important because it is associated with economic mobility.

Rather than focusing on the role of ethnicity, ethnic group membership, and the ethnic group's reception context in provoking entrepreneurialism among specific, highly entrepreneurial groups, this chapter investigates how multiple dimensions of identity and belonging, embedded within an unequal social structure, may inform the motivations for and expectations of business ownership among Latino/a, White, and Black entrepreneurs. In keeping with previous research, my findings suggest that the majority of entrepreneurs engage in business ownership for two primary reasons: to make more money than they could as wage workers and to achieve autonomy. These motivations and expectations transcend social location and structural inequality. There are, however, differences in motivations and expectations across race, ethnicity, class, and gender, and which appear to be conditioned, at least in part, on structural inequality. For example, lower-class Latinos/as and Blacks are disproportionately relegated to the low-wage, low-skilled labor market. This labor market sector is characterized by jobs at the bottom of the economic ladder, where exploitation, occupational gender segregation, discrimination, exposure to environmental hazards, and unemployment or underemployment are common, and for the Mexican-origin population in particular, these jobs are often dirty, dangerous, and difficult. In this labor market context, lower-class Latino/a and Black men and women pursue business ownership for different reasons than their middle-class counterparts or Whites. Disadvantaged workers express a strong desire to escape the harsh conditions associated with low-skilled and dirty, dangerous, or difficult wage work through enterprise. In contrast, middle-class Latinos/as, Whites, and Blacks are more likely to voice their excitement at pursuing entrepreneurship as a means to fulfill a dream or to challenge themselves. Rarely, if ever, do they suggest that the working conditions associated with their previous employment influenced or facilitated their decision to open a restaurant.

Moreover, early exposure to family-owned businesses, or entrepreneurial capital, is associated with entrepreneurialism among many of the respondents. Yet, there are differences in the way in which entrepreneurial capital matters for those from different social locations. Latino, White, and Black men, in particular, seem to benefit from family business experience; they see entrepreneurship as a natural and comfortable alternative to wage work. Furthermore, their family history of business is often directly tied to their own ability to open a business. Women may possess business experience from their families as well; however, their ability to translate entrepreneurial capital into entrepreneurial activity is constrained. Instead, women entrepreneurs who espouse its importance often rely on their husbands' entrepreneurial capital and associated networks to establish their businesses, rather than their own. So although entrepreneurial capital is commonly remarked upon as an important factor in shaping respondents' entrepreneurial endeavors, race, class, and gender mediate its influence differently. Finally, disparities in wealth creation and its reproduction are observed in the propensity of White middle-class men to not only possess entrepreneurial capital, but actually *inherit* lucrative family-owned businesses.

The embedded market approach maintains that Latino/a entrepreneurs' motivations for and expectations of business ownership must be understood in the context of their hierarchical and intersectional position within the unequal American social structure. While all entrepreneurs hope to increase their earnings and "be their own boss," there are also differences in their motivations for and expectations of business ownership associated with systems of oppression and privilege rooted in race, ethnicity, class and gender. Racism, sexism, and classism—in residential and occupational segregation, discrimination in the labor market, and wealth creation and inheritance—create different conditions for individuals and groups from different social locations within the social structure. Hence, middle-class men are more likely to "fall into" entrepreneurship through inheritance; entrepreneurial succession is more prevalent among middle-class Latino men than among middle-class Latino women;

lower-class Mexican men and women are likely to seek an escape from toxic working conditions through enterprise; and Black entrepreneurs pursue their commitment to social justice in lieu of the opportunity for economic mobility. In other words, distinct social locations based on multiple dimensions of inter-sectionality, embedded within an unequal structural context, combine to influence different expectations and motivations for engaging in entrepreneurship.

# 4 Intersectionality, Market Capacity, and Latino/a Enterprise

*My financial status was good; I didn't need to depend on a bank. [I started with] personal savings first [$250,000] and then the resources from my partners [brother, $150,000; sister-in-law, $65,000] and then a credit line [$100,000]. You don't start making money the first day [or] the first month. . . . You need capital for the first six months.*

—Rob, thirty-seven years old, naturalized citizen, Hispanic Italian

*It's as if you were drowning in a river; you reach out for the nearest branch to help you out. What you want is to not drown; you just got to reach up to catch a breath. You have to learn how to live; you need to hold on to anything, to the wings of a fly . . . you hold on and you borrow some money. . . .*

—Don José, sixty-six years old, long-term U.S. resident, Mexican

RECALL THAT ROB is a thirty-seven-year-old middle-class "Hispanic Italian" immigrant from El Salvador with a family history of business ownership. Two years ago, he left his job as the manager of his brother's successful restaurant in Boston to start his own business. With ample sources of economic and social support, Rob was well-positioned to open his lucrative Italian restaurant, A Taste of Venice, with relative ease. For middle-class Latinos/as like Rob, a strong class position facilitates greater opportunities and access to market capital resources related to class background. Such resources, which include education and work experience (including managerial experience), substantial personal savings, and access to financial capital through formal money lending institutions, are valued in the American market economy (Valdez 2008b). Although middle-class Latinos/as may still confront a negative reception context in the form of ethnic, racial, or gender discrimination, and, if they are foreign-born, an anti-immigrant sentiment, access to market capital may help to alleviate the detrimental impact of discrimination that is based on multiple dimensions of intersectionality. Rob's substantial market capital appears to have mediated any disadvantages in the market that he may have experienced due to his race, ethnicity, or nativity.

In stark contrast, Don José dreamed of owning a Mexican restaurant but did not have the means to do so. As an unauthorized immigrant with a grade-school education, he worked in the construction industry as a roofer for ten years. After painstakingly saving $4,000 over several years, Don José turned to three Mexican men in his community who were known to lend money at an inflated rate of interest to other co-ethnic men. He borrowed $5,500 from these semiformal lenders, and with the modest sum of $9,500 he started his own business. For lower-class and sometimes unauthorized Latinos/as like Don José, limited access to market capital hinders their chances for business ownership.

The difficulties that lower-class Latinos/as confront in starting and maintaining their businesses belie their greater market insecurity, a consequence of their disadvantaged class position within the highly stratified American social structure. Such class disadvantage is likely intensified by a negative societal reception context. As indicated by the ethnic entrepreneurship approach, being unauthorized and unskilled, residing in a co-ethnic community of concentrated poverty, and working in a discriminatory and "ethnicized" labor market represent combined "modes of incorporation" that hinder enterprise (Portes and Rumbaut 2001, 2006). Nevertheless, and contrary to the predictions of the ethnic entrepreneurship approach, Don José overcame these obstacles. Access to additional financial capital gotten from co-ethnics provided him with just enough support to realize his dream. Investigating the extent to which disadvantaged Latino/a entrepreneurs transcend market uncertainty and structural inequality reveals the compensatory role of nonmarket, social capital resources.

In the American market economy, social and government capital offset a lack of market capital. Social capital based on ethnic, racial, gender, or family ties creates opportunities for informal lending, unpaid family or low-wage labor, and business information channels and networking opportunities to assist disadvantaged Latinos/as in enterprise. Likewise, government capital, or access to state-sponsored resources, such as subsidized business loans or tax relief for minorities and women, facilitates entrepreneurial activity among members of the polity who are historically underrepresented in business. Although the ethnic entrepreneurship approach underscores the essential role of social capital in facilitating ethnic minority business, as typified by middle-class and male members of entrepreneurially oriented groups, the embedded market approach reconsiders social and government capital as nonessential, or supplementary forms of support in the market economy that are especially relevant for disadvantaged groups. After all, access to substantial market capital among quintessential entrepreneurial groups, such as middle-class Korean or Cuban men, largely trumps the compensatory support available through social or government capital. Likewise, for middle-class Latinos/as, the use of social or government capital is probably helpful *but largely not essential*, given their stronger market position at business start-up. For disadvantaged Latinos/as like Don José, however, social or government aid, or both, may be more salient, as these nonmarket resources augment negligible market capital to foster business ownership.

## Market Capacity in the Embedded Market

*Market capacity* is comprised of the sum total of market, social, and government capital resources that would-be entrepreneurs bring to the market. In the American market economy, market capital has a direct and positive impact on business ownership and economic progress (Valdez 2008a, 2008b). In particular, researchers observe a positive relationship linking human capital attainment, class background, entrepreneurial participation, and economic success (Bates 1990, 1994; Portes and Rumbaut 2001; Sanders and Nee 1996; Valdez 2008a, 2008b). Although social capital and government capital may facilitate the entrepreneurial activity of ethnic-, racial-, and gender-affiliated group and polity members, respectively, especially when compared to those without such resources, the impact of this nonmarket capital is largely indirect and compensatory.

Middle-class Latinos' use of substantial market capital, such as education and skills, personal savings, and access to bank loans, indicates the strength of their class position alone. Latinos/as with access to considerable market capital are primed for business entry in the market economy. Moreover, their strong market position renders social capital or government capital somewhat superfluous, as such resources are not required to compensate for market uncertainty, although they may provide additional, nonessential support. In Rob's case, his personal savings and line of credit were such that he did not require social or government capital resources. Although he invested a substantial amount of money provided by members of his family, a social capital resource rooted in kinship ties (Nee, Sanders, and Sernau 1994; Sanders and Nee 1996; Valdez 2008b), he acknowledged that he did so only as a "favor to them," not because he needed it, but so that they might reap the rewards of an excellent investment opportunity.

For Latinos/as who face market uncertainty, however, the combined use of market, social, and government capital may facilitate business ownership to a greater extent than market capital alone. In general, lower-class Latinos/as do not possess high levels of human capital or personal savings, nor do they qualify for business loans from national banks. In the absence of substantial or multiple sources of market capital, social or government capital may mediate market disadvantage. In the case of Don José, the compensatory financial support provided by his co-ethnic and male networks allowed him to gain a foothold in business. For others, government-backed small-business loans targeting minorities and women may provide the supplementary capital to start a business.

Taken together, market capital rooted in class background, social capital rooted in family, gender, racial, and ethnic group affiliation, and government capital rooted in polity membership combine to determine Latinos' overall *market capacity*, or the economic resources and social and government support that they bring to the market. In the context of the American market economy, market capital is likely to have a stronger, positive effect on business startup than that of social or government capital. Although reciprocal relationships rooted in family, gender, race, and ethnicity generate social capital, and polity membership produces government capital, this aid may be only compensatory, contingent, and ultimately insufficient, especially in the face of market uncertainty or disadvantage. Consequently, while social and government capital matter, they are generally less effective than market capital in fostering business ownership in the market economy (Valdez 2003, 2008b). Ultimately, the market capacity of Latinos/as conditions in large part their experiences in starting and maintaining businesses.

## A Note on the Primacy of Class in the Embedded Market

An intersectional approach recognizes that classes, or the hierarchical placement of groups of individuals based on common economic interests and power, are shaped by ubiquitous, multiple, and interlocking systems of oppression and privilege. Structural inequality that is founded on gender and racial hierarchies, for example, has consistently resulted in unequal access to education, property ownership, and employment across gender and racial classifications. Consequently, the class position of an individual is inextricably linked with the individual's gender, racial, and ethnic classifications, as they are "created, maintained, and transformed simultaneously and in relation to one another" (Weber 2001:104). Scholars of intersectionality generally agree that these multiple dimensions fuse "within an individual's identity." They disagree, however, on the extent to which they converge "at the level of the social system" (Brewer 1993:15; Browne and Misra 2003:494).

In the embedded market, the intersection of class, gender, race, and ethnicity in America is both ubiquitous and contextually contingent. It is ubiquitous in that these multiple dimensions of intersectionality, or intersecting oppressions (Collins 1997:18), "cannot be understood independently of one another" (Weber 2001:104). It is contingent in that each dimension may be more or less salient under specific market conditions and within particular local and historical contexts (Browne and Misra 2003:492; Glenn 1999). In the modern American market economy, class takes precedence over gender, race, and ethnicity in facilitating business ownership. This assertion does not attempt to undo the interdependence of intersectional group formations, or imply that gender, race, and ethnicity are less important, irrelevant, or subsumed somehow under the rubric of class. Nor does it reject a "working hypothesis of equivalency between oppressions" (Collins 1997:14). Rather, this perspective maintains that in the modern market economy, market capital, which is rooted in class background, is essential and has a direct impact on the American economy, whereas social capital, which stems from reciprocal, social relationships rooted in gender, race, and ethnicity, and government capital, the centralized redistribution of resources rooted in polity membership, are not always essential, although each may be especially relevant in the face of market disadvantage. Under conditions of market uncertainty, government or social capital may provide financial or economic resources or social support, or both. These economic and noneconomic resources may facilitate business ownership; however, they do not have the same influence on the market as those resources that are rooted in market capital. After all, the access to and use of market capital resources represent a strong market position, while the use of social or government capital resources—economic or otherwise—generally reveals a weaker market position.

## Essential Market Capital and Nonessential Social and Government Capital

All Latino/a entrepreneurs possess, access, and use market capital, such as personal savings, to start and maintain their businesses, regardless of their class, gender, race, or ethnicity. Market capital may be used alone or in combination with social capital and government capital resources, such as ethnic- or gender-based informal lending networks, or a government-backed loan, respectively. As Table 4.1 shows, a modest portion of Latinos/as in my sample rely on market capital alone (21 percent), although the majority (71 percent) report the use of both market and social capital for business start-up and maintenance. Social or government capital is always used in concert with market capital and never alone, and only 3 percent of Latinos/as indicate the use of any form of government capital. The widespread use of market capital, the uneven use of social capital, and the almost nonexistent use of government capital suggest the primacy of market capital and the secondary, compensatory role of social and government capital, in keeping with the embedded market approach.

A closer look at the types of market, social, and government capital that Latinos/as use to start and maintain their businesses reveals the specific resources that are of central importance in facilitating their business entry and

**Table 4.1**  Percentage Market, Social, and Government Capital Used by Latino/a, White, and Black Entrepreneurs to Start and Maintain Their Businesses

|  | Latino/a | White | Black |
|---|---|---|---|
| Market Capital Only | 20.6 | 10.0 | 30.0 |
| Market and Social Capital | 70.6 | 10.0 | 40.0 |
| Market and Government Capital | 0 | 10.0 | 0 |
| Market, Social, and Government Capital | 8.8 | 20.0 | 10.0 |
| Social Capital Only (family inheritance)* | 0 | 40.0 | 0 |
| Social Capital Only (nonfamily inheritance)* | 0 | 10.0 | 0 |
| Government Capital Only | 0 | 0 | 0 |
| Refuse to Answer | 0 | 0 | 20.0 |
| Total | 100 | 100 | 100 |

* I distinguish between social capital that consists of family inheritance and social capital that consists of nonfamily inheritance. This distinction is especially important for Whites, since they are the sole racial group that relies on social capital alone, in any form, to start and maintain a business.

**Table 4.2**  Percentage Market, Social, and Government Capital Sources Used by Latino/a, White, and Black Entrepreneurs

|  | Latino/a | White | Black |
|---|---|---|---|
| Market Capital |  |  |  |
|   Personal savings | 94.0 | 30.0 | 50.0 |
|   Property (sold, refinanced) | 35.3 | 10 | 0 |
|   Credit cards, credit line | 29.0 | 0 | 10.0 |
|   National bank loan | 41.2 | 20.0 | 10.0 |
| Social Capital |  |  |  |
|   Family inheritance | 11.8 | 40.0 | 10 |
|   Other family resources or support | 58.8 | 40.0 | 20.0 |
|   Co-ethnic resources or support | 17.6 | 0 | 0 |
|   Co-racial resources or support | 5.9 | 10 | 10.0 |
| Government Capital |  |  |  |
|   Government loan, subsidy | 11.8 | 30.0 | 10.0 |
| Refuse to Answer | 0 | 0 | 20.0 |

NOTE: Multiple responses were possible so columns do not total 100.

longevity. Table 4.2 shows that almost all Latino/a entrepreneurs (94 percent) rely on personal savings to start and maintain their businesses. No other market, social, or government capital resource comes close to the importance of personal savings. More than half (59 percent) depend on the second-most important resource, family-based social capital and support, such as informal or semiformal lending or the use of unpaid family labor. Even fewer Latinos/as report the use of other market, social, or government capital resources. Regarding other forms of market capital, 35 percent of Latinos/as sell or refinance property, 29 percent report the use of credit cards or a credit line, and almost 41 percent indicate the use of a bank loan to accumulate the financial capital necessary to start and maintain their businesses. Notably, the use of these market capital resources is more prevalent than the use of ethnic- or racial-based social capital, the latter tied to resources generated by co-racial membership based on Latino/a or Hispanic group affiliation, for instance, moneylending between a Mexican-origin and a Nicaraguan-origin immigrant. In this sample, only 18 percent of Latinos/as rely on co-ethnic social capital and 6 percent on co-racial social capital. Regarding state-sponsored government capital, only 12 percent rely on this form of support to help them with their businesses (see Table 4.2).

It is clear from Table 4.2 that market capital resources trump social capital and government capital resources in facilitating Latinos'/as' entrepreneurial activity. Latinos'/as' resource-mobilization strategies—where their resources come from, what they consist of, and how they are used—comprise crucial pieces of the puzzle that reveal their overall *market capacity*, or the cumulative market, social, and government capital resources that they bring to the market. The multiple dimensions of class, gender, race, and ethnicity are ubiquitous in shaping Latinos'/as' market capacity. Market capacity, however, is contextually contingent, as it is circumscribed by relations of market exchange, reciprocity, and redistribution, or the three forms of economic integration that constitute the market economy. In this economy, market capital has a greater impact on business start-up and maintenance than social or government capital; nevertheless, social or government capital may serve to compensate for market uncertainty. Because Latino/a entrepreneurs' market capacity is conditioned by their hierarchical position within the social structure, understanding its composition exposes structural inequality at the starting gate of business ownership. Ultimately, this position determines, in no small part, their standing at the finish line.

## *Market Capital*

The case of Arturo Mendez exemplifies the primacy of market capital in starting and maintaining a business. Arturo is a sixty-one-year-old naturalized U.S. citizen of Mexican descent who lives and works in Little Mexico, the historic Mexican enclave in eastern Houston. Before migrating, he pursued an economics degree in Mexico, but he did not graduate. Fearing that his job prospects in Mexico were limited, he came to the United States for "a better life." He soon found work in a Mexican restaurant, where he was employed as a full-time manager for more than twenty years. During that time, he married Lisa, a college-educated, U.S.-born second-generation[1] Mexican American. The Mendezes can be characterized as middle-class before owning their restaurant, since they were college-educated, were employed in management and white-collar work (Lisa worked in real estate), and had acquired some wealth in the form of personal savings and real estate. In 1988, Arturo quit his job to open a restaurant, which he financed with market capital only, specifically, $25,000 from the sale of an investment property.

El Rancho is located on the other side of the freeway, across from most of the businesses in the area. The large, bright-pink-and-maroon-trimmed building is old, as are the interior furnishings, which consist of wooden tables and chairs, some booths, and displays of Mexican tchotchkes (maracas, sombreros, and the like). With live bands on the weekends and a few colorful and private rooms set aside for special occasions, this friendly, full-service Mexican restaurant caters to large crowds and families. Arturo has owned El Rancho for more than twenty years. For well over a decade, Lisa has worked as the restaurant's full-time, salaried bookkeeper. In 2001, Arturo opened a second restaurant, again using market capital resources exclusively. Specifically, he financed this second business with $50,000 in personal savings, $60,000 from a bank loan, and a $200,000 credit line.

Likewise, Martín, a fifty-one-year-old Salvadoran naturalized U.S. citizen, financed his first and second restaurants with market capital only. After migrating to the United States in 1971, Martín, who at that time held a bachelor's degree in business and spoke English fluently, was hired to work at a medical supply company. He was promoted to manager after five years. Unfortunately, the business folded in 2002, and after a year of looking for work with no luck, Martín decided to go into business for himself. With $16,000 in personal savings, he established his first Salvadoran-food restaurant in Little Latin America, a Latino/a enclave located in southwestern Houston. Pupusa Tienda, named for the popular Salvadoran flatbread made from cornmeal and stuffed with cheese, pork, or beans, caters to a Salvadoran crowd. Pupusa Tienda occupies a small space in a busy strip mall near the freeway. There are no more than four tables and a counter that seats eight in the whole restaurant. It is generally busy and louder than you'd expect, as Spanish-speaking men raise their voices to be heard over the competing sounds of the television and jukebox, the entertainment staples of many Central American restaurants. With the success of this first business, Martín opened a second restaurant, Sabroso, in 2007. He financed this newer restaurant with $35,000 in personal savings and a $60,000 bank loan (using his first restaurant as collateral).

Unlike his first business, Sabroso caters to "Anglos" and a "high-class clientele." It is located on the border between Little Latin America and Houston Heights, the latter a predominately White middle-class community. Sabroso is at least twice the size of Pupusa Tienda, with an interior that is well lit and professionally painted bright yellow. Its walls are hung with several oil paintings depicting colorful birds and landscapes (painted by his daughter), and its floors are made of Spanish tile. An unopened bottle of red wine sits at every table, while the pleasant sound of Spanish classical guitar completes the ambiance.

In sum, Arturo and Martín possessed the skills, work experience, and wealth to start their first and second businesses with relative ease. During their initial foray, they counted on one type of market capital only (the sale of an investment property and personal savings, respectively). By the time they opened their second businesses, however, both enjoyed stronger market positions. Their improved economic conditions granted each of them access to considerably more financial capital, this time from multiple sources of market capital. For these middle-class Latino men with sufficient access to market capital, social capital resources were not sought out or required to start their businesses. Even when Arturo experienced some unexpected financial trouble, he continued to rely on market capital alone to maintain his businesses.

Arturo did not expect to run into money troubles, as he had prepared a careful and thoughtful business plan before starting his first restaurant. Unfortunately, his financial expectations were not met and the business took a loss in the first year. He attributed this financial crisis to the recession of the 1980s. During that time, business was slow, and although his wife worked as a real estate agent, her income did not cover their household expenses. To make ends meet and keep the struggling business afloat, Arturo refinanced their home. The following year the business broke even and has since generated a modest profit. That financial crisis was not his only close call with business failure. In a second instance of market vulnerability, Arturo's second and most recent business ran out of money in the wake of 9/11, which occurred just two weeks after opening. To weather that storm, he quickly secured an emergency bank loan in the amount of $20,000 using his first business as collateral. The bank loan kept the restaurant going until it could turn a profit nine months later. In each of these financial emergencies, Arturo restored economic stability with the use of market capital resources alone.

The salience of class in shaping the market capital resources available to Arturo and Martín is clear. For these middle-class Latino men, their class position granted them access to substantial market capital that allowed them to start and maintain their businesses. It is important to note that gender, racial, and ethnic group affiliations may indirectly contribute to the class position that Arturo and Martín enjoy; for example, men are more likely than women to advance to management positions in the American labor market, and both Arturo and Martín possessed this valuable experience before becoming restaurateurs. In this way, intersecting nonclass dimensions may affect Latinos' class position. Once established, however, it is their class position—rather than their gender, ethnic, or racial group affiliations—that is directly related to market exchange and the consequent market capital that they possess and use to engage in enterprise. In contrast, gender, ethnic, and racial group affiliations have a more direct influence on reciprocity, and the social capital that stems from such relationships. Social capital, however, was not sought out or used by these more privileged, middle-class Latinos.

Middle-class Latino men are not the only entrepreneurs who start their businesses with market capital alone. Before owning her business, Rita, a forty-seven-year-old middle-class naturalized citizen, was a stay-at-home mom. Her husband provided financially for their family, and with his middle-income earnings, they lived a comfortable, middle-class lifestyle. Rita decided to go into business for herself after the loss of her daughter, who died of cancer five years earlier. She started her business with $50,000 drawn from her family's household savings and $50,000 in equipment and supplies purchased through credit cards. Her restaurant, Amigos y Comidas, is a small and welcoming space decorated with Mexican artwork and lush, indoor plants. Freshly painted walls in autumn colors, comfortable tables and chairs, and a coffee bar that offers free Internet access complete the interior decor.

As a high school graduate, Rita did not possess the education and work experience reported by Arturo or Martín; however, her middle-class lifestyle through marriage granted her access to sufficient market capital from which to start and maintain her business. Rita is an exception rather than the rule, however, as most stay-at-home moms, middle-class or otherwise, do not choose to start businesses, nor do they have the kind of access to market capital that Rita enjoys. That being said, she, alongside Arturo and Martín, are representative of the 21 percent of Latino/a entrepreneurs in my sample who started and maintained their businesses with market capital alone (see Table 4.1).

Disadvantaged Latinos/as, in contrast, generally have substantially less market capital to invest in businesses than their middle-class counterparts. For example, lower-class Latinos/as—those would-be entrepreneurs who did not attend college, work in low-wage, low-skilled occupations, and possess limited or no wealth—often lack the skills and financial support to participate competitively and securely in the market economy. Additionally, gender discrimination and inequality persist in the American economy and society, increasing disparities between men and women in labor force participation, occupational attainment, earnings, and opportunities for advancement or promotions. Women, in particular, have fewer opportunities to accumulate the necessary market capital resources from which to start and grow their businesses. Nevertheless, recent studies indicate that Latinas are one of the fastest-growing entrepreneurial subgroups. These more disadvantaged business owners, however, are especially susceptible to market fluctuation and uncertainty and are therefore at greater risk of experiencing financial duress or complete business failure. For them, social and government capital may provide the additional resources and support to help them start and maintain their businesses, without which their businesses might not get off the ground.

### Market and Social Capital

Although the use of social capital in small business is certainly not unique to ethnic minorities, the classic theory of ethnic entrepreneurship maintains that its use is more prevalent among entrepreneurially oriented ethnic groups than among Whites, who are more likely to emphasize nuclear family cohesion (Bonacich 1975; Bonacich and Modell 1981; Light and Bonacich 1988), or disadvantaged nonentrepreneurial ethnic or racial groups, such as Mexicans or Blacks (Portes and Rumbaut 2001, 2006). According to that traditional approach, ethnic-based social capital consists of close-knit family ties and co-ethnic networks that engender solidarity, reciprocal obligations, and enforceable trust between members through social closure (Kim and Hurh 1985; Yoon 1991). These reciprocal relationships generate material goods and social supports that facilitate enterprise, such as providing a source of cheap or unpaid labor, informal lending, or sharing business information. For example, studies have shown that Korean and Chinese entrepreneurs benefit from co-ethnic mutual aid, such as that provided by rotating credit associations (Light and Bonacich 1988). Similarly, researchers observe that Cuban entrepreneurs sometimes acquire co-ethnic financial capital from informal "character loans," money that is borrowed by new arrivals to the United States, based solely on their family's reputation in Cuba (Portes and Stepick 1993).

Correspondingly, this approach characterizes ethnic groups with negligible rates of entrepreneurship as disadvantaged; these groups are perceived as concentrated in "socially isolated" communities with limited access to resources and structural opportunities (Fratoe 1988; Lee 2002; Light 1972; Logan, Alba, and McNulty 1994; Portes and Bach 1985; Wilson 1987). In particular, Black-owned businesses within the Black community have been depicted as derelict and undercapitalized (Silverman 2000:83). Moreover, Lee (2002:121) contends that Black business owners "have historically experienced and continue to experience co-ethnic disadvantages in serving their own." Likewise, Portes and Rumbaut (2001:278) claim that the Mexican-origin population is comprised of "weak communities that have emerged under their precarious conditions of arrival and settlement." This group's social and economic disadvantages are presumed to constrain members' ability to mobilize resources for enterprise. Portes and Bach (1985:245) conclude that the lack of entrepreneurial activity among the Mexican-origin population relegates its members to low-wage labor and economic stagnation.

The ethnic entrepreneurship paradigm selectively highlights the role of ethnic-based social capital in facilitating enterprise; however, it overlooks the role of social capital that may stem from nonethnic social group formations, such as those rooted in gender or race. It is likely that membership within these neglected groups generate additional sources of social capital, which may or may not intersect with ethnicity. Moreover, the classic approach often conflates family-based social capital (such as unpaid family labor) with that of ethnic-based social capital (such as a source of low-wage labor). This imbrication masks the distinct contribution of family-based social capital that, although "synonymous with ethnic entrepreneurship" (Sanders and Nee 1996:233), is nevertheless a separate form of social capital that is more accurately synonymous with family-owned businesses more generally, regardless of ethnicity. A clear understanding of the emergence and type of social capital that facilitates entrepreneurship requires an attempt to separate these distinct social groupings and the social capital they produce.

Finally, the embedded market approach reconsiders the role of social capital, which may stem from ethnic, racial, gender, or family ties, as a secondary aspect of *market capacity*, which is comprised of market, social, and, to a lesser extent, government capital. Accordingly, social capital is not essential for enterprise, nor is it absent from those groups that are characterized as nonethnic or nonentrepreneurial, such as women or Mexicans, respectively. Whereas market capital is essential for entrepreneurial activity, social capital is nonessential in the presence of significant market capital. That said, social capital may compensate for market uncertainty among disadvantaged groups. The extent to which social capital may affect enterprise, however, is shaped, in the first instance, by the intersecting and multiple dimensions of race, ethnicity, gender, and family. In other words, the strength of the social capital that is produced is itself circumscribed by the individual and collective social location of the members themselves. *Thus, it is the quality and type of social capital that varies across dimensions of race, ethnicity, gender, and family rather than its presence or absence, that determines its effect on enterprise.* This is no more apparent than in the case of Michelle Silva and her mother, Theresa.

At twenty-two, Michelle co-owns Casa Picante, a tiny Mexican restaurant located in a Greater Houston–area strip mall, with her mother, Theresa. Michelle and her parents are unauthorized, having migrated clandestinely to Houston from Mexico in 1991. Michelle speaks English and Spanish and has a high school diploma, unlike her mother and father, who speak Spanish only and did not complete elementary school. After her father, Jesús, fell ill and could not work, Michelle suggested to her mother that they go into business for themselves. Although they each worked as cashiers and customer service assistants in retail sales prior to Jesús's illness, Michelle wanted "to rise up in life." She also wanted her mother to "have a job where nobody is going to bug her, where she's her own boss . . . something a little bit more laid back for her."

I characterize Michelle and her mother as lower-class because they both possess a limited education and, before going into business, worked in the low-wage service sector. With Michelle's personal savings ($10,000) and the help of Jesús, who sold his investment property in Mexico for $25,000, Michelle and Theresa went into business. The $35,000 that they had to invest in the business covered the cost of the restaurant's lease and some equipment and supplies but did not meet all of their expenses. To make up the difference, Michelle and Theresa turned to their family and co-ethnic friends for additional support. However, because their friends and family share their same class position—they are all lower-class—the social capital generated by these co-ethnic and family ties consisted mainly of nonfinancial, compensatory support:

> Michelle: We had a lot of help from family at first. I had my uncles that do the painting, the walls, you know. My brother-in-law did the floor. . . . I worked at the furniture store so I have good [Mexican] friends that [work there and] would give me good prices.

The social capital provided by family and co-ethnic friends allowed Michelle and Theresa to complete the needed repairs and furnish the restaurant.

In stark contrast to Rob's elegantly styled A Taste of Venice and Martín's brightly decorated Sabroso, Casa Picante, which is flanked by a dry cleaner on one side and a Domino's Pizza on the other, is sparsely furnished with five tables and chairs, a self-serve soda dispenser, and a home stereo system. It is painted an institutional green, the paint provided by one of Michelle's uncles, who works as a janitor at an elementary school. In lieu of menus, which Michelle and Theresa could not afford to purchase, customers walk up to a buffet-style counter and simply order the items that they can see through a glass partition. A typical morning's options include rice, beans, eggs, bacon, *chicharrón*, fresh tortillas, *pico de gallo*, salsa, and tortilla chips.

Michelle and her mother are not alone in starting their business with very little financial capital. The majority of Mexican-origin restaurateurs in my sample, and nationally, lack substantial market capital from which to start their businesses (Valdez 2008b). When market capital falls short, would-be Latino/a entrepreneurs generally compensate with the use of social capital from family, ethnic, and racial group members, which often includes a gendered component (as discussed in the next section). In Michelle and Theresa's case, the social capital generated by family and co-ethnic friends was nonfinancial in character. Their case highlights an aspect of the limits of social capital that is often overlooked in studies of ethnic enterprise: that the social capital provided by family ties and co-ethnic and racial networks is largely constrained by the intersectional social location of the members themselves. After all, Michelle and Theresa's sources of social capital are not unlike themselves—low-wage workers at the bottom of the hourglass economy. As such, the social capital generated from these relationships is limited, which may ultimately reduce its effectiveness or restrict requests for such resources or their use in facilitating the entrepreneurial dreams of economically disadvantaged Latinos/as.

The line between market capital and social capital is not always clear-cut. For Manuel Ortega, a bilingual twenty-five-year-old Mexican immigrant with a high school diploma, a bank loan of $70,000 provided the only source of financial capital from which to start his sandwich and yogurt shop, Manuel's All Natural. At first glance, the use of this modest bank loan seemingly indicates an obvious form of market capital, one that is readily available to those who qualify (that is, individuals with sufficient collateral or creditworthiness). For Manuel, however, this was not the case, as his class position is decidedly lower-class (given his limited education and lack of personal savings or property). His immediate family is also lower-class: His mother, Doña Paz, is a sixty-year-old Spanish-speaking immigrant with a second-grade education; his Peruvian immigrant wife, Carmen, works primarily in the informal economy as a babysitter. To secure the bank loan, the only resource that he used to start and maintain his business, Manuel relied on his uncle, Doña Paz's brother, who agreed to be the cosigner.

Perhaps not surprisingly, Manuel experienced financial trouble right from the start. Without much work experience and no prior business experience, he did not think about a business plan or budget, which contributed to his selling of high-quality products without a sufficient profit-making margin. Because his customer base, though loyal, was small, customer traffic and volume did not offset the too-low prices. To keep the shop from going out of business in those first critical months, he depleted the last $10,000 from the loan. Manuel also turned to his mother and his wife for additional social capital support in the form of full-time, unpaid family labor: "We worked more and I laid my employees off to cut down on costs. . . . We just paid for our meals to keep the business going." For Manuel, securing a bank loan did not signify a strong market position in the absence of a strong class position. On the contrary, and as I have shown in previous research (Valdez 2008b), the use of a bank loan among ethnic minorities often reveals a weaker market position than that held by those who possess substantial personal savings or multiple forms of market capital, or who can rely on a combination of substantial market and social capital support. Fortunately for Manuel, the compensatory social capital he received from his mother and wife provided just enough support to keep his business open.

In the examples described here, limited market capital is mediated by the contributions of social capital. Restricted access to market capital, however, is not a precondition for the use of social capital. On the contrary, the more market capital a would-be entrepreneur has, the better the social capital resources are from which to draw. Predictably, middle-class Latinos/as face few if any obstacles to business start-up. As discussed in this chapter's opening, Rob financed his restaurant, A Taste of Venice, with substantial personal savings ($250,000) and a line of credit ($100,000). Nevertheless, he accepted additional financial aid from his family ($215,000). In Rob's case, a strong class position provided him with ample market and social capital, minimizing his need or desire to acquire additional financial resources from market-based institutions such as a bank. What separates Rob from his disadvantaged counterparts is not his use of market and family-based social capital, but rather his access to substantial financial capital accumulated from these sources, rooted primarily in his class position.

## Gender and Social Capital

Previous studies find that gender has a negative effect on women's social capital accumulation (Aaltio, Kyro, and Sundin 2008; Healy, Haynes, and Hampshire 2007). I also observe gender differences in Latinas access to and use of social capital. Specifically, Latina entrepreneurs who rely on social capital resources to borrow financial capital are overwhelmingly more likely to depend on family ties only; they do not generally borrow from ethnic- or racial-based (that is, Hispanic or Latino) networks. In contrast, Latino men are likely to borrow money from all potential sources of social capital they have at their disposal, including family and ethnic- or racial-based networks. Thus, Latino men appear to have more social capital sources from which to draw financial support, which contributes to disparities between men and women in the amount of financial capital they access and use to start and maintain their businesses. The stark difference between men and women in the financial support that is available to them from social capital resources is especially apparent in the cases of Ruben, Marta and Javier, and Michelle and Theresa.

In 1976, sixteen-year-old Ruben and his undocumented lower-class parents migrated to the United States. Ruben attended an American high school, where he learned English and excelled in his coursework. After graduation, he enrolled in college and eventually earned a bachelor's degree from a state university. Although a college degree is associated with being middle-class, neither he nor his parents had sufficient market capital to open a restaurant. Moreover, as an unauthorized immigrant, Ruben assumed he was ineligible to apply for a national bank or government-subsidized loan (and lacked the collateral to do so). Still, he had a network of middle-class Latino friends from college that provided him with the financial capital he needed:

> I approached my [wealthy Guatemalan male] friend with my idea. I knew his father very well and I put a business plan together and it looked good. I was in a conversation with this friend of mine and another [Guatemalan] friend. . . . The other guy approached me later and said, "You know what, I want to do it with you." He didn't have any money so he went to his father.

That friend's father contributed half of the $60,000 initial investment, and they went into business together (Ruben and his friend used their combined personal savings for the other half). While running the business, Ruben met and married a White American woman and became a U.S. citizen. Several years later, he sold his share of the restaurant to his partner and started his own business. This time, he had access to substantial market and family-based social capital. Along with $40,000 in personal savings, he borrowed $30,000 from a bank and $30,000 from his father-in-law. All in all, Ruben had acquired some skills, wealth, and middle-class connections in college, which granted him access to a middle- and upper-class network of Latino men. Although he was undocumented and possessed no collateral from which to borrow from market-based institutions, his middle-class Latino male network and, later, his extended family ties provided the financial capital he needed to start his first and second businesses.

Access to financial capital from co-ethnic, co-racial, and male-based social capital sources is not relegated to middle-class Latino men. Lower-class Latino men benefit from such networks as well. Don José, the undocumented Mexican immigrant introduced earlier, migrated to the United States in the early 1970s. With five years of schooling in Mexico and no knowledge of English, he found work as a roofer before starting his business. With his meager earnings, Don José managed to save $4,000 over several years. In search of additional aid, Don José resorted to borrowing $5,500 from "three old [Mexican] men from the neighborhood" who were known to grant loans to other Mexican men "with lots of interest." He also counted on an initial investment of property and a line of credit from another co-ethnic male friend. With these co-ethnic and male networks in place, Don José accumulated sufficient financial capital to start his business.

Likewise, Marta and Javier Gomez acquired resources from Javier's ethnic and male networks. After they were married, Marta quit her job as a cashier because her husband "didn't let me work anymore. He said, "No more, I'm going to support you.'" Refusing to stay at home for long, however, Marta started selling tamales and fruit door-to-door. Eventually, Javier's co-ethnic male friend advised him to open a business for her, "instead of having your wife selling on the streets." In Marta and Javier's household, traditional gender roles dictated that Marta quit her job at the request of her husband, and, later, that *he* was responsible for getting *her* "off the street." Javier elected to do just that, and opened a business (for her). Javier used their personal savings ($30,000) and borrowed $15,000 from his co-ethnic friend and $5,000 from his brother to open a butcher shop and restaurant. Although Marta was the original entrepreneur, albeit in the informal economy, it was her husband's ethnic and male networks (in addition to their class position) that generated the resources for Marta's formal business.

Latino men acquire financial support from their ethnic-, racial-, and gender-based social capital networks. Such group affiliations, however, generally supply noneconomic aid to Latinas. For financial help beyond that provided by market capital resources, Latinas usually turn to their families only. Recall that Michelle and Theresa started their business with $35,000 (from the sale of an investment property and Michelle's personal savings) and noneconomic compensatory support (unpaid family labor, a discount on furniture) from family- and ethnic-based social capital sources. Upon opening their restaurant, Michelle and Theresa did not make a profit, which led to mistakes that caused them further economic distress. In particular, Michelle, following a friend's flawed advice, did not pay the payroll taxes during a slow month (she was wrongly advised that she could instead pay those taxes in one lump sum at the end of the year). Two weeks later, two IRS agents showed up at the restaurant during business hours and took money out of the cash register ("It was embarrassing. . . . They took all the fives, tens, and twenties and left the ones"). Michelle was warned that continued nonpayment would result in legal action. At the time, her savings were wiped out, and she knew her ethnic networks could not provide the financial support she needed, so she did not approach them for help. Claiming that she had "no alternative," she asked her grandfather for help:

> It was the only time we were [in financial trouble], when I didn't pay my taxes. So I had to ask my grandpa for money [approximately $1,000]. . . . It was hard; he's a great man. . . . You never go ask your grandparents for money. But I borrowed it and I paid it [back].

In contrast to Michelle and Theresa, Don José, whose initial market capital resources generated far less financial capital, was able to seek out the extra cash he needed from his ethnic and male networks. Similarly, Marta's husband secured financial support from his co-ethnic male friend. In these examples, economically disadvantaged men acquired financial support from social capital rooted in their ethnic and gender affiliations. Latinas generally do not have access to such resources for financial aid; they instead count on their family only.

It is clear that Latinos'/as' social location is critical in establishing their market capacity. Especially salient is the class position of would-be entrepreneurs, which determines most of the market capital that is contributed to business start-up and maintenance. Although Latinos/as may rely on market capital alone, disadvantaged Latinos/as are more likely to depend on a combination of market and social capital. Specifically, access to family, ethnic, and racial-based social capital facilitates business ownership with the additional support of economic and noneconomic resources beyond that from market capital alone. Yet, not all Latinos/as enjoy access to the same resources from the same sources. In particular, Latinas do not benefit from ethnic-, racial-, and gender-based networks to the same extent that men do. Although monetary support is available to men from such networks, women's borrowing is relegated to the family. Latinas' lack of ethnic-, racial-, and gender-based networks from which to accumulate financial support disadvantages them disproportionately, as these resources often generate substantial financial capital, at times matching or doubling the amount that is invested without such networks. From this perspective, Latina entrepreneurs, especially lower-class women like Michelle and Theresa, appear to experience a "triple disadvantage" (Browne and Misra 2003) that limits their overall market capacity. For them, social capital is restricted to economic resources or social support provided by family and noneconomic resources provided by ethnic-based social capital networks.

### Government Capital

Previous research suggests that ethnic and racial group differences in government aid are linked to disparities in business start-up (Fairlie and Robb 2008; Oliver and Shapiro 2006; Portes and Rumbaut 2001, 2006). Although the percentage of small businesses in Texas that rely on guaranteed government lending programs is small overall, at just over 8 percent, researchers observe that the lack of access to and use of such resources hinders minority enterprise disproportionately (Fairlie and Robb 2008; Valdez 2008b; Verdaguer 2009). In my sample of Latino/a, White, and Black business owners, approximately 9 percent reported the use of government capital resources, or close to the state average; yet, there are substantial differences across race. Specifically, 30 percent of Whites, 10 percent of Blacks, and less than 3 percent of Latinos/as report the use of government support to start and maintain their businesses.

Although the explicit role of the government in facilitating ethnic entrepreneurship through lending, tax breaks, or other incentives is understudied (Curry 2008:20–21), the observed lower rate of borrowing among Latino/a immigrant entrepreneurs when compared to that of U.S.-born Whites and

Blacks may indicate a disproportionate lack of access based on polity membership, specifically relating to nativity, legal, refugee, or citizenship status (Portes and Rumbaut 2006), and the failure of the Small Business Administration (SBA) and other government organizations to effectively aid would-be Latino/a immigrant entrepreneurs.

In a special report to the Finance Commission of Texas regarding government and commercial market-based lending in Texas, researchers conclude that the "loan evaluation process *appears* to be the same" across minority and nonminority firms (Johnson, Schauer, and Soden 2002:19–20; my emphasis).[2] Apart from that indeterminate supposition, researchers nevertheless concede that "minority-owned firms are denied credit at a higher rate," are "more likely to pay higher interest rates," and experience "credit discrepancies" more frequently (2002:19–20). Such disparities between minority and nonminority firms are presumably attributed to differences in market capital resources, such as education, work experience, and creditworthiness, rather than racial or ethnic discrimination, per se. Yet, numerous studies provide evidence that challenges the report's unsubstantiated claim of racial equality in lending (Blanchard, Yinger, and Zhao 2004; Blanchflower, Levine, and Zimmerman 2003; Cavalluzzo, Cavalluzzo, and Wolken 2002; Cavalluzzo and Wolken 2005; Coleman 2002, 2003; Robb and Fairlie 2006:26). These studies demonstrate that the higher rate of credit denials and higher interest rates for minority-owned businesses persist "even after controlling for differences in credit worthiness and other factors" (Robb and Fairlie 2006:26). Fairlie and Robb (2008:114) conclude that "the evidence from the literature is consistent with the existence of continuing lending discrimination."

In addition to racial disparities in lending, recent research also suggests that many would-be or current minority business owners fail to apply for government and nongovernment loans, as minorities' expectations of being turned down often prevent them from applying in the first place (Curry 2008; Fairlie and Robb 2008; Verdaguer 2009; Wainright 2006). In this study, only Don Francisco, the 1.5-generation Mexican entrepreneur who took over his parents' business, applied for and was granted an SBA loan. He readily complained about the bureaucracy and hidden costs associated with the loan and vowed never to borrow from the government again. For other Latino/a entrepreneurs, their status as unauthorized immigrants, their expectations of being denied a loan, and their lack of knowledge about or confusion with the substantial paperwork involved prevented them from applying or pursuing a loan, in keeping with previous research (Verdaguer 2009). It is likely that this lack of government capital is partly responsible for Latinos'/as' lower rate of business ownership (Verdaguer 2009).

## Racial Group Differences in Market Capacity

The ways in which class, gender, ethnicity, and family generate dissimilar resources that are nevertheless shared by Latinos/as from similar backgrounds suggest that individual Latinos'/as' collective social location influences their market capacity, and thus their business opportunities, from the start. Likewise, racial group classification determines placement within the racial hierarchy, which influences the resource-mobilization strategies and allocation of resources among Whites, Blacks, and Latinos/as. For example, White entrepreneurs sometimes rely on social capital alone, and benefit from family inheritance, to a greater extent than Latinos/as or Blacks do, while Black entrepreneurs are more limited in the types of resources that are available to them than either Whites or Latinos/as.

Although Latinos/as and Blacks did not report the use of social capital alone to start or maintain their businesses, the largest percentage of Whites benefited from family-based social capital only (Table 4.1). Specifically, 40 percent of White entrepreneurs inherited their businesses from their parents. Moreover, these heirs did not require additional resources or support from market, social, or government capital, or some combination of the three, for upgrades or other investments to make the restaurant profitable; they took over the business "as is." For example, Tony Frank, the fifty-one-year-old owner of Lonestar Burger, took over his parents' business with no additional costs: "There was already money in the bank, and I had been here long enough to know that the money in the bank was sufficient." Conversely, only 12 percent of Latinos/as and 10 percent of Blacks inherited the family business. Moreover, unlike the majority of White heirs, these entrepreneurs required additional market capital funds.

Although the class position of Black and Latino/a entrepreneurs is weaker than that of Whites, fully 30 percent of Black entrepreneurs started their businesses using market capital alone, which is 10 percent higher than the percentage of Latinos/as that do so. In contrast, only 10 percent of White entrepreneurs started their businesses with market capital alone. Most Latinos/as use a combination of market capital and social capital resources; however, only 10 percent of Whites and 40 percent of Blacks reported the use of these combined sources. Additionally, while 20 percent of Whites relied on government capital in combination with market or social capital, or both, only 10 percent of Blacks and 9 percent of Latinos/as reported the use of any government capital. Findings reveal distinctly different access to such resources, especially among Whites, in the use of family-based social capital and government capital, secondary resources that appear to provide substantial compensatory support to this group. In contrast, the greater reliance on market capital only or market and noninheritance-based social capital hints at a greater self-reliance and more limited secondary resources available to Black and Latino/a entrepreneurs.

Nevertheless, Table 4.2 demonstrates that Latinos/as make use of a diverse set of resources stemming from market, social, and government capital. On the other hand, Blacks do not rely on co-ethnic resources or the selling of property, whereas Whites do not access credit or co-ethnic resources; instead, Whites rely almost exclusively on family-based social capital, personal savings, and national or government-backed bank loans. For example, John Riley, fifty-three, is representative of many White entrepreneurs who relied on a combination of bank loans and personal savings.

> We bought this with an SBA loan [in the amount of $320,000] . . . and the rest was from my personal savings [$100,000]. . . . You know, it wasn't all borrowing.

By stating that "it wasn't all borrowing," Mr. Riley implies that he recognizes the importance of a strong class position. He suggests further that the combination of personal savings and loans puts him in a more secure position.

> So many people do all borrowing [when they start a business]. [For me] it wasn't all borrowing, and I think that gives [those of us who have both] a little more leeway.

He makes a good point. Would-be entrepreneurs who are more market integrated—who have the collateral to qualify for a bank loan *and* who have excess financial capital to contribute to a new business venture— generally outperform those who cannot qualify for a bank loan or who contribute negligible personal savings only (Valdez 2008b). Like John, the majority of White entrepreneurs possess substantial market capital resources and rely heavily on family, particularly on the transmission of intergenerational wealth through inheritance. White entrepreneurs' disproportionate access to these market-friendly avenues of resource mobilization and the consequent accumulation of substantial resources underscore this predominately middle-class and male group's superior position in the market, which goes a long way toward ensuring their success in starting and maintaining their businesses with relative ease. White entrepreneurs, like Mr. Frank, also benefit from government capital in the form of small-business loans.

Although previous studies have shown that Blacks and other racial minorities, immigrant refugees, and women benefit from government capital when starting new business ventures (Portes and Rumbaut 2001; Valdez 2008b), my sample shows that Whites are more likely to secure a government-backed loan from the SBA than Blacks or Latinos/as. While some members of these minority groups did not know of or seek out information regarding government support, or believed they would not qualify for such loans due to unauthorized status, others reported that they tried to apply but were confused by the application, they were turned off by "too much red tape" and the size of the application, or their application was rejected due to a lack of experience or insufficient collateral. Andre, a forty-six-year-old Black entrepreneur, captured the sentiments of many Black entrepreneurs when he stated that government loans are more trouble than they are worth because at the end of the day, "they seem like they *don't* want to help you. They *say* they want to help you but they want you to be perfect. If I'm perfect then I don't need you."

The frustration Andre expressed is indicative of the many and varied attempts by Black entrepreneurs to accumulate resources from market, social, and government capital sources, and the constant rejection that greets them. In the face of unceasing denials, most Black entrepreneurs opt to fund their businesses with limited resources and from fewer sources. For example, Renee Tate, forty-two, started her business with $35,000 in personal savings alone. She admitted that she had tried to apply for a government loan initially, because she knew "there are some good opportunities out there for minority women." In the end, however, she realized that she lacked the skills to complete the application; there was "too much to go through to get to the meat." When asked if she turned to any family or friends for additional aid before starting her business she replied, somewhat wryly, "Normally *I* give money to *them*!" Because she started her business with less than she needed but with all that she had, she quickly fell behind on her lease. To keep the business open, she withdrew $10,000 from her husband's 401(k) (for which he paid a significant penalty for early withdrawal).

The disadvantages that most Black entrepreneurs experience do not apply to all Black entrepreneurs. Keith Malone, a forty-five-year-old Black business owner, started his South Ward sandwich shop eight years ago. He established his business with the help of an SBA loan, after getting turned down by "every [national] bank, by the best of them." With $144,000 from that SBA loan (he asked for but did not quality for $200,000), $33,000 from his own personal savings, and $15,000 from friends and family, Mr. Malone started his business with just enough capital from a variety of sources. His ability to access multiple sources of capital is rooted in his previous managerial experience, college education, personal savings, and co-racial and kin networks with access to financial capital, a fairly advantageous position and one that is unique when compared to the majority of Black entrepreneurs.

## Conclusion

The classic theory of ethnic entrepreneurship adopts Granovetter's notion of embeddedness (1985:487), that the economy is embedded in its social relationships. For example, Portes and Sensenbrenner (1993) argue that ethnic group membership generates social capital that facilitates "actions within a collectivity that affects the economic goals and goal-seeking behavior of its members" (1323). Similarly, Light (1972) argues that ethnic group affiliation provides the basis for the development of ethnic-based resources that contribute to ethnic enterprise. Although evidence reveals support for this traditional approach, the ethnic entrepreneurship paradigm neglects to consider whether or to what extent nonethnic or nonentrepreneurial groups might also foster reciprocal ties from which to mobilize resources that facilitate entrepreneurship. Moreover, the emphasis on the role of ethnicity (for example, "ethnic entrepreneurship," "ethnic resources," "ethnic strategies") to explain economic action is likely overstated, as social relationships are often fragile and unpredictable rather than robust (Nee and Ingram 1988:22). Accordingly, economic activity or behavior that is rooted in such relationships is likely to be inconsistent or constrained. Explaining precisely how group affiliation affects entrepreneurship, in the context of enduring structural inequality in the modern market economy, requires an alternative approach.

The embedded market approach reconsiders the role of group affiliation within the social structure of the American market economy. From this perspective, intersecting group affiliations (gender, race, ethnicity) have the potential to generate resources and opportunities that facilitate or constrain

enterprise. These social groupings, however, are comprised of distinct classifications endemic to the American capitalist system—a hierarchical system that
is inherently rigid and unequal. Under these conditions, group affiliation may
provide the basis for reciprocal relationships to emerge that foster compensatory support in the face of market disadvantage; to a lesser extent, polity membership offers an additional or alternative source of lending. These group-based
resources and support, however, are ultimately shaped, maintained, and reproduced in the American social structure.

Intersections of class, gender, race, and ethnicity are embedded in the unequal American social structure and shape the overall market capacity of
Latino/a entrepreneurs through the production of market, social, and government capital. Although market capital is conditioned largely by one's class position, the context of nonclass group formations (race, gender) within interlocking systems of structural oppression and privilege influences the mobilization
of market capital resources, regardless of the class position of individuals and
groups. For example, immigration policy may restrict noncitizen immigrants
from securing a bank loan; traditional gender roles of masculinity and femi-
ninity may increase men's business networks and prospects over women's. At
the same time, structural forces that create, maintain, and reproduce inequality along class, gender, and racial hierarchies provide the foundation for the
emergence of social capital based on relationships of reciprocity, which attempt to compensate for market disadvantage. By situating reciprocal relations within the context of the American social structure, its emergence reveals agency, in terms of the individual and collective action of actors to
respond to structural inequality with social capital compensation (albeit that
which is circumscribed by those same structurally unequal hierarchies).

Thus, individuals and groups with a strong class position are more likely
to acquire and use market capital alone or in concert with social capital. In
the face of market disadvantage, however, Latinos/as may reach out to their
family-, gender-, ethnic-, or race-based networks to support them in economic and noneconomic ways. Although the compensatory aid that is generated always helps would-be entrepreneurs to get started and maintain their
businesses, the support is itself bounded by members' hierarchical position
within the social structure. Thus, middle-class Latino men, along with White
middle-class and male entrepreneurs, enjoy a stronger market position within
the American economy. Specifically, middle-class Latino and White entrepreneurs' access to substantial market capital resources—and for Whites, the

transmission of intergenerational wealth through family-based social capital—allows them to start and maintain their businesses with relative ease. Similarly, middle-class Latina women entrepreneurs, albeit a disproportionately smaller subset of the Latino/a entrepreneurial population, enjoy access to market capital resources that facilitate business start-up. For these more privileged Latinos/as, social capital is a nonessential resource.

In contrast, lower-class Latinos/as experience a weaker position in the American market economy due to their limited access to market capital resources, as do the majority of Black entrepreneurs. In the absence of a strong class position, these disadvantaged groups seek out compensatory social capital support based on their gender, ethnic, and racial group affiliations. Unlike their male counterparts, however, Latinas' disadvantaged gender classification as women restricts their social capital resources to a greater extent than experienced by men. Specifically, in the advent of a financial crisis, Latinas have fewer sources of social capital to keep their businesses going. Similarly, Black entrepreneurs, regardless of gender, are particularly disadvantaged with respect to their capacity to access social capital and government capital, leaving the majority to start their businesses with limited market capital only. Ultimately, middle-class White entrepreneurs and middle-class Latinos/as outperform lower-class men and women in their ease of business entry and maintenance; lower-class Latinos/as benefit from compensatory social capital resources to overcome obstacles that would prevent business ownership, although Latinas possess fewer social capital resources overall from which to draw. Black entrepreneurs, in contrast, lack significant sources of market, social, and government capital support, so start their businesses with limited resources and fewer sources of support. By revealing the conditions under which class, gender, race, and ethnicity intersect among individuals and groups from distinct social locations, and how such intersections influence entrepreneurial outcomes through the access to and use of market, social, and government capital, this chapter identifies the ubiquity and contextually contingent aspects of intersectionality on entrepreneurship.

# 5

# By What Measure Success?

## The Economic and Social Value of Latino/a Enterprise

*Do you consider your business a success?*
*Well, yes, I'm still alive.*

—**Don José, sixty-six years old, long-term U.S. resident, Mexican**

**THIS CHAPTER** investigates the entrepreneurial success of Latino/a entrepreneurs. From the perspective of the embedded market, entrepreneurial success must be understood in the larger context of Latinos'/as' individual and collective placement within the unequal American social structure, in which Latino/a entrepreneurs from different social locations are embedded. Accordingly, Latinos'/as' social location within that structure shapes their notions of entrepreneurial success, as well as their capacity to attain it. Understanding their reasons for business ownership is critical in resolving whether or to what extent Latinos/as achieve success through enterprise, as their entry into business and perceptions of success vary by their social location and are not determined wholly by economic concerns.

Most Latinos/as engage in entrepreneurial activity to achieve economic progress, regardless of their social location. For these economically minded entrepreneurs, making money, or at least more money than they made as wage workers, is the goal. As a measure of economic progress, success is easily equated with an entrepreneur's take-home earnings, a commonly used indicator of economic success in the American market economy. This goal is achieved for some (albeit modestly and with considerable sacrifice) but not all, which calls into question the presumed positive relationship between enterprise and economic mobility (Valdez 2008b). For example, middle-class Latinos earn more than lower-class Latinos or Latinas, the latter group regardless of class. This observation suggests that middle-class Latinos benefit disproportionately from their more privileged class and gender positioning. Although economic success to the extent that middle-class Latinos achieve it may lie beyond the reach of many Latinas and lower-class Latinos, these more disadvantaged entrepreneurs do not concede that it has eluded them entirely. Instead, they offer alternative measures of success. For example, lower-class men often emphasize indirect measures that proxy economic success, such as business survival or longevity (Valdez 2003; van Praag 2003:3). By underscoring their ability to stay in business, these entrepreneurs declare success, even as they shift its meaning away from a purely monetary or financial measure and toward a more indirect measure of economic progress.

Latino/a entrepreneurs also define success using a number of noneconomic indicators, as some are motivated not only by money, but also by a yearning for autonomy, which ranks as high as economic mobility as the main reason for deciding to go into business. They also embrace business ownership as a means to escape wage work or to achieve job satisfaction. For these independent-minded entrepreneurs, being their own bosses or enjoying their work brings rewards that rival purely economic considerations. These alternative objectives allow disadvantaged Latinos/as, in particular, to claim that success has been achieved, even in the face of economic stagnation or decline. Still, it is easier for middle-class Latinos to make this argument. After all, they are in a better economic position to start with, so even if they fail to achieve economic progress through enterprise, a fairly uncommon scenario, they are better positioned to shift the meaning of success convincingly from earnings to autonomy as a sufficient goal. For lower-class Latinos/as, achieving autonomy may take center stage in their discourse of success, especially in the absence of economic mobility or longevity. Unlike middle-class Latinos/as, however, their economic insecurity and vulnerability are not forgotten or set aside as easily.

In the end, all Latino/a business owners characterize themselves as successful. This discourse of success, however, may not reflect their initial expectations of and motivations for business ownership or their actual work experiences, practices, and socioeconomic outcomes. Many confront marked disparities between their expectations and practices and their actual outcomes, which at times contradict their claims of success. Even so, such disparities are not sufficient to alter Latino/a entrepreneurs' wholly positive discourse of success. That being said, it is clear that Latino/a entrepreneurs from diverse social locations experience success very differently, and from a socioeconomic standpoint, at times not at all. In keeping with the embedded market approach, it appears that the intersection connecting class, gender, race, and ethnicity

converges to shape (and reshape) a shifting meaning of success among entrepreneurs, as they modify their expectations to align more closely to their
economic and social reality.

For example, the emphasis on business longevity in the absence of profitability among lower-class Latinos/as is a direct response to their inability to
generate that profit. Lower-class Latinos'/as' less-than-desirable economic returns are conditioned initially on their disadvantaged position within the
embedded market. From that initial position as lower-class, low-skilled workers
attempting to escape the harsh conditions of dirty, dangerous, or difficult work,
to their inability to generate sufficient market capacity from which to start
their businesses, lower-class Latinos/as carry their vulnerable status with them
throughout the entrepreneurial process; in this way the embedded market
ensures that inequality is reproduced among disadvantaged Latinos/as, even
in entrepreneurship. This finding challenges the assumption of the ethnic entrepreneurship approach that entrepreneurship facilitates economic mobility
among immigrant minorities.

## Entrepreneurship and Economic Mobility

Previous literature on ethnic entrepreneurship generally equates entrepreneurial participation with economic success. Whether within the borders of
the ethnic enclave economy, such as in the case of the Chinese in San Francisco's Chinatown, or outside of it, such as in the case of the Korean middleman entrepreneurs who work in predominately Black communities (see Lee
2002), researchers observe that ethnic entrepreneurs increase their earnings relative to those of their co-ethnic wage worker counterparts (Light and
Bonacich 1988; Portes and Rumbaut 2001, 2006; Waldinger et al. 1990). The
positive relationship between entrepreneurial participation and economic
success, however, is challenged by studies that provide contradictory evidence. For example, Hamilton (2000:628) finds that it is wage workers who
earn more and outpace the earnings growth of similarly skilled entrepreneurs, while Borjas (1990) concludes that all things being equal, the earnings of
entrepreneurs are not markedly different from the earnings of wage workers.
In a study that compares workers' earnings with those of entrepreneurs across
different Latin American national-origin groups, I show that the earnings of
self-employed Latinos are generally higher than those of wage workers. The
earnings for self-employed Latinas, however, are not as favorable or clear-cut.
Latina entrepreneurs do not always exceed the earnings of their wage worker

counterparts and always earn less than men (Valdez 2008b). In a more refined study that focuses on high- and low-skilled Mexican entrepreneurs in the Southwest, I find some evidence of divergent trends in earnings by skill and gender. For men, the earnings of foreign-born Mexican entrepreneurs are not markedly different from those of their wage worker counterparts, regardless of skill. Among women, I find that high-skilled foreign-born Mexican women outperform their wage worker counterparts. For this group, self-employment is associated with higher earnings. In contrast, low-skilled foreign-born Mexican women entrepreneurs earn less than similarly skilled wage workers (Valdez 2006). These mixed findings challenge the assumption that entrepreneurship is generally associated with economic success.

Moreover, the ethnic entrepreneurship approach tends to minimize the social costs associated with enterprise. For example, many Korean entrepreneurs concentrate in low-skilled, low-wage industries where they may average an eighty-hour work week and suffer from physical and mental exhaustion (Light and Bonacich 1988:278). Ethnic entrepreneurs' self-exploitation calls into question their presumed upwardly mobile trajectory (Bates 1997; Valdez 2008b). Nowikowski (1984) echoes this sentiment. Regardless of high participation rates, Indian and Pakistani entrepreneurs in Britain remain managers of small workshops and petty traders, not members of the bourgeoisie proper. Still others argue that some ethnic groups favor entrepreneurship as a "survival strategy" or "economic lifeboat" only (Light and Roach 1996:193; Valenzuela 2003), that is, a last-ditch alternative to unemployment or joblessness rather than an avenue of upward mobility. As Hakim states, "It cannot be assumed that the self-employed are invariably entrepreneurs who are building businesses that will eventually employ more people than themselves. The evidence to date suggests that most of the self-employed are only providing themselves with an alternative to the employee job" (1988:430). Related to the question of economic progress through entrepreneurship is the indicator itself. Previous attempts to measure the earnings of ethnic entrepreneurs regularly disregard zero (break-even) or negative earnings returns (see Portes and Zhou 1996). However, the loss of this information is significant in that its absence may dismiss from the analysis those individuals for whom entrepreneurial participation is not synonymous with economic progress. Taken as a whole, the relationship between entrepreneurship and economic mobility is unclear, as Latinos/as from diverse ethnic, gender, and class backgrounds may engage in enterprise for a variety of reasons and with divergent economic outcomes.

Nevertheless, most Latino/a entrepreneurs engage in enterprise to improve their economic circumstances.

## Entrepreneurial Earnings as Economic Success

Table 5.1 displays Latino/a entrepreneurs' annual earnings by gender for the year before the interviews were conducted, between 2005 and 2007.[1] Owners were asked to report their take-home earnings for the previous year. The overwhelming majority of business owners revealed this information (only 6 percent refused); however, most preferred to present their earnings using a range of income categories from a card that was provided (from $0 to more than $130,000) rather than reporting a specific dollar amount. I use median annual income guidelines provided by the federal government to approximate lower-, middle-, and upper-middle-income ranges.[2]

Column 1 of Table 5.1 shows that a quarter of the Latino/a entrepreneurs in my sample are low-income earners (24 percent), taking home less than $29,000 in annual earnings. Another quarter of the population falls on the lower end of the middle-income distribution, reporting earnings in the range of $30,000 to $49,000; in other words, almost half of Latino/a entrepreneurs earn $50,000 or less. In contrast, only 15 percent of Latinos/as fall between the mid- to upper-middle-income ranges ($50,000 and $89,000). Only one-

**Table 5.1**  Latino/a Entrepreneurs' Annual Household Income from Business, by Gender, 2005–2007

|  | All (%) | Men (%) | Women (%) |
|---|---|---|---|
| Low |  |  |  |
| $0–$29,000 | 23.5 | 17.6 | 29.4 |
| Middle |  |  |  |
| $30,000–$49,000 | 23.5 | 23.5 | 23.5 |
| $50,000–$69,000 | 14.7 | 11.8 | 17.6 |
| $70,000–$89,000 | 5.9 | 5.9 | 5.9 |
| Upper |  |  |  |
| $90,000–$109,000 | 17.6 | 23.5 | 11.8 |
| $110,000–$129,000 | 0 | 0 | 0 |
| $130,000+ | 8.8 | 11.8 | 5.9 |
| Refuse to Answer | 5.9 | 5.9 | 5.9 |
| Total | 100 | 100 | 100 |

NOTES: Household business income is reported twice for co-owners who live in the same household. Annual income is reported for the year before the interview took place. Interviews were conducted between 2006 and 2008.

quarter qualify as upper-income earners (earning more than $90,000). When asked about their expected earnings for the current year (the year in which the interview took place), the vast majority of entrepreneurs predicted that they would earn the same amount they reported for the previous year. In a follow-up question, when asked why they did not expect a growth in earnings, most attributed their predicted earnings stagnation to the ongoing economic recession, which has increased costs and decreased customer traffic considerably.

As demonstrated earlier, middle-class Latinos enjoy greater access to resources and thus experience fewer hardships in starting and maintaining their restaurants than do their Latina and lower-class Latino counterparts. Correspondingly, differential access to resources by class and gender appear to impact Latinos'/as' earnings. As Table 5.1 shows, 12 percent more women than men are low-income earners (29 percent of women compared to 18 percent of men), whereas twice as many men are upper-income earners (35 percent of men compared to 18 percent of women); half as many women as men reach the highest income-earning range of $130,000 or more (6 percent of women compared to 12 percent of men).

Among the Latino/a business owners I spoke to, there is a general consensus that they are earning more as entrepreneurs than they did as wage workers in the general labor market. These findings confirm previous research on ethnic enterprise, which suggests that business ownership fosters economic mobility among ethnic minorities (Portes and Zhou 1996). Yet, Latino/a entrepreneurs, like the majority of small-business owners, also report working well in excess of the standard American work week (forty hours per week, fifty weeks per year). Entrepreneurial activity, then, may increase earnings only by allowing entrepreneurs to work more hours than they were able to as wage workers. For example, one Latino entrepreneur in my sample reported an annual income of $20,000, for which he put in a fifty-hour work week. This entrepreneur's hourly wage averages $6.66 per hour, or close to the 2008 federal hourly minimum wage of $6.55.[3] In contrast, an entrepreneur who earned $50,000 in the previous year but worked the same number of hours (fifty hours per week) earned substantially more, or $20 per hour. Yet 50 percent of Latino/a entrepreneurs earn below $50,000 (see Table 5.1). This latter scenario is unlikely to represent more than a few fortunate Latino/a entrepreneurs. A more common scenario is that of Don Francisco, who, after asking his wife for a calculator, eagerly computed his hourly wage during our interview.

After crunching a few numbers, he concluded that he made a whopping $4.50 an hour, at which he remarked somewhat tongue in cheek, "Wow, that much?" It is also important to consider the not insignificant proportion of Latino/a entrepreneurs who break even only, or essentially work for free. These entrepreneurs usually rely on their spouses or take on an extra job to make ends meet. As Michelle, the twenty-two-year-old lower-class Mexican who co-owns a restaurant with her mother, explains:

> We've had some hard times. So I had to go back to work. That's why I have another job. . . . My mother is the one that brings in all the income, you know? So if [the restaurant makes a profit] I have enough to pay her but . . . if I have to pay the lights [that is, pay the electricity bill], she's like, well, pay me Wednesday when we have a little more money. So, it's hard. . . . I don't get paid from here.

Surprisingly, of all the entrepreneurs who do not report an income or who just break even, most are not disadvantaged, lower-class Latinos/as like Michelle. Rather, the more vulnerable the entrepreneur, the more likely he or she is to report a profit, albeit a low-income profit, when compared to his or her middle-class counterparts. This counterintuitive finding has less to do with disadvantaged entrepreneurs' economic prowess and more to do with their economic insecurity—they are unable to work for too long for free, as they lack a safety net, typically in the form of an additional job held or a second household income.

Middle-class entrepreneurs with access to sufficient sources of support may opt to work in an unprofitable business for some time, and often for nonpecuniary reasons. As Rita, the middle-class restaurateur who started a business "for herself," acknowledges, she "doesn't need a check," nor does her business need to "put food on the table." Her husband supports the family financially, while she runs the business primarily as a "challenge" to herself. Likewise, Don Julio, a middle-class Mexican restaurateur of twenty-five years, explains that he took a job as a manager in another restaurant to keep his business going when it fell on hard times:

> [During the 1980s recession] I had to leave the business in the hands of my wife. I had to go work elsewhere because we weren't making much business here, but it just stuck; it kept going because of the customers until we had better times. I retired from that other company [in 1994], and from then on I've been working on my own.

In this way, middle-class entrepreneurs' use of additional resources offsets or mediates their income, which allows them to keep unprofitable businesses open longer, while lower-class entrepreneurs like Michelle are not so lucky. In fact, at the time of this writing (and in the face of a nationwide economic recession), Michelle and Theresa's restaurant closed its doors, less than one year after opening.

Overall, entrepreneurship may provide for increased earnings when compared to previous wage work; however, it may do so only by allowing entrepreneurs an opportunity for self-exploitation through additional hours worked, with hourly earnings actually hovering at or below minimum wage (which nevertheless results in increased earnings overall). That said, it is important to note that earnings, although an obvious starting point, may not capture the complete meaning of "success" among the entrepreneurs themselves, as the noneconomic benefits of business ownership may sometimes trump entrepreneurs' economic concerns. Although this observation has been demonstrated in previous research (Blanchflower 2004; Butler and Greene 1997; Douglas and Shepherd 2000; Hamilton 2000), I find that the extent to which noneconomic or social factors matter varies by entrepreneurs' intersectional social location.

## The Economic and Social Value of Success

One of the more surprising findings of this study is that all Latino/a entrepreneurs share a universal belief in their success, regardless of their intersectional social location. Without fail, Latino/a entrepreneurs from diverse ethnic, racial, gender, and class backgrounds characterize themselves and their businesses as successful, despite marked differences that include salary earned (breaking even to more than $130,000 annually), hours worked (twenty to seventy-plus hours per week), length of time owning a business (less than a year to more than twenty years), and amount of stress and other health problems experienced that they attribute to business ownership (for the vast majority, without health insurance for themselves or their workers). The observed ubiquity of success among this diverse group of Latino/a entrepreneurs corroborates previous research, which demonstrates that nonpecuniary benefits, such as being one's own boss, flexible hours, and job satisfaction, often trump economic or other concerns (Benz 2009). On the other hand, when entrepreneurs fall short of their socioeconomic expectations, they sometimes contradict this discourse of success or alter its criteria to more closely align with the reality of their lived experience. In other words, expectations are reconfigured to reflect diminished socioeconomic outcomes—outcomes that are associated with class, gender, ethnic, and racial hierarchies, and that require disadvantaged entrepreneurs, especially, to develop a situational, contingent, or shifting meaning of success.

### The Ubiquity of Success

Rita, a forty-seven-year-old, petite Mexican naturalized citizen, works full-time in her restaurant, a small and welcoming space decorated with Mexican artwork, plants, and tchotchkes, freshly painted walls in autumn colors, comfortable tables and chairs, and free Internet access. In addition to being a restaurateur, she volunteers at her church and holds a part-time job teaching spinning classes at the neighborhood gym several times a week. Although her two-year-old business is not profitable—she breaks even every year—this economic reality did not deter her from recently opening a second and larger restaurant across town with an expanded menu. Notwithstanding her frenetic schedule, she is toying with the idea of writing a memoir about the loss of her daughter, who died of cancer seven years ago after a three-year battle.

Recall that Rita characterizes her decision to go into business as a way to achieve autonomy and as a challenge to herself. Her decision was made easier because she knew that her husband's occupation provides her family with a middle-class lifestyle and economic security. When asked whether she is a successful business owner, she replies that she considers herself to be a success because she enjoys her business, is excited about the new store opening, and can "do whatever I want." While she has certainly achieved her goals of autonomy and passion through business ownership, she nevertheless expresses some regret about the unexpected, negative consequences of being her own boss:

> If you ask me now, even though I like my business a lot, there's a lot of things that . . . that need to be done and you . . . I bring my problems home, you see. And I can't relax sometimes, whereas working for somebody else, you work your hours and you go home and you're done. Now that I think about it, it would have been nice just to work for somebody else. . . . I would be making money, I guess, and not bring my problems home.

Rita believes that owning a business fulfills her need for independence but at the same time acknowledges that it increases her anxiety and likely decreases her income. She also imagines that instead of working for herself, it "would have been nice just to work for somebody else." Although these sentiments seem to contradict her earlier characterization of herself as a successful entrepreneur, she goes on to extend her definition of success to the business itself. Through that extension she is able to strengthen and reinforce her initial claim of success:

> Success [comes from] my products, customer service, and just the environment . . . the scenery. . . . It's very important for people. . . . It's not about making money or me getting a check, you know. Because I don't need to. And here, you know, I see sometimes my customers all bummed out, and I ask them, "Hey, what's wrong?" There's something wrong, so I kind of make them at least live better.

Upon further reflection, Rita is not at all certain that owning a business has been beneficial to her; yet, she is certain that her business is a success because it has improved her customers' lives. By equating success with happy customers whom she helps to "live better," Rita rearticulates a notion of success that reflects her lived experience as one who helps others.

Similarly, Doña María, a forty-four-year-old Mexican long-term U.S. resident, became an entrepreneur to earn more money and be her own boss. Unfortunately, her business does not generate a profit. She reasons that her lack of work experience and limited education (she concedes that she is "bad with numbers" and points out that she quit school after second grade) prevent her from being "more [economically] successful." Still, she concludes that her business is a success because "success comes from how you treat clients, your enthusiasm . . . when people finish eating and you ask them how the meal was and they tell you it was great." In the face of economic uncertainty, Doña María emphasizes the nonpecuniary rewards associated with customer satisfaction, which she equates with a new meaning of success. At the same time, she implicates her lack of human capital, a shared feature of the Latino/a lower class, to explain why her business does not generate a profit.

Rita's and María's discourse regarding the noneconomic or social meaning of success is common among Latina entrepreneurs, regardless of class. Financially successful Latinas are also likely to highlight interpersonal relationships and other noneconomic factors to indicate success that transcend economic outcomes, such as a love of cooking, the loyalty of the staff ("I treat them like family") and the presence of a regular customer base. These findings support previous research demonstrating that women frequently articulate or rearticulate a meaning of entrepreneurial success in terms of noneconomic criteria, such as personal growth, interpersonal relations, and a concern for others (Eagly and Wood 1991; Travis et al. 1988; Unger and Crawford 1992). Although these objectives seem to reinforce gender-role or sex-role stereotypes— that in the process of gender socialization, women entrepreneurs are oriented toward noneconomic markers of success—it is interesting to note that such goals are mentioned by Rita, a middle-class Latina, and María, a lower-class Latina, only after they acknowledge that they are not making any money. This subtle transition, from economic to noneconomic expressions of success, uncovers a discourse that is not simply reducible to traditional gender roles or the social construction of gender. It exposes instead a more complex strategy of justifying and laying claim to success, even in the face of economic decline, which is more accurately linked to their social location.

Unlike Latinas, Latinos rarely emphasize such noneconomic markers of success. For them, prosperity is generally equated with the bottom line. Rob, one of the most financially successful entrepreneurs in this study, affirms his success by stating simply that he met his economic expectations by breaking even the first year and increasing his profit margin every year since. Similarly, Don Fernando (who reported annual earnings in excess of $75,000) claims that the recession did not affect his successful business, which grows at a steady and enviable monthly rate of 2 percent.

In contrast, success among disadvantaged Latino entrepreneurs who experience economic stagnation or decline is not markedly different from that described by Rob or Don Fernando—Latino entrepreneurs who experience economic mobility. Most Latinos equate success with their economic conditions, regardless of their income, although those who earn less offer a more nuanced and relative or indirect notion of economic progress that reflects their more vulnerable socioeconomic status. As mentioned earlier, Don José started his restaurant to improve his economic conditions and to escape a physically demanding job. As an entrepreneur, however, his earnings have not improved (his income continues to fall below the poverty line as it did when he was employed as a roofer). Still, he regards his business as an economic success without hesitation. He explains:

> I'm still alive. I provided for my family. I never had to go asking for food stamps or anything, thank God. . . . For someone who has studies and education that's nothing, but for me it's a lot. For an educated person, it doesn't take long to move up, because they have computers and they can click here and

there and everywhere. I on the other hand look at a computer and I don't know where to click. That's the problem for the person who doesn't have an education; it's very hard; it's pure work, work, work.[4]

Don José readily concedes that he has not met his expectations of economic progress through enterprise. Moreover, like María and other lower-class Latinos/as, he suspects that his lack of skills and education has had a negative impact on his earnings. Unlike Latinas, however, he does not underscore the nonpecuniary benefits associated with enterprise, such as customer satisfaction. Instead, he rearticulates a relative meaning of economic gain, specifically, that he is "still alive" and has provided for his family without resorting to welfare. Although this notion of success does not resemble his initial expectations of monetary gain, it accurately reflects his current and more modest economic circumstances, which, in the end, allow him to stay in business and thus declare his business a success.

## Racial Group Differences in Success

For the most part, success in Latino/a entrepreneurship, as measured by economic and noneconomic indicators, appears to be correlated with the individual and collective market capacity of Latinos/as from different social locations. Middle-class Latinos enjoy substantial access to market and social capital; consequently, their income returns are generally higher than those of lower-class men and women, the latter group regardless of class. In contrast, Latinas and lower-class Latinos have less access to market, social, and government capital. Their businesses generally reflect this discrepancy and generate less income.

Moreover, Latinos often express success in terms of monetary gain. Although some lower-class Latinos concede that their earnings fall below their expectations, they rearticulate a meaning of success that captures relative or indirect economic success, as measured by their ability to survive in difficult economic circumstances and against all odds. Latinas, in contrast, generally hope to increase their earnings or improve their economic conditions through enterprise; however, in the absence of economic progress, they are likely to equate success with a number of noneconomic measures, such as being their own bosses or satisfying their customers' needs.

In a similar fashion, the annual income of White and Black entrepreneurs is associated with each group's access to and use of market, social, and government capital resources. Black entrepreneurs have less access to social or government capital; in their absence, they instead rely heavily on the limited amount of market capital they can accumulate, such as a small investment of personal savings. Consequently, Black entrepreneurs report substantially lower annual earnings, on average, than White or Latino/a entrepreneurs. As Table 5.2 shows, the majority of Black entrepreneurs (60 percent) earn $29,000 or less, the lowest-income-earning category. In contrast, only 10 percent of White entrepreneurs fall into this same range, which suggests that White entrepreneurs clearly benefit from their substantial access to and use of market, social, and government capital resources. Latinos/as fall in between, at 24 percent. The greater overall market capacity of White entrepreneurs likely contributes to their higher income returns when compared to those of Latino/a and Black entrepreneurs. This appears to be the case, as almost one in three White entrepreneurs earns $130,000 or more per year, a significant percentage of that population (30 percent), especially when one considers that less than 10 percent of Latinos/as and 20 percent of Black entrepreneurs reach that highest-income-earning category. Although this sample of Black and White entrepreneurs is very small, reported earnings roughly correspond with those reported in previous research. For example, in a sample of almost six thousand Black and thirteen thousand White business owners across the United States, 50 percent of Blacks reported earnings that fell below $25,000, while 40 percent of White entrepreneurs reported earnings above $75,000 (Valdez 2008b).

White entrepreneurs' notion of success, much like that of middle-class Latinos, closely aligns with their economic conditions. For example, Tony Frank, the fifty-one-year-old owner of Lonestar Burger, equates success with his profit margin alone, and was fairly aggressive in his response regarding his own economic progress.

*Do you consider yourself to be a success?*
Yes.

*Why is that?*
Why am I successful? You mean besides that my business makes money? I mean, is there another answer to that?

*There are no right or wrong answers; I'm just trying to get a sense of what success means to you.*
This business is profitable. If a business is profitable, then you know it's successful. If you know it's not, then it's not. [long pause] I get a lot more out of it than just money; there's a lot of satisfaction too.

**Table 5.2**  Latino/a, White, and Black Entrepreneurs' Annual Household Income
from Business, 2005–2007

|  | Latino/a (%) | White (%) | Black (%) |
|---|---|---|---|
| Low |  |  |  |
| $0–$29,000 | 23.5 | 10.0 | 60.0 |
| Middle |  |  |  |
| $30,000–$49,000 | 23.5 | 10.0 | 0 |
| $50,000–$69,000 | 14.7 | 20.0 | 0 |
| $70,000–$89,000 | 5.9 | 10.0 | 0 |
| Upper |  |  |  |
| $90,000–$109,000 | 17.6 | 0 | 0 |
| $110,000–$129,000 | 0 | 0 | 0 |
| $130,000+ | 8.8 | 30.0 | 20.0 |
| Refuse to Answer | 5.9 | 20.0 | 20.0 |
| Total | 100 | 100 | 100 |

NOTES: Household business income is reported twice for co-owners who live in the same household.
Annual income is reported for the year before the interview took place. Interviews were conducted between
2006 and 2008.

Like Tony, Sam Christensen, the fifty-eight-year-old owner White of Don Juan's
Mexican Restaurante, equates his success with economic indicators. Mr. Christensen has managed his full-service Mexican restaurant, located in the Greater
Houston area, for more than forty years. He takes home more than $130,000
each year. When asked whether he is a success, he replied simply, "Yes, by all
measures of the industry."

In contrast, Black entrepreneurs, whose earnings generally lag far behind
those of their White and Latino/a counterparts, often equate success with
nonpecuniary factors, such as being their own boss, giving back to their community, and performing a job and tasks that they enjoy, such as a "love" of
or "passion" for cooking. Notably, the discourse of success among Black men
and women entrepreneurs mirrors that of Latinas, specifically in highlighting
the social aspects of enterprise. Yet, while Latinas acknowledge that they strive
for economic success but concede that they often fall short of this goal, Black
entrepreneurs are likely to disregard economic considerations altogether, and
often from the start of their entrepreneurial activity. Because Black entrepreneurs are more likely to start a business for noneconomic reasons, it follows
that they do not appear to be overly concerned with the profitability of the
business. In fact, some Black entrepreneurs volunteer that they don't expect
their business to ever generate a profitable return. In some cases, they antici-
pate the need to rely on the income of their spouse or acquire a second job to

get by financially. Renee Tate, a forty-two-year-old Black, French Haitian, and Creole business owner, is representative of many Black business owners in the South Ward.

After moving to Houston from Louisiana in 2000, Ms. Tate decided to go into business to satisfy a passion for cooking. She started her business with limited market capital, only $35,000 in personal savings that she accumulated over several years of working in real estate (a job she has held since 1996). After earning an associate's degree in food service management and a chef's certificate, she opened The Creole Seafood Shack in 2004. Her restaurant does not generate much revenue, but she is not overly preoccupied with its negligible returns. Early on she decided that she would continue her job as a Realtor, a job she characterizes as "financially rewarding," adding, "As for the restaurant, I just love to cook." Similarly, Keith Malone, the forty-five-year-old owner of a South Ward sandwich shop, manages some rental property on the side. He says he keeps that job "to supplement my income like when it's slow, like right now." Mr. Malone went into business because he believes that it is the best way to "control your own destiny" and do "what you want to do," even though he concedes that it "isn't the quickest way" to make money.

> If you want to make money, [owning a business] probably isn't the quickest way. But I think it's really just doing what you want to do [that matters]. If you can make money doing it, fine. If you make money doing something that you don't want to do, it's not as good.

For Ms. Tate, the restaurant gives her the opportunity to do something she loves; for Mr. Malone, it offers an opportunity to achieve autonomy. These owners are like many other Black entrepreneurs who express expectations of their businesses that are noneconomic in character, such as a desire to give back to their community, to be their own bosses, and to enjoy their work. These nonpecuniary measures of success are often the primary reasons Black entrepreneurs turn to entrepreneurship in the first place. They do not appear to privilege the economic aspects of success that are often shared by White and Lantino middle-class entrepreneurs, nor do they underscore a notion of relative economic success via business survival and longevity, as emphasized by lower-class Latinos. The ways in which Black entrepreneurs stress the social aspects of entrepreneurship are more in line with those expressed by Latina entrepreneurs, although Black entrepreneurs go even farther, often dismissing economic considerations completely. This is not to suggest that Black entrepreneurs' economic concerns are trivial or nonexistent; rather, they find other ways to meet their financial obligations, including additional employment. These findings reflect those found in previous research on Black enterprise, which suggest that Black business owners are primarily motivated by "personal happiness," "freedom from harassment," and a "desire to contribute to their community" (Richtermeyer 2002; Woodward 1997:220).

To assume too quickly that Black entrepreneurs and poor Latinas embrace the nonpecuniary benefits of enterprise in lieu of economic ones, however, misses the connection to their initial social location, which shapes in large part the economic outcomes that they can expect to receive and what they actually receive as entrepreneurs.

From the perspective of the embedded market, Black entrepreneurs' emphasis on the social aspects of entrepreneurial success at the outset, and poor Latina entrepreneurs' shifting meaning of success from economic to social concerns, belie their disadvantaged social location within an unequal structural context. In particular, the intersection of race and class among Black entrepreneurs who live and work in geographically concentrated areas of racial segregation and poverty ensures that the disadvantages they confront at the bottom of the racial and class hierarchies are transmitted to their entrepreneurial outcomes. For poor Latina women, the intersection of gender and class limits their access to the market capital resources that are available to middle-class Latinos, and the social capital available to lower-class Latinos—resources that help secure a stronger foundation from which to start a profitable enterprise. In this embedded market, where discrimination, disrespect, and dirty, dangerous, or difficult jobs at the bottom of the hourglass economy give rise to entrepreneurial dreams that are realized with only a fraction of the resources that are needed, *success* becomes a relative term. Thus, the meaning of success among disadvantaged groups is, predictably, significantly different from the meaning assigned to it by those who are more privileged, such as middle-class White and Latino men, whose motivations for and expectations of entrepreneurship are, like those of Blacks or poor Latinas, also mediated by their social location. Ultimately, it is not that Black entrepreneurs reject economic measures of success or that poor Latinas come to the realization that success means that their customers are satisfied; rather, it is that their position within the embedded market, from which they are jockeying for a new social location through enterprise, is so far away from one in which economic growth is possible that their expectations of enterprise become necessarily and more narrowly tailored. In the case of Black entrepreneurs, the meaning of success is replaced at the onset of enterprise, while in the case of poor Latinas it shifts over the course of their business tenure, from economic to social aspects that constitute reachable, if diminished goals.

## Conclusion

The majority of Latino/a entrepreneurs articulate success in terms of financial or economic considerations, regardless of class background. The outcomes for those who seek economic prosperity, as the vast majority of Latino/a entrepreneurs do, are not clear-cut. Economic progress is achieved for many Latino/a entrepreneurs, especially middle-class Latinos, but not without considerable sacrifice. On the other hand, lower-class Latino/a entrepreneurs sometimes earn less than they did previously as wage workers, which requires them to rely on their spouses or other family members, or to take on an extra job to make ends meet. Still others, especially lower-class Latinos and Latinas, the latter regardless of class background, experience economic stagnation or questionable financial gains (that is, working more hours to generate negligible increases in earnings).

Regardless of these diverse financial outcomes, Latino/a entrepreneurs' discourse of success is wholly confirmatory, even as their actual work experiences and practices reveal a more complex and less optimistic story. For middle-class Latinos, the economic and social aspects of success are indisputable, as they enjoy comparably profitable businesses and a deep satisfaction in their work, although they fail to reach economic parity with their White racial counterparts. In the absence of economic progress, however, the meaning of success requires a fundamental shift away from its initial economic objectives. Correspondingly, Latino/a entrepreneurs who do not generate a profitable return develop an alternative, noneconomic meaning of success that includes business survival and longevity, prioritizes autonomy, or emphasizes job satisfaction. For example, the earnings of lower-class Latinos are likely to fall short of their economic expectations, leading them to rearticulate a meaning of success that captures *relative* economic success.

For Latinas, the majority of whom are lower-class, the social benefits of ownership, such as the development of interpersonal relationships or customer satisfaction, trump economic concerns in the face of economic stagnation or decline. Notably, however, lower-class Latinos/as sometimes implicate a lack of skills or education to justify a poor economic performance; such statements implicitly acknowledge that class differences in enterprise might impact their economic outcomes. What is overlooked by lower-class Latinas, however, is how class intersects with gender to dampen their socioeconomic outcomes even further.

Black entrepreneurs provide a remarkable comparison to Whites and Latinos/as, as they generally disregard economic measures of success from the outset. For Blacks, the meaning of success includes the social aspects mentioned earlier, along with an additional one, that of building up or giving back to the community. These admirable goals do not necessarily reflect a greater philanthropy on the part of Black entrepreneurs when compared to their White and Latino/a counterparts, however, as much as they highlight the intensity of the Black entrepreneurs' disadvantage. The adversity associated with Black entrepreneurs' social location is such that it often eliminates from consideration even the possibility that their economic actions might influence their socioeconomic outcomes in positive or even neutral ways.

The diversity of economic outcomes among Latinos/as from different class backgrounds, compared to those of White and Black entrepreneurs, reveals the salience of social location in conditioning the life chances of American entrepreneurs. Regardless of extreme disparities in socioeconomic outcomes, all entrepreneurs believe in their success. Yet, success is not the same for all entrepreneurs; its meaning shifts from purely economic to purely social aspects, which superimpose positions of privilege and oppression within the embedded market. Such findings challenge the ubiquity of success, as its shifting meaning contradicts its universal relevancy among entrepreneurs who are differently positioned within the unequal social structure.

# 6 Ethnic and Racial Identity Formation Among American Entrepreneurs

THE LONG HISTORY of racial oppression against Blacks, Native Americans, Latinos/as, and Asians in America is well established. The dominant position of Whites in the United States has been maintained historically through coercion and, perhaps more recently, consent (Omi and Winant 1994). From its inception, White privilege and power have been readily exercised in the United States, observed early on in the blatant, forced removal of Native Americans from tribal lands and the enslavement of multiple generations of Africans and their descendants from the sixteenth to mid-nineteenth centuries. Later, the aggressive recruitment of immigrant minority labor during the Industrial Revolution and the exclusionary immigration policies that followed on its heels, such as the Chinese Exclusion Act (1882) and the Gentleman's Agreement (1907–24), demonstrated the continuing power of the dominant racial group to control immigration and, thus, the racial and ethnic demographic profile of the country. Additionally, the forced internment in 1942 of 110,000 Japanese, including American citizens (Okihiro 1994:137), and today's clarion call to dismantle birthright citizenship for the children of unauthorized immigrants, and the recently passed anti-immigrant bill in Arizona that essentially clears the way for racial profiling of Latinos/as, remind us of the persistence of foreignness and the nagging question of belonging that is too often leveled against non-White immigrants and their descendants. While the civil rights movement sought an end to de facto and de jure racism in public places, such as the segregation of Black and Mexican Americans in public schools, housing, and parks (Perea 1997), institutional racism, statistical discrimination, and everyday, "common sense" racial ideologies and "controlling images" (Espiritu 2008:14) continue to undermine the civil rights movement's "triumph of liberalism" (Omi and Winant 1994:15), thereby ensuring the maintenance, persistence, and reproduction of racial inequality in the United States. From ideology to practice, racism and its effects are observed in a multitude of socioeconomic, cultural, political, physical, and psychological outcomes in America, including racial disparities in education, wealth, occupational attainment, housing, lending, business ownership, incarceration and death penalty rates, infant mortality, health, mental health, and general well-being.

The U.S. racial hierarchy is not symbolic, cultural, or ideological. It has a structural foundation that develops out of a racialized social system (Bonilla-Silva 1994:23). Under conditions of (largely unacknowledged) systemic racial oppression, power and privilege are ascribed to those at the top of the racial hierarchy (Whites), while oppression and disadvantage are ascribed to those at the bottom (Blacks), with other groups (Latinos/as, Asians) "positioned *by Whites*" in between (Feagin 2006:21; Feagin's emphasis). The racial hierarchy captures the "reality of divergent racial group interests" that defines systemic racism, or the pervasive and persistent racial inequality that characterizes U.S. race relations (Bonilla-Silva 1994; Feagin 2006:21). Although Feagin (2006) does not specify which "groups of color" are positioned in between Whites and Blacks, their ordering or ranking is dynamic, varying from one sociohistorical and regional or geographic context to another. Historically, Native Americans (2006:22), Mexicans (2006:286), and Chinese and Japanese (2006:287) have all been ascribed a racial status; for example, the Mexican-origin population in Texas was characterized as an inferior, "mongrel Spanish-Indian and negro race" by Stephen F. Austin, a colonizer of Mexican Texas (Feagin 2006:286). Similarly, at the turn of the previous century the Chinese and Japanese were typified as "yellow races" that would bring peril to White Americans and irreparably tear apart the fabric of the United States (Daniels [1988] 1995:116).

Today, the Mexican, Chinese, and Japanese racial classifications of the past comprise ethnic rather than racial categories, although these distinct categories of identity and belonging are not mutually exclusive. For example, the Mexican-origin population is typically defined as belonging not only to the Mexican *ethnic* group but to the Latino/a (or Hispanic) *panethnic*[1] or *racial* group as well, while the Chinese and Japanese *ethnic* groups are commonly classified *racially* as Asian. Under current sociohistorical conditions, then, it is more accurate from a conceptual standpoint to define the U.S. racial hierarchy as one that is exclusively comprised of racial groups only (for example,

Whites, Asians, Latinos/as, Native Americans, and Blacks). Although ethnicity may indicate an ethnic classification and an associated racial classification (for example, *Mexican* is affiliated with *Latino/a*), the ethnic classification itself is not included in or required to determine Latinos'/as' position within the racial hierarchy. All that is required is a racial classification. This begs the question as to the distinct roles of ethnicity and race within the social structure, and the relationship between them.

The embedded market approach conceptualizes the distinction between ethnic identity and racial identity as one that rests along a *continuum* of agency and structure integration. Along this continuum, ethnic identity is socially constructed as fluid and is presumed to be determined more by individual and collective agency than by structural forces (Bonilla-Silva 1997). In contrast, racial identity is socially constructed as fixed and is understood to be constrained by structural forces rather than determined by individual or collective action. Furthermore, and as mentioned earlier, ethnic and racial identities are not mutually exclusive; with respect to the racialized social structure, ethnic identity is an "optional" classification, while racial identity is not.[2]

Because ethnicity does not establish an ethnic group member's position within the U.S. racial hierarchy, ethnic group members (for example, Mexicans, Hondurans) require a racial classification to determine placement. The label *Latino/a* serves this purpose by providing a new racial category for those Latin American–origin ethnic group members who are socially constructed as neither White nor Black. This process of racialization compresses distinct ethnic groups into one overarching group—thereby establishing Latino/a *racial* group members' positioning within the American racial hierarchy.

This process of Latino/a racialization constitutes a recent transformation of American race relations in the contemporary post-1965 period, following immigration policy reforms that substantially increased U.S. migration from Latin American sending countries. Since power and privilege are conferred to Whites who enjoy the top position of the American racial hierarchy, it is unlikely that non-European, Latin American national-origin immigrants and their descendants would be allowed to encroach upon this privileged position and "become White," as the Irish did before them (Roediger 2007). Conversely, non-Whites are likely to resist structural incorporation into the other available racial category, Black, and the consequent oppression that such a racial classification confers. Nor would they fit easily into the American race relations conception of who is White or Black, with respect to phenotypical characteristics and features that are commonly ascribed to those traditional racial groups. Because non-White, non-Black groups do not correspond to preconceived notions, and since these groups are likely to resist ascription as racially oppressed Blacks, the development of additional racial categories to situate these newer immigrants of color within the American racial hierarchy is warranted. The emergence of the label *Latino/a* reflects structural forces that externally impose a racial classification upon members of new and distinct ethnic groups.[3]

From the perspective of the embedded market, the emergence of this racial classification reveals human agency, in terms of the individual and collective response by Latin American–origin ethnic group members to resist incorporation into preexisting non-White racial categories (for example, Asian, Native American, Black). To the degree that this resistance is conscious and rational, the development of the Latino/a racial identity represents agency on the part of individual and collective ethnic group members who seek a non-White, non-Black racial classification for members of Latin American–origin ethnic groups. Moreover, the emergence of a Latino/a racial group also allows for the formation of a new social group that provides the basis for the development of social capital across ethnicity. In this way, the Latino/a racial identity, like ethnicity, can facilitate economic action. At the same time, however, its emergence constitutes a recognition of and response to structural forces that impose racial classifications upon ethnic group members.

A closer examination of the process of identity formation reveals the complexity involved in determining Latinos'/as' ethnic and racial classifications, even by the members themselves. For example, the 2000 census collects information on four (to six) racial groups: American Indian or Alaskan Native, Asian or Pacific Islander, Black, and White. Among Latino/a respondents, 48 percent self-identify racially as White and 2 percent identify as Black. Only 6 percent report belonging to two or more racial groups. Yet, fully 42 percent self-identify as "some other race." Of those respondents, the overwhelming majority report a panethnic or ethnic or national-origin identity rooted in Latin America (Swarns 2004).

Rodríguez and Cordero-Guzmán (1992) have argued that the selection of "some other race" among Latinos/as suggests that ethnicity or national origin and culture provide the basis for a racial group that is separate from traditional (White or Black) groups. In a recent study of racial identity formation among Latinos/as, I find support for this claim, as fully half of those surveyed

believe that Latinos/as form a distinct racial group (Valdez 2009). Using the
2007 Latino National Survey, which includes questions on race and ethnic
identity that replicate the U.S. census categories as well as questions on Latinos'/
as' "primary identity," the majority of Latino/a respondents identify racially as
White. However, when asked to identify their "primary identity," 44 percent
of Latinos/as identify themselves panethnically or racially (that is, as Latino
or Hispanic), while 7 percent identified themselves nationally (that is, as Mexican, Cuban, and the like). In a separate question that asked whether Latinos/as
constitute a racial group, roughly half of all survey respondents answered yes,
regardless of their reported ethnic, panethnic, or racial primary identity (Valdez 2009). Building on this previous research, this chapter explores ethnic and
racial group identity among Latino/a entrepreneurs, specifically, the conditions under which Latinos/as identify themselves or others by ethnicity (Mexican, Salvadoran) or by race (Latino/a, Hispanic). It further investigates the
relationships that link identity, market capacity, and entrepreneurial success.

Latino/a business owners overwhelmingly self-identify ethnically, or
what Joan Moore (1990) refers to as an "anchoring" identity.[4] Additionally,
Latino/a entrepreneurs sometimes self-identify racially, as Latino/a or Hispanic, to demonstrate cohesion or a sense of community that crosses ethnic
group affiliation. At other times, they may self-identify ethnically but invoke
a racial label to classify other, non-co-ethnic Latinos/as to stereotype or express bias against them. This process of racialization effectively hinders resource mobilization between non-co-ethnics. In contrast, all Latino/a entrepreneurs, regardless of ethnicity, report the use of ethnic-based social capital
to help them with their businesses. Findings expose the dynamic and contextually contingent process of ethnic and racial identity formation, which reproduces different aspects of the social structure to help (or hinder) Latino/a
enterprise.

## Theorizing Ethnic and Racial Identity Formation

Research on ethnic identity formation is generally concerned with self-
identification; that is, this research largely examines the conditions under
which individuals claim membership in a particular ethnic group. A precondition for ethnic group membership is the awareness of one's own ethnicity,
which is generally and initially conditioned by national origin. From that
point on, however, ethnic identity is adaptable, embedded in notions of similar and shared history, culture, and kinship. Thus, ethnicity provides a salient

basis of group identity that is nevertheless fluid, with respect to members' socially constructed and contested meanings of *similar* and *shared*. Once collectively established, ethnicity provides a powerful basis of group association that facilitates members' circumstantialist (that is, economic, political, legal, or symbolic) objectives (Cornell and Hartmann 1998; Waters 1991; Yancey, Erikson, and Juliani 1976).

In contrast, racial identity is characterized as a secondary form of group identity that is externally imposed and other defined (Bonilla-Silva 1997; Feagin 2006). Research on racial identity formation commonly focuses on the unavoidable and compulsory placement of individuals into racial groups based on socially constructed ascribed characteristics, such as skin color or ancestry, regardless of self-identification. This process of race making relegates those individuals who are recognized as members of a given racial group to that group's positioning along the American racial hierarchy (Bashi 1998; Bonilla-Silva 1997; Feagin 2006). In a society where race matters, racial classification is nontrivial; it is structurally important, as it confers greater or lesser privilege or oppression to facilitate or constrain members' life chances. Whereas Bonilla-Silva (1997:469) concedes some similarities between ethnicity and race, he ultimately underscores their differences:

> Ethnicity and race are different bases of group association. Ethnicity has a primarily sociocultural foundation, and ethnic groups have exhibited tremendous malleability in terms of who belongs; racial ascriptions (initially) are imposed externally to justify the collective exploitation of a people and are maintained to preserve status differences. Hence scholars have pointed out that despite the similarities between race and ethnicity, they should be viewed as producing different types of structurations.

In other words, ethnic identity is distinct from racial identity in the United States; each reproduces different aspects of the social structure.

Research on ethnic and racial identity formation generally supports this view, as scholars presume and preserve the distinction by investigating *either* racial *or* ethnic identity formation separately.[5] However, as Loveman (1999:891) cautions, "the attempt to theorize the former [race] in intellectual isolation from the latter [ethnicity] . . . limits our understanding of whether or to what extent these analytical categories actually capture theoretical and conceptual differences." Yet, rather than concluding that a distinction between race and ethnicity is "unwarranted" or "unfounded" as Loveman suspects (1999:891), I suggest that it does indeed reflect a conceptual distinction, one that is rooted in the differential integration of agency and structure.

### Ethnic Identity Among Latinos/as

When asked about their background and ancestry, the overwhelming majority of Latino/a business owners identify themselves ethnically.

- "I'm one hundred percent Mexican." —José
- "I consider myself to be Cuban American." —Rubén
- "My parents were from Chile. . . . I'm Chilean." —Carla

Latino/a business owners often associate their entrepreneurial activity with some aspect of their ethnicity. Martín, the fifty-one-year-old Salvadoran owner of two restaurants in Little Latin America, expressed a typical sentiment.

> *Earlier, you said that your ethnic background is Salvadoran. How important is being Salvadoran to your business?*
> It's important because the people from El Salvador are used to working hard. I would say it's very important.

Martín identifies himself as Salvadoran and American. He states that he loves El Salvador and the United States equally but implies that being Salvadoran has helped him in his business because of Salvadorans' strong work ethic.

Furthermore, when asked about how they got started in their businesses, Latinos/as often mentioned the importance of ethnic-based social capital, or the capacity to access resources based on ethnic group membership, in contributing necessary resources, such as cheap, co-ethnic labor or informal lending. They also attributed their success to co-ethnic information networks.

- "I always ask for advice from other Salvadorans [who own businesses]. I learn from their experience." —Martín (Salvadoran)
- "I ask about why their [other Hondurans'] businesses closed because it helps me not to make the same mistakes." —María (Honduran)
- "I trade business cards with other Mexican owners; we share advertising and pass the word around. If someone wants dessert, I send them down the street [points in the direction of a Mexican-owned frozen yogurt shop]." —Miguel (Mexican)

Such statements are consistent with the classic theory of ethnic enterprise that has demonstrated the importance of ethnic solidarity and close-knit ties in generating ethnic-based social capital, which facilitates entrepreneurship (Light and Bonacich 1988; Portes and Rumbaut 2006; Waldinger et al. 1990; Zhou 1992). Although the ethnic entrepreneurship paradigm implies that ethnic-based solidarity and resources are generally available to specific, entrepreneurially oriented groups only, my findings reveal that all Latinos/as, regardless of ethnicity or self-employment participation rates, use ethnic-based social capital to facilitate business ownership.

### Ethnic Identity Among White and Black Entrepreneurs

Notably, White entrepreneurs who self-identify ethnically *also* attribute their business success to ethnic group characteristics and features and ethnic-based social capital. Like Martín and José, Stavros Loukas, a thirty-seven-year-old, second-generation Greek American, attributes his success in business to a strong work ethic and close-knit, co-ethnic ties.

> [Being Greek] is important to my business because Greeks work hard and Greeks help Greeks. . . . We stick together and help each other out.

Mr. Loukas inherited his family's business, Dimitri's BBQ House; he never worked anywhere else. Although he acknowledges that he "fell into" the family business, he connects his family's interest in business ownership to being Greek (notably, not the other way around). His sentiment about the salience of ethnicity in business ownership is echoed by his friend, Alec Dukas, a co-ethnic business owner who owns Dukas' Seafood and Steaks, a fine-dining restaurant located nearby. Alec, a forty-year-old second-generation Greek American, also inherited the family business. Like Mr. Loukas, he attributes much of his success to his ethnic background, stating that Greeks are "usually successful" in business and claiming that being Greek is important because "Greeks own businesses . . . [somewhat jokingly, he added as an afterthought] either restaurants or gas stations."

In contrast to Latino/a and White entrepreneurs who may prefer to self-identify either ethnically or racially, Black entrepreneurs are just as likely to identify ethnically (for example, African American, Caribbean) as racially (for example, Black), and often use these terms interchangeably—sometimes in the same sentence. Renee Tate, the forty-two-year-old business owner who moved to Houston from Louisiana in 2000, offered her perspective on identity. She indicated that although ethnic and racial identities are conceptually different, each identity describes her accurately.

*How would you describe your background, your ancestry?*
I would say Black, but it's mixed with French Haitian and Creole.

*Do you think there's any difference . . . say, between Black, Creole, or African American?*
I think there is a difference. If you're speaking in reference to Nigerian or African Blacks, it's a different category. Even though it all derives from the same thing. We came from the continent, so all soul food is a derivative of African food, but for some reason we like to make distinctions.

*Do you prefer one term over the other?*
Well, I am both; they both describe me, so I use them interchangeably.

Stacey Holmes, introduced earlier as a thirty-five-year-old soul food restaurant owner, also confirms this common sentiment among Black business owners.

*How would you describe your background, your ancestry?*
I'd say African American.

*Is that different from Black to you?*
They're the same to me. . . . I'm proud to be Black, African American, colored, whatever you call it. . . .

Whereas ethnic-identified Latinos/as and Whites tend to link their ethnicity with group-based resources and support, Black entrepreneurs are often as likely to associate social capital with ethnic or racial group membership. Ms. Tate, who identified herself as Black mixed with French Haitian and Creole, states that being Black helps her with her business, as it is characteristic of being a good cook.

It helps because Black people can cook, and people know we can cook; that's something we've known how to do if you go back to slavery years, where'd they [Whites] have us; in the kitchen.

Ms. Tate observes that her customers know they will get a good meal because "Black people can cook." She also believes that once potential customers find out that a Black woman is preparing the food, they will come for that same reason. Renee Tate's acceptance of this relatively positive stereotype is similar to other entrepreneurs' assertions that their ethnic or racial group features and attributes facilitate their businesses in distinct ways, such as the claims that Salvadorans "work hard" or that "Greeks help other Greeks."

As a self-identified African American, Andre also associates his African American ethnic identity with social capital accumulation. Originally from

Chicago, where Andre owned a popcorn shop for less than one year (the business folded due to a lack of revenue; he also claimed to have "burned out" given the long hours), Andre moved to Houston eight years ago to work as a caseworker with the Houston Housing Authority. At forty-six, Andre quit his job to try his hand in business one more time. He opened Chicago Dogs in December of 2007. His restaurant is located on the corner of a residential street, across from an apartment building and next to a Laundromat in the predominately Black South Ward. Chicago Dogs and the Laundromat share a building and parking area that runs alongside the building, which accommodates a dozen or so cars. During the afternoon, several Black men can be found gathering in the parking lot, sometimes huddled under the hood of a car but most of the time talking and socializing in the friendly atmosphere. The restaurant is tiny, consisting of a couple of tables and a few barstools at a counter that faces a short-order-style kitchen. Andre and his adopted son face away from their customers, preparing the food. A television sits precariously on top of the soft drink refrigerator case, and a working pinball machine takes up a corner of the perfectly square space.

Andre believes that knowing other African American business owners helps him to build networks that encourage him and other African American entrepreneurs to run businesses and increase their profits. He offers one example of how he benefited from reaching out to others.

> There was this young [African American] lady opening a club around here, and I went over to introduce myself. I went to speak to her about how to get her business set up because I had some problems with mine, because nothing was in here; so I got her in touch with the people that helped me, and now he's workin' with her. Now she's agreed to let me cater some events, and now I told her that as long as the club is open, I'll stay open. . . . So building that network helps.

Unfortunately, for Andre, his fledgling business did not have sufficient economic and social resources and support outside of a few new, co-ethnic business owners and the unpaid labor of his adopted son to keep the business afloat; it folded after eight months, less than two months after this interview.

These examples illustrate that although the majority of Black entrepreneurs may draw a distinction between the meaning of ethnicity and race, they do not apply that distinction when they self-identify but, rather, use these concepts interchangeably. Regardless of their choice of self-identity, Black entrepreneurs report that co-ethnic and co-racial ties facilitate their businesses through the use of group-based social capital. In contrast, White and Latino/a entrepreneurs are more likely to identify as one or the other, that is, as a member of either a specific ethnic or a specific racial group. Moreover, those who identified ethnically (for example, as Mexican or Greek) were more likely to report the access to and use of ethnic-based social capital than those who identified racially (as Latino/a or White, respectively).

### Racial Identity Among Latinos/as

Latino/a entrepreneurs' statements about the benefits of being a member of a specific ethnic group, however, are sometimes combined with negative sentiments regarding non-co-ethnic Latinos/as. In making such claims, ethnic-identified Latinos/as often refer to the non-co-ethnic group in question as "Latinos/as" or "Hispanics," invoking a racial classification rather than an ethnic-specific one, even when they know the ethnic or national origin of the person or group to whom they are referring. Martín, the Salvadoran American who believes that his Salvadoran work ethic contributes to his success in business, volunteered a comparison between Salvadorans and "Latin people" more generally, portraying the latter group in a decidedly negative light.

> I can say, though, that the Latin people, in general, don't have loyalty with anyone. If someone gives them good service, good food, or a good price, they will buy from the Chinese, they will by from Middle Easterners. . . . They don't have loyalty to anyone. Latin people are like that. On the other hand, the Chinese don't. They don't buy from anyone that's not Chinese. The Middle Easterners, the same. They are faithful to their own people. Latin people *do buy* from people who are not Latin. The Latin people are not faithful to anyone.

In the context of an explicit discussion about the benefits of being Salvadoran, Martín offers a contrasting group, "Latin people," and expresses negative sentiments toward this (non-co-ethnic) racial group. By suggesting that "Latin people . . . will buy . . . from people who are not Latin," he characterizes "Latin people" as lacking in group solidarity. Importantly, however, he does not ascribe such negative characteristics to the Salvadoran-origin population. When these comments are contextualized within the American embedded market, the racial hierarchy is exposed. Moreover, the process of racialization is captured here, as distinct Latin American–origin ethnic groups are compressed

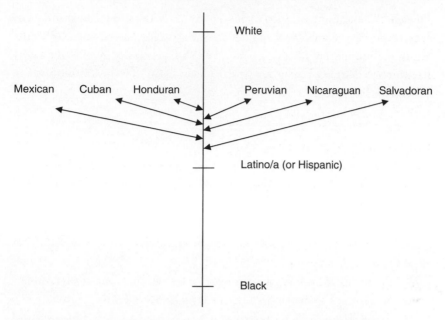

**Figure 6.1** The Contested Position of Latin American–Origin Ethnic Groups: Externally Positioned "Outside" or Internally Positioned "Within" the American Racial Hierarchy

into one subordinate *racial group*—"Latin people." Notably in this account, the externally imposed racial classification is invoked *from within*, that is, from a self-identified Salvadoran American, who in any other context might be just as likely to share that same racial classification. Lastly, the owner's perceived benefits of being Salvadoran when compared to the detriments of being Latino/a suggest a contestation of membership in the latter (racial) group, an attempt to exclude or distance Salvadorans from "Latin people's" subordinate placement along the racial hierarchy (see Figure 6.1).

The use of the Hispanic/Latino label to racialize non-co-ethnics is fairly common among Latino/a entrepreneurs who self-identify ethnically. In another example, Carla, a fifty-four-year-old self-identified Chilean woman, attributes her business acumen to her Chilean identity. She also makes the ubiquitous reference to her ethnicity as providing a strong work ethnic. She explains that when she moved to Little Latin America from New Jersey in the mid-1980s, it was a Mexican ethnic enclave in transition, as many Salvadorans and other Central Americans were beginning to migrate to the area. She opened a

Salvadoran restaurant to cater to the newly arrived Salvadoran immigrant community. She readily identifies her business, staff, and customer base ethnically (Salvadoran). Additionally, however, she specifically invokes the racial classification *Hispanic* when contrasting her "clean" restaurant with other restaurants in the area.

*You are Chilean, but the food is Salvadoran?*
Yes, because in 1986 when we [Carla, her mother, and her brother] came here, there were only Mexican restaurants. When I saw the area, there's a lot of Salvadorans. . . . So we decided to make it a Salvadoran restaurant. All of the cookers, all the employees, except us, are Salvadoran. But this question, everyone asks. Sometimes Salvadorans are surprised. They say this is the best!

*Why do you think that is?*
For the quality of the food, the way we treat the customers, and the cleaning. Do you see that? [points to the kitchen] My pots. Tell me if they have any black stuff on them? On the bottom.

*No, I don't see any black stuff anywhere.*
I keep my restaurant clean. You know, you can go to many Hispanic restaurants around here, and the pots are all black. [She points to the street where a Tex-Mex restaurant and a Salvadoran restaurant are located nearby.] I don't like any of that! *I'm* not like that!

Carla attributes her drive and ambition to her Chilean ethnicity, while invoking a racial classification to negatively stereotype (non-Chilean) Hispanic restaurants as dirty. In Martín's and Carla's accounts, the use of the racial classifications *Latin people* and *Hispanic*, respectively, serve to racialize and subordinate non-co-ethnic Latino groups; this process of "othering" neutralizes the distinct ethnic group differences that exist across those Latino/a subgroups, while at the same time subordinating and distancing those Latinos/as identified as such from their own ethnic group identity. In this way, ethnic-identified Latino/a business owners invoke a racial classification to identify non-co-ethnics to characterize them in a negative light. In so doing, they also signify their own ethnic-specific superiority.

This process of racialization is possible only in societies that are structured racially, that is, where race matters. Latino/a entrepreneurs that self-identify ethnically invoke a Latino/a *racial* classification to characterize non-co-ethnics with inferior or subordinate features, which allows the group in question to be positioned within the racial hierarchy. By self-identifying ethnically, however, these Latino/a entrepreneurs resist their own placement within the racial hierarchy.

## Racial Identity Among Black and White Entrepreneurs

Black entrepreneurs also expressed negative perceptions of the Black community, regardless of whether they self-identify ethnically or racially. In these instances, Black entrepreneurs might refer to other Blacks ethnically (for example, African American), racially, or both, again, underscoring the ambiguity between ethnic and racial identity for Blacks, which is absent among Latinos/as and Whites. Black entrepreneurs who shared such sentiments maintained that Blacks did not always mobilize resources or build community; in fact, they suggested that some Blacks actively hurt their businesses or contributed to making their economic situation worse.

Ms. Holmes has owned Stacey's Kitchen in the South Ward since 2007. The restaurant, a white, brick, and wood duplex with peeling paint, a black wrought-iron security door, and a hand-painted sign hanging over the door, is located off the main street, but there is precious little pedestrian or car traffic in the area. Stacey's shares the building with a Black-owned barbershop. On one side of the business is an empty lot, which serves as the parking lot for both businesses; the other side is peppered with older residential homes, some of which have boarded up windows and are clearly vacant, many more empty lots, and a church. The Houston cityscape is clearly visible in the distance.

Ms. Holmes relied on her husband's savings to start her business (he is a welder), and her niece works full-time in the restaurant. Although she acknowledges that her family has helped her in her business, she complains that the wider Black community is not cohesive and is filled with "haters" (a term that connotes envy and the desire to see others fail, somewhat akin to schadenfreude), who do not want to see other Blacks succeed. Her assessment is analogous to Martín's take on "Latin people," as she specifically contrasts the lack of Black co-racial solidarity with the ostensibly more supportive and unified Asian community.

> Hell, our race, our people don't stick together. Other races will put ninety people in one house and pull in together, but we can't do it. The Chinese work

together even if they have to have thirty-five in a room. Kim Son brought all those people here, and they went in and bought one house, and all those people lived in one house, and now they all have mansions. They worked together until everybody had a house.

Stacey characterizes the Black community as disconnected, at the same time referencing Kim Son, a famous Vietnamese restaurant in Houston that started with one small restaurant located in downtown Houston, but which has grown to astronomical, or at least Texas-sized, proportions. Kim Son now boasts several locations, one of which is a twenty-two-thousand-square-foot space that was built at a cost of $2 million. The newest, located in Chinatown, is more than thirty-five thousand square feet, with marble floors and wrought-iron banisters (a far cry from the wrought-iron security doors at Stacey's Kitchen). Stacey's belief that Kim Son's success is attributed to Vietnamese co-ethnic solidarity, however, may not be completely or perhaps even partially accurate. Kim Son is owned and operated by a middle-class family of Vietnamese immigrant war refugees, who, prior to fleeing their country of origin, owned a successful restaurant in Vietnam. With market capital resources in the form of financial capital, skills and knowledge, family-based social capital in the form of unpaid family labor, and, as refugees, access to government loans that encourage business ownership, the Kim Son "dynasty" was reborn in America. Kim Son's middle-class Vietnamese owners' access to substantial market and social capital resources cannot be overstated; in contrast to Stacey's assessment of the importance of co-ethnic solidarity, Kim Son was well positioned to succeed, arguably regardless of co-ethnic or racial solidarity.

Beyond the indication that the Black community lacks co-racial solidarity (which is thought to hinder Black-owned businesses and their socioeconomic success) is the opposite complaint: that those Black community members who embrace or seek to establish co-racial solidarity *also* initiate negative consequences for Black business owners. Andre, the forty-six-year-old self-identified African American owner of Chicago Dogs, mentioned earlier that building networks among African American entrepreneurs has helped him to expand and promote his business. Nevertheless, he also expressed some resistance to African Americans thinking of themselves as a racial group, an identity that he associates with negative outcomes for his business. When asked to explain, he described a sense of entitlement that

Black customers convey to him, their demands for him to give them "something for nothing." Andre's grievance is not without merit, as researchers observe the same phenomenon among ethnic entrepreneurs. The traditional approach to ethnic entrepreneurship acknowledges the tensions surrounding the benefits and detriments of group-based solidarity, termed "reciprocal obligations" (Portes and Sensenbrenner 1993). Although this type of obligatory social capital may foster enterprise among co-ethnics, for example, by providing a source for informal lending or a supply of low-wage labor, it is also associated with negative consequences that may emerge between group members to the detriment of employers. For example, entrepreneurs may feel an obligation or pressure to lower prices, hire co-ethnics unnecessarily, or pay employees more rather than less, in response to the pull of reciprocal obligation. For Andre, the negative consequences associated with his customers' frequent requests for reciprocity hinder his success and cause him to question the benefits of "racial unity."

> African Americans come in, and they want something for nothing; and they do it solely on race, because I know they wouldn't do it at McDonald's or anywhere else, but they come in here lookin' for the hookup. . . . They want me to do something special for them cause we took a boat ride six hundred years ago together, so now I owe them for life, and I think that that's wrong. Helpingwise, some people who are African Americans come in, and they smile 'cause they see me in business, and they smile and you can see the pride. Usually when somebody comes in and the first words they say are about loving to support their Black people, it makes me cringe because to me that means that they're going to try to mess me up as much as they can. I don't need you to tell me that you're going to support me, just come, because to hear it is condescending. And every time somebody has said that, they didn't come back.

Andre's perspective on the negative consequences associated with co-racial solidarity was shared by several Black entrepreneurs and is similar to the sentiments shared by some Latino/a entrepreneurs. In these instances, Black and Latino/a business owners impose a racial classification on group members, which is used to express a negative (or anti-Black or anti-Latino/a) sentiment by the members themselves. In contrast, White entrepreneurs did not characterize other Whites in a negative light, regardless of how they self-identified (ethnically or racially). The absence of co-racial prejudice by Whites does not indicate a stronger racial unity among members, as White entrepreneurs do not connect their racial identity to fostering business through co-racial net-works, social capital, or a cohesive community either. Rather, the absence of White racial talk may suggest a color-blind ideology; in other words, the privileged position of Whites within the American racial hierarchy may allow them to overlook or dismiss race, or the effects of race, from their discourse (of business ownership, the mobilization of resources, success, and so forth). Individual merit takes center stage in White business owner accounts, whereas White racial identity and its consequences remain invisible.

## White Supremacy in the Racial Hierarchy

Latino/a business owners in America live and work within a social structure that is stratified by race. As members of that society, they understand what the American racial hierarchy looks like, and their position within it. They also recognize where other groups are located, and whether their position, in comparison, is superior or inferior. In this context, it is not surprising that Latinos/as might resist racial group membership by self-identifying ethni-cally; it is not surprising that they may express sentiments about their own racial groups that are prejudicial, as they reinforce and reproduce that which exists in the greater society; and finally, it is not surprising that Latino/a en-trepreneurs may recognize, acknowledge, or even accept their inferior posi-tion relative to Whites. Not only are these circumstances *not surprising*; they are *predictable* and *expected* in a society that is stratified by race.

Martín, the self-identified Salvadoran American, made clear his ethnocen-tric preference for Salvadorans and his negative attitudes toward "Latin people." Nevertheless, he recognizes that Salvadorans and "Latin people" are in a sub-ordinate position relative to "Anglos." Specifically, and when comparing his customer base in the two restaurants he owns in the area, he clearly situates "Anglos" above "regular" Salvadorans.

> *Now, I'd like to ask you about this restaurant. It's Salvadoran as well. . . .*
> Yes, it's a Salvadoran restaurant, but it's not like the other one. This one is
> for a high-class clientele. The other one is a like a café, with counters only. It
> has loud music; it's full of men, *machos* [tough guys]. Regular Salvadoran
> people. . . . *This* restaurant is nicer. I can bring my American friends in and
> show them this is a nice place, with good Salvadoran food. They always ask,
> "Take me to a good Salvadoran restaurant," and before, I was embarrassed . . .
> ashamed . . . there was no place to go. Now I can take them here.

Martín distinguishes his two restaurants by clientele. He characterizes one of his restaurants as serving "regular Salvadoran people" and the other restaurant (the one in which this interview took place) as serving his "American friends"[6] and "Anglos." This Anglo-friendly Salvadoran restaurant is located in a new strip mall. It is painted bright yellow and decorated with several paintings on every wall (mostly large oil paintings of birds and landscapes in bright primary colors, painted by Martín's daughter). The floors are Spanish tile, and each of the glass-topped tables has its own vase of fresh flowers and unopened bottle of red wine. Soft music, Spanish classical guitar, can be heard in the background. At the time of this interview, a young White man and woman were in the restaurant, and another White couple entered as I left. A young, light-skinned Salvadoran waiter was working. It is significant that Martín expresses his own embarrassment and shame at the prospect of taking "Anglos" to the "regular Salvadoran restaurant." His words acknowledge (consciously or not) the superior position of Whites within the racial hierarchy relative to his own. Notably, Martín makes an allowance for some Salvadorans to rise above their position by introducing class to his Salvadoran customer profile; although "regular Salvadorans" are not included alongside Whites, there is room for "high-class" Salvadorans to join Anglos in frequenting the "nicer" restaurant. A class distinction was rarely introduced by Martín or anyone else in discussions of racial or ethnic identity, which underscores the perceived homogeneity associated with these group memberships.

During my next visit to the area, my curiosity was piqued, so I stopped by Martín's *Salvadoran* Salvadoran restaurant. It was located in a dilapidated strip mall, next to a discotheque. A Spanish record store, a vacant storefront, and a liquor store shared the same parking lot. The restaurant was small, with linoleum floors and a total of four small tables, each with its own large glass jar of marinated cabbage, a traditional topping used for *pupusas* (a traditional Salvadoran dish made from deep-fried cornmeal and stuffed with cheese and beans or meat). A map of El Salvador was taped to the wall behind the cash register. A jukebox was prominently displayed in the center of the small space. Four men were sitting at two tables that had been pushed together and were eating, drinking beer, and speaking Spanish loudly in order to be heard over the music. One employee was visible behind the counter, and another was behind a partition separating the counter space from the kitchen. The counter employee, a young Latina woman, greeted me in Spanish and then continued to carry on a conversation in Spanish with two other men who sat at the counter. After a moment, she turned her attention to me and asked in Spanish if she could help me. The contrast between the two restaurants was striking. Differences included the restaurant location, space, furniture, music, employees, language, and customer base. Certainly Martín correctly identified these two restaurants as serving different clientele; interestingly, the differences for him were rooted in a distinction between Anglos and "high-class" Salvadorans on the one hand and "regular Salvadorans" on the other. In his assessment is the suggestion of the superiority of the former and the inferiority of the latter.

These examples highlight the implicit (and sometimes explicit) recognition of Whites at the top of the racial hierarchy and the subordinate position held by non-Whites. These accounts contrast with attempts made by self-identified ethnic group members to distinguish their ethnic group from an associated racial group, in an attempt to position their own ethnic group above the racial group with which they are associated. The attempt to contest their racial group membership, while at the same time challenging their ethnic or racial standing relative to Whites, reveals a clear awareness of the American racial hierarchy.

Ruben, a fifty-seven-year-old Cuban restaurateur, revealed his recognition of the racial hierarchy in a brief discussion of voluntary segregation by Hispanics from "Anglos" (notably, not the other way around). In this account, Ruben highlights the demographic changes that have taken place in Little Latin America, specifically, the transition of Little Latin America from a working and middle-class, predominately White community to a well-known area of Salvadoran immigrant settlement.

> *When did they start moving out? Was this around the time of the oil bust?*
> I would say it was . . . the 80s, when things started changing. It was a lot
> of immigration from Salvadorans. Over here, they called it Little Central
> America [laughing]. That's why you see so many Salvadoran-related
> businesses. I don't know whether the owners are Salvadoran or not. You also
> have a lot of Anglos who come here. From Houston Heights. I got to tell you;
> about ninety-five percent of my clientele are Anglo. You see the Anglos coming
> in for lunch during the work week. But, you know, the weekend comes and it's
> all Hispanic. The Hispanics don't like to be around the Anglos—it makes them
> uncomfortable—but on the weekends, when they want to relax and have a nice
> meal, then you see the people from around here.

In discussing Little Latin America's transition from a White, working, and middle-class community to one of new immigrant settlement, Ruben does not hesitate to identify these new immigrants by their Salvadoran origin, and implies that the Little Latin America community is now majority Salvadoran (at 29 percent, it is decidedly not; Mexicans still make up the majority, at 41 percent). However, when he discusses the interracial tensions among Whites, Salvadorans, and Mexicans, he compresses Salvadorans and Mexicans into "Hispanics." Racial classification is invoked to equate and racialize distinct Latin American–origin groups, which are then compared to Whites.

Additionally, Ruben discusses the discomfort that Hispanics feel in the presence of Whites, which suggests that Hispanics recognize their position as one of subordination. A cursory look at the customers on this Thursday afternoon supported Ruben's statement, as the vast majority of the customers appeared to be well-dressed and office-attired non-Hispanic Whites. Although I did not have another chance to drop by Ruben's restaurant on the weekend, Little Latin America restaurants were generally very busy during weekends, and the vast majority of customers appeared to be Latinos/as.

Notably, Latino/a entrepreneurs recognize further that their racial group position is superior to that of Blacks. At the end of a two-hour interview, Miguel, a forty-five-year-old Mexican business owner, asked me why I was interested in Little Latin America anyway. I responded that I was interested in how business owners like him got started and succeed in business. I then mentioned that I was especially interested in learning about Latino/a entrepreneurs, who often have to settle in high-poverty or high-crime areas of the United States, and finally told him that after I had talked with some Houston community organizers, the Little Latin America area was mentioned as a good place for me to start my study. Miguel then replied,

> You know, many people have a very bad perception of this area. It's in the apartments. They have crime. If you really think about it, it's crimes of passion. You see all these killings. It's somebody who doesn't like somebody killing each other. It's not like they're going and robbing somebody. . . . I live two minutes away from here. I live in Houston Heights. It's not any different than living in this area. I've been there for eighteen years in that house. I don't even know anybody in that street being broken in. So the bad people are not here. They don't live here. You see people walking down the street.

These people are not wealthy. They take the bus, they have a job, and they're hard working.

*They're just poor. . . .*
They're not walking around because they're trying to get into trouble. I would say that is West of here more so than here. I would say in that Black neighborhood [waves a hand in the direction of the South Ward] . . . I have never been—well, I was robbed here one time at gunpoint. I was at a bank, and it was a couple of Black men that did it. I was at a bank two or three miles away from here. They were waiting for someone to come out with a bank bag. I had a bank bag full of coins when they saw me. And I ran errands for about forty-five minutes until I got here. These guys followed me from this bank. That was the only incident that we had, and I've been here for twenty-four years.

Houston Heights is the predominately White, middle-class area that is adjacent to Little Latin America. Miguel lives in Houston Heights and works in Little Latin America. He admits that "crimes of passion" occur in Little Latin America, but he maintains that the community, albeit a poor one, is hardworking and that "the bad people are not here. They don't live here." Following this exchange, Miguel offered a contrasting example of a community with residents who "get into trouble." Not only does Miguel characterize the South Ward as a Black community that is plagued by crime; he offers a personal vignette of getting robbed at gunpoint by two Black men who came into Little Latin America from the South Ward to commit the robbery. Explicit in his account is the contrast in the communities—Little Latin America is made up of poor but hardworking people who occasionally commit "crimes of passion" but are generally good. He goes so far as to equate the residents of Little Latin America with the predominately White and middle-class residents of Houston Heights. In contrast, his assessment of the South Ward is dire indeed—a Black community that is rife with troublemaking criminals and murderers. In this account, the American racial hierarchy is reaffirmed in the negative portrayal of Blacks and the contestation that Latinos/as who live in Little Latin America are poor but good—and even in some ways comparable to Whites, even as Miguel acknowledges their inferior status relative to Whites.

Andre, the forty-six-year-old African American owner of Chicago Dogs, understands that the racial hierarchy is endemic to the American society but suggests that it is more salient and overt in the South than in the Midwest. He claims that Blacks in Houston treat Whites with more deference, that through their behavior they submit to or believe in their inferior position within the racial hierarchy.

> The South is . . . not like us in the Midwest. We didn't see White people as being anything that great, just regular folks. We didn't bother them, and they didn't bother us. But down here they [Blacks] still glorify them. They walk with their heads down and mumble and stuff.

Although Andre's claims are more explicit than those made by Latinos/as, these examples show that both groups concede that their position within the racial hierarchy is inferior to that of Whites.

## Conclusion

This chapter explores the contingent use of ethnic and racial identity among Latino/a, White, and Black business owners. For Latinos/as, self-identifying ethnically or racially is associated with aiding in enterprise through the mobilization of social capital. Racial classification is not always connected to resource mobilization, however, as it is sometimes invoked by ethnic-identified Latinos/as under certain conditions: (1) when negatively stereotyping or expressing bias against non-co-ethnic Latinos; (2) when distancing one's own ethnic group from the negative stereotypes or prejudices associated with Latinos; or (3) when discussing social interactions or relationships with traditional (White or Black) racial groups. For Blacks, ethnic and racial identities, such as African American or Black, respectively, are generally used interchangeably. Like those associated with Latinos/as, these classifications provide the basis for the mobilization of social capital or to express an anti-Black sentiment toward other Blacks. For Whites, however, ethnicity alone is associated with resource-mobilization strategies among ethnic-identified Whites (for example, Greeks). Racially identified Whites do not link their racial group identity with the mobilization of resources, nor do they invoke a White racial identity to express prejudice or discrimination against other Whites.

What is clear from this analysis is that Latino/a, Black, and White entrepreneurs do not conceptualize ethnic and racial identities in the same way, nor is the distinction between these categories always obvious. For Whites, the distinction between ethnicity and race is clear. Ethnic-identified Whites engage in boundary maintenance and social closure, which facilitates enterprise through the development of social capital among co-ethnics, in keeping with the literature on ethnic enterprise. For these ethnic-identified Whites, ethnic identity is more salient than racial identity. Racially identified Whites do not report benefits or detriments associated with White racial group membership or belonging. The absence of social capital or anti-White sentiment among White entrepreneurs—in fact, the lack of awareness of their own racial identity—underscores their privileged racial group position within the American racial hierarchy, a privilege that equates being White with the invisible norm (McKinney 2004:13–14, 75). Moreover, in the context of a social structure whose institutions favor Whites, the compensatory social capital rooted in co-racial networks is not essential or necessary to the degree that it is for more disadvantaged ethnic and racial minorities such as Blacks or Latinos/as. The lack of a racial identity among Whites and their color blindness in "seeing" race in themselves or others are likely an attempt, whether conscious or not, to neutralize or contest the White privilege that they enjoy in the American racial hierarchy.

For Blacks, in contrast, the distinction between ethnicity and race is blurred. Black entrepreneurs may offer conceptually different definitions of ethnicity and race—for example, that ethnicity is linked to ancestry or culture, whereas race is linked to color; however, their experience as Black entrepreneurs living and working at the bottom of the racial hierarchy serves to compress these distinct, conceptually different identities into a single and salient racial identity. Blacks who self-identify as African American or French Haitian *always* identify as Black as well. Moreover, and regardless of how they self-identify, Black entrepreneurs benefit from co-racial networks that transcend ethnicity, even as they may espouse, at times, an anti-Black (or anti–African American) sentiment. Finally, Latinos/as appear to have a more nuanced notion of group identity than Whites or Blacks. Latinos/as may identify ethnically or racially or both, and benefit from membership in these groups through the development of social capital. When Latinos/as express an anti-Latino/a sentiment, however, most self-identify ethnically, as the racial classification *Latino/a* or *Hispanic* that they invoke becomes synonymous with a (negative) racial identity. By self-identifying ethnically in these instances, they attempt to resist or contest their membership in that racialized group.

Overall, this chapter reveals the process of racialization that is inherent in a society where race matters. Although agency is revealed in individual or collective action, for example, in one's ability to self-identify ethnically or racially, the racialized social structure prevents actors from being identified ethnically only; the imposition of race is always required—it is not an option. The pattern of recognition, resistance, and reproduction underscores the interdependence of agency and structure: agency in the attempt by individuals to resist the process of racialization through the use of ethnicity and in the creation of new, non-White, non-Black racial categories; and structure in the reproduction of the racial hierarchy, endemic in the American social structure.

# 7  Rugged Individualists and the American Dream

*I came to this country, and I came here—excuse my words—I came here with one single piece of underwear just like everybody else. But I came here, and I knew I liked the good life. I wanted a car; I wanted good clothes. So, I worked day and night. After three to four months after coming to this country, I had a brand new car. What's the difference? Those people [Latinos/as who don't work hard] don't have intelligence. . . . You can't just say, "No, no I can't." How is it that you can't? Being able to is wanting to. I came to work and fight because I wanted to improve myself. I wanted everything that was available, I was in the country of opportunity, but I also had to work. Why don't others do it? Because they don't want to. Wouldn't you agree?*

—Concepción Cortez, fifty years old, Salvadoran

THE AMERICAN CREED affirms that America is the land of liberty, justice, and equal opportunity for all (Myrdal 1944). This ideology is widely held among the people of America and among many who live outside of its national borders. The belief in the American creed is "supported by such broad cultural themes as individual responsibility, materialism, unfettered competition and an undying belief in the economic system as fair and meritocratic" (Wells and Crain 1997:11). Latino/a entrepreneurs from diverse social locations convey their trust in the American creed. They readily and regularly espouse the mantra that hard work, dedication, a positive attitude, and courage are all one needs to succeed in America. This commitment to rugged individualism complements the creed and reinforces the certainty of its authenticity, as do the resolute claims of success that are made by all Latino/a entrepreneurs despite observed economic stagnation or decline.

Latino/a entrepreneurs' conviction in the American way of life seemingly undermines a central tenet of this book, that the American social structure is inherently unequal. For how can classism, racism, and sexism exist in a society that engenders human agency through equality of opportunity, rewards individual achievements, and is rife with successful entrepreneurs from all walks of life? If American entrepreneurs' life chances are not wholly determined by individual agency but, rather, are conditioned in part on structural forces outside of an individual's control rooted in the socially constructed reality of rich or poor, White or non-White, man or woman, then the American creed ideology is a myth and its sidekick rugged individualism an illusion.

The majority of White entrepreneurs fervently deny—or, more accurately, overlook—any and all forms of structural inequality. In contrast, most Latino/a and Black entrepreneurs acknowledge that classism, sexism, and especially racism exist; yet, they do not generally connect unequal treatment based on race, ethnicity, class, or gender to their life chances. It is likely that White, middle-class, male entrepreneurs' passionate belief in the American creed, individual responsibility, and rejection of structural inequality is related to their position at the top of racial, class, and gender hierarchies, while those same ideologies reinforce Black and Latino/a entrepreneurs' belief in their ability to transcend it.

Latino/a entrepreneurs frequently bring up examples and experiences of unequal treatment based on race or ethnicity, though not on class and gender; however, such experiences are almost never associated with socioeconomic inequality. Instead, racial inequality is viewed through a color-blind lens, a subtle but no less effective form of race relations discourse and practice that justifies racial inequality through nonracial means. Simply put, color-blind racism constitutes the "common sense" notion that contemporary racial inequality has nothing to do with racism (Bonilla-Silva 2006).

Color-blind racism is intimately linked with the American creed and rugged individualism ideologies. Latino/a immigrant entrepreneurs put their faith in these ideologies well before leaving their countries of origin. Upon their arrival to the United States, their experiences with racial and ethnic discrimination do not alter their belief in these ideologies and, in some ways, reinforce them. They trust that with hard work and determination they can overcome the effects of systemic racism on their life chances. Notably, Black entrepreneurs, regardless of class or gender, show little conviction for the American creed when compared to Whites or Latinos/as; nevertheless, their belief in the principle of rugged individualism surmounts the implications of their ideological reservations to the creed. Although Black entrepreneurs acknowledge that structural inequality based on race exists, they, like Latinos/as, reject the notion that it may negatively impact their life chances; this is due, in large part, to their trust in overcoming inequality through individual agency.

## Class Inequality

Even when class inequality is connected to differences in economic success, it is often attributed to individual shortcomings rather than viewed as a structural force—the outcome of an unequal society that privileges and reproduces a class hierarchy. When class concerns are raised, those individual Latinos/as who possess few skills, limited education, or not much money expect, and are expected by others, to underperform. Rob, the upper-class Hispanic Italian who runs a successful business, understood the attempts by desperate lower-class Latinos/as to start a business but vented his frustration that they would take that far-fetched shot without the proper credentials or capital:

> A lot of people [in my experience] that have lower economic [status] and education; they open their own business. . . . In business, it's not about who you think you are, you know? You can't open a business because you think Juan, Pedro, John, Mrs. X, open a business—"Okay, I'm gonna open one too!" That's the most . . . [He sighs.] Especially when you're low-income, you know; when you have less education, your mind can only take you so far. The way we live these days with the economy so bad, anybody will take that gamble . . . but they *have to have* the capital. At least forty percent if not more of their own money before they start a business. Anybody that starts with less than that, they have a greater chance of struggling and not making it through.

Rob does not think that lower-class Latino/a entrepreneurs' outside chance of success is worth the risk of losing whatever capital they can scratch up to invest in a business. Additionally, whereas lower-class entrepreneurs may recognize that their vulnerable economic conditions make it harder to start a business or keep it going, they do not characterize themselves as unsuccessful, even when they may just break even. Recall that Don José, the sixty-six-year-old unauthorized Mexican immigrant, concedes that he does not make much money (his household income falls below the poverty line), nor does he think he has the right skills "to move up." Still, he considers himself to be a success because he did not have to resort to welfare and his business is still open. He concludes, "For someone who has studies and education that's nothing, but for me it's a lot." For many lower-class entrepreneurs like Don José, the certainty and acceptance of relative success lend credence to their belief in personal responsibility and the American creed, thereby weakening the perceived role of class in shaping or reproducing economic inequality.

In these examples, social class is reduced to individual skills and resources. Yet, low-skilled entrepreneurs share a class position, one that constrains their individual and collective access to those skills and resources that are generally associated with the middle and upper classes. By reducing social class, a capitalist social formation endemic to the unequal market economy, to individual shortcomings, entrepreneurs ignore the class position of individuals and collectivities and its role in shaping and reproducing inequality within the stratified American economy (Gimenez 2007:111).

## Gender Inequality

It is revealing that gender inequality is almost entirely ignored as influencing Latino/a entrepreneurs' economic outcomes. As Rhode (1999) suggests, gender inequality is a "'no problem' problem" that "prevents Americans from noticing that on every major measure of wealth, power, and status, women are still significantly worse off than men" (1999:1–2). Although Rhode (1999) argues further that different forms of denial explain perceived gender inequality, for example, that women make choices that lead to unequal outcomes or that discrimination against women is (like racism) a thing of the past (3), Latino/a entrepreneurs do not offer such rationales. Rather, they dismiss charges of gender inequality altogether and at times argue that women often have it better than men. Perhaps not surprisingly, their reasoning sometimes reinforces cultural stereotypes of the innate biological differences between the sexes.

Concepción Cortez, a fifty-one-year-old Salvadoran immigrant, claims that from her cultural perspective, women not only produce a superior product when compared to men, but are the sole group who should do so.

> *Some owners believe that being a woman has helped them in their business. Others feel that it has hurt them. What do you think?*
> For me, yes [it has helped], because like I told you, in the kitchen I can do anything. If I were a man, I don't think I would be capable of doing everything in a kitchen. For us, in the type of food we make, it has to be made by women because, first, we make tortillas by hand and, second, because *pupusas* need to be made by hand, not with a machine. In our culture, it is looked down upon for a man to make *pupusas*. I'm not saying that they can't do it. If I see a man making *pupusas*, I won't eat there. . . . I have felt that because I am a woman, people who come here, the men that come here, like the food more!

In a similar vein, Sylvia Delgado, a petit, thirty-nine-year-old, middle-class woman who co-owns a restaurant with her husband (the chef), suggests that women have a way with customers that men do not:

> I think that being a woman is a very good thing to bring more customers. Because of our way of being, if there is good management and a good relationship between the customer and the owner, women will bring more fruit.

In a departure from such sentiments, Florencia Molina, the forty-three-year-old, middle-class Honduran owner of Las Palmas, is clear about her negative experiences with sexism. Unlike the majority of women who dismissed gender inequality from consideration altogether, or those who suggested that being a woman actually helped them in business, Doña Florencia identifies experiences with gender discrimination and connects her personal experiences to unequal gender relations more generally. From her social location, Doña Florencia suggests that the effects of gender inequality and sexism are more salient and harder to overcome than racial or ethnic discrimination (which she experienced but did not connect to structural inequality).

> *You mentioned that you did not experience discrimination based on race. What about discrimination based on gender?*
> Oh, yeah, I call that a normal thing. Every time I have the opportunity it's the first thing I tell them [men in business]: "Don't undermine me." You always experience the discrimination, and it's always put to the fact that as women, you should not know and you do not know certain things. Business is supposedly a man's world.
>
> *So you have to remind them?*
> Yes, I still do. I have to find my place, and I have to make my place, and I have to assure them that I know my game to be able to establish a business relationship. . . . The owner of Green Peppers is a dear friend; however, when he comes down for business, it's a different level: "I am a male; you are a female." I have to prove to them, yes, that you walk the walk, not just talk the talk, like we say. They challenge you in every aspect. Even if I go to the bank and I happen to have a male financial adviser or loan officer, they are not comfortable with speaking business to business with a woman.

Doña Florencia is a middle-class woman who has connections with the male-dominated, upper echelons of the Latino/a restaurant industry, such as being a member of Houston's Hispanic Business Association. She also has ambitions to grow her business and hopes to open several more locations in the next five years, so she often attends business conferences, where she networks with successful, predominately male, restaurateurs. Because she is the sole owner and operator of her business, she is also responsible for the ordering of all supplies and materials, again from largely male distributors. For these reasons, she is exposed to male-dominated environments more frequently than the other, largely lower-class women in this study, or those middle-class Latinas whose husbands take over such responsibilities and duties, as in the case of Sylvia Delgado. Doña Florencia's unique experience is in keeping with previous research, which suggests that different groups of individual women face different gender relations, or "regimes," based on their social location, including class (Walby 1997:6). For Doña Florencia, gender inequality is a daily, salient, and inescapable reality that influences her entrepreneurial strategies, opportunities, and outcomes in sometimes negative ways.

## American Entrepreneurs and Color-Blind Racism

Mainstream and even more critical approaches to understanding race relations generally focus on the binary relationship between Whites and Blacks only. Racial inequality and oppression among non-Black racial minorities is often characterized as an equivalent or perhaps a somewhat contracted version of that which is experienced by Blacks. Based on this general consensus, non-Black minority race relations are thought, presumably, to be based on the same fundamental organization and principles as those that typify White-Black race relations. Specifically, the structure of the racial hierarchy and racial classifications are thought to be based on phenotypical characteristics and features, such as skin color. As Feagin, Vera, and Batur (2000) argue, in keeping with many who emphasize this relationship, the White-Black binary "is an archetype for other subsequent patterns of *white treatment of people of color*" (Feagin, Vera, and Batur 2000:111; their emphasis; see also Perea 1997).

A critical race approach generally maintains that racism is unidirectional, perpetrated by Whites against Blacks (and by extension, non-Black racial minorities). This perspective implicates Whites in the reproduction and persistence of racism because as the group at the top of the racial hierarchy, they alone possess the power and capacity to support or dismantle systemic racism in America (see Bonilla-Silva 2006; Feagin, Vera, and Batur 2000; Moore 2007:114–115; Tatum 1997). Critical race scholars have demonstrated convincingly that the American social structure serves to protect the interests—material, political, and otherwise—of the dominant racial group (Whites), and furthermore, that to achieve a fundamental change in American race relations would require a social movement that includes Whites who are willing to recognize and compromise on their position of privilege. Yet, the emphasis on the White-Black binary and, specifically, on *White racism against Blacks* does not necessarily capture racism against Latinos/as, as new or different arrangements may develop, for example, the racialization of Latinos/as based on a lack of English proficiency or possessing a foreign accent (Perea 1997). Furthermore, the emphasis on Whites' agency alone in reproducing racism shifts the focus away from the agency of non-White racial minorities, concealing or minimizing their role in maintaining or altering American race relations.

Although Blacks and Latinos/as do not enjoy the privileged position of Whites at the top of the racial hierarchy, they too are embedded within the racialized American social structure. It is therefore imperative to consider the role of non-White groups in reproducing the American racial hierarchy, however tangential or central. The emphasis on White racism against Blacks, however, does little to provide the space to develop or entertain complex relations among multiple racial groups at different positions within the racial hierarchy. The agency of racial minority groups in reproducing or transforming racism is unclear but cannot be presumed to reflect that of Whites, given their comparatively subordinate position and thus their limited capacity to shape or alter the existing racialized social structure.

Understanding whether or to what extent minorities reproduce racism is especially salient in the post–civil rights era, a period in which de facto and de jure Jim Crow racism—a form that was clearly and almost exclusively used by the White dominant majority to oppress and subjugate all racial minority groups—has, for the most part, given way to color-blind racism, a more subtle but no less effective form of race relations discourse and practice that justifies racial inequality through nonracial means. Simply put, color-blind racism constitutes the "common sense" notion that contemporary racial inequality has nothing to do with racism (Bonilla-Silva 2006). This presumption is based on the dramatic sociopolitical changes that have taken place in the history of American race relations, especially since the 1960s. Following the civil rights movement, race-equity laws and policies were passed that made it illegal to discriminate against racial and ethnic minorities in America's institutions

and public life. Their legal access to the American mainstream, however restricted or incomplete in practice, provides the potential for racial minorities
to gain knowledge of the dominant discourse and ideology on race relations,
and participate in its maintenance and reproduction, if not its substance. In
the present context, racial minorities are no longer on the sidelines of race
relations; they engage in race relations directly: specifically, maintaining, reproducing, and possibly even altering the dominant ideology of color-blind
racism.

White, Black and Latino/a business owners consistently express a color-
blind view of American race relations. As I argue earlier, racial minorities are
embedded in a society where the dominant race relations ideology is that of
color-blind racism. Thus, it should not be surprising, and indeed should be
expected, that racial minorities would share to some degree in Whites' under-
standings and conceptions of race relations. In keeping with this prediction, I
find that all White, Black, and Latino/a entrepreneurs use the four components
or frames of color-blind racism identified by Eduardo Bonilla-Silva (2006).
These include abstract liberalism, or the assertion that all people are treated
equally in America (which disregards racial group–based structural oppression and disadvantage); cultural racism, or identifying racial inequality as the
by-product of a group's cultural deficiencies or excellence; the naturalization
of racial group differences; and minimizing racism (Bonilla-Silva 2006). This
color-blind arsenal provides various justifications and explanations for racial
group differences in America that share the same basic premise: Racial inequality in America is the result of "anything but racism" (Bonilla-Silva and
Baiocchi 2001:117).

My findings confirm a recent study on Black color blindness, even as it challenges its conclusions. Bonilla-Silva and Embrick (2001) observe that Blacks in
Detroit engage in color-blind racism when discussing affirmative action and
residential and school segregation. They suggest, however, that Blacks do so to
a lesser extent or in a more indirect manner than Whites do. In particular,
they concede that some Blacks employ color-blind racism, such as their use
of cultural stereotypes to explain racial differences (for example, "Blacks
are lazy") or their belief that racial segregation is "natural" or "no one's fault"
(Bonilla-Silva and Embrick 2001:52). Nevertheless, Black Detroiters also recognize that racial inequality is partly an outcome of structural forces, whereas
their White counterparts generally do not. Thus, they conclude, somewhat un-
convincingly and uneasily, that "many Blacks" are only "slightly color blind"

(62). Yet, does the recognition of systemic racism lessen a belief in color blindness, as Bonilla-Silva and Embrick (2001) suggest? If, as they observe, a Black man justifies racial inequality by stereotyping Blacks as possessing a cultural deficiency, does his concession that structural inequality matters offset his conviction of that particular cultural stereotype for that specific outcome? Does it lessen the impact of cultural racism in reproducing racism in society?

For the Black and Latino/a entrepreneurs in my study, this seeming contradiction (a belief in both systemic racism and color-blind racism) is ubiquitous. Their expression and use of color-blind frames are as common and compelling as those of Whites, and just as effective in rationalizing and justifying racial inequality, even as Black and Latino/a entrepreneurs acknowledge that racial inequality is rooted in structural disadvantage (whereas White entrepreneurs generally do not). I argue that this ostensible paradox among racial minority entrepreneurs and perhaps racial minorities in general may be due, in part, to their unshakable belief in the American creed.

## American Entrepreneurs and the American Creed

White, Black, and Latino/a business owners convey their trust in the American creed, which affirms that America provides liberty, justice, equality, and opportunity for all (Myrdal 1944). White and Latino/a entrepreneurs, in particular, are especially likely to repeat the refrain that America is the "land of opportunity." Martín, the fifty-one-year-old Salvadoran immigrant owner of Sabrosa, shares this common philosophy.

> People have a chance when they cross the border. You're coming to this country because this country is prosperous; this country is the "Neverland." The people are good. The people are generous. So many good things about this country. You can accomplish anything here.

In addition to their own belief in the American creed, Latino/a entrepreneurs also report that they were often encouraged or urged to go into business by Whites. Recall that Doña Toña decided to go into business after a White man, the owner of a company that contracted the cleaning service that she worked for, told her that she "lived in a country where [she] could do anything." Similarly, Señor and Señora Gomez attended English-language night classes at a community college where their "Anglo" teacher told them "that if we had a chance to open up a business in this country that we should, that this is one of the best countries to open a business."

Although Black entrepreneurs are less likely to suggest that America offers equality of opportunity for all, they, like White and Latino/a entrepreneurs, nevertheless share the related rugged individualist mantra. Rugged individualism complements the American creed ideology; they are both intimately linked to color-blind racism. After all, if racism against minority groups exists, then the American creed ideology falls down because it would mean that an individual's life chances are not determined by individual agency, but, rather, are conditioned on structural forces outside of an individual's control, namely, membership in a racial group. As entrepreneurs, however, Whites, Blacks, and Latinos/as view their opportunities and outcomes, and those of others, through a rugged-individualist lens. Unlike Whites, however, Black and Latino/a entrepreneurs recognize that racial minorities often confront structural disadvantages. Nevertheless, their faith in rugged individualism ultimately reinforces their belief that through hard work and determination they can overcome the effects of systemic racism on their entrepreneurial outcomes, a belief that ultimately contributes to and reinforces their color-blind ideology.

### Abstract Liberalism

Abstract liberalism, or the notion that every individual is equal and enjoys a level playing field, ignores systemic racial oppression in America. This color-blind frame is closely associated with the American creed and rugged-individualist ideologies, as each highlights the role of individual agency in determining one's life chances. White, Black, and Latino/a entrepreneurs generally agree with this common premise, regardless of their class or gender. Although the majority of Black and Latino/a entrepreneurs readily identify instances of discrimination or racism that they or others experience, they do not necessarily connect those experiences to their life chances. Rather, they express a confidence in their individual agency. This belief is often expressed in the most common frame of color-blind racism, that of abstract liberalism.

Recall that Francisco Pinto is a fifty-eight-year-old, 1.5-generation Mexican American who took over his parents restaurant, Cocina Pinto, in Little Mexico. Francisco is well aware of racism against the Mexican-origin population. He readily shared personal experiences of overt Jim Crow racism in public places as a child, as a student at college, and as a janitor (a job that he held to pay his way through college). For example, growing up in Texas and Utah, Francisco recalled how legal segregation in public places divided the population into Whites and non-Whites (Mexicans and Blacks).

> I remember going to Texas in the summertime from Utah for our vacations, and we couldn't go to the ice cream shops. We would have to go to the ice factory and get *raspas* [shaved ice] and make our own snow cones, because Mexicans couldn't go to the ice cream shops. This was in Texas in the sixties. . . . In Utah, at the theater they had Mexican Night. . . . This wasn't that long ago, and we'd walk in, and I'd start walking to the front and my cousins go, "Wait, wait, you gotta sit upstairs," and I go, "All right! We get to sit up in the balcony!" and my cousins would say, "What do you mean you *get to*; you *have to*!" "What do you mean you have to?" And they'd say, "Mexicans and Blacks sit in the balcony."

It is instructive that Francisco feels the need to underscore that these experiences with legal racism in the Southwest took place in the past, even as he reminds us that it "wasn't that long ago." A decade later, then-illegal racial discrimination was still occurring in Central Texas.

> This is true. I ain't making this up. This is shocking because this is in my lifetime. And I'm sure that racism and discrimination hasn't been cleaned up. Gonzales [a city in Texas] had a "Whites only" [public] swimming pool in the seventies! . . . Some lawyer from Corpus goes in there and he says to the city of Gonzales, you gotta let the Blacks and Mexicans into the public swimming pool. You know what the city of Gonzales did? Instead of opening up the swimming pool, they covered it up and they put a [cattle]-roping arena there, which was for the Anglos.

Francisco recalled many other instances of racism and discrimination, including dropping a college course on the first day of class after the professor threw a brown paper bag on his desk and stated, "If your skin is darker than this bag, you're gonna flunk this class." (He and a Black student looked at each other and walked out of the classroom.) Given these overt examples of racism and discrimination, and Francisco's assertion that "racism and discrimination hasn't been cleaned up," it is telling that he does not believe that racial discrimination affects his business. As this discussion continued, he offered his philosophy on confronting discrimination and racism, a viewpoint that emphasizes individual agency.

> You know, by the time I got out of college, by then I already figured it out. Just do your own thing and don't worry if you're Mexican or if you're White or what you dress like. Just do your own thing and everything's always okay. . . . I always used to have arguments with some of my friends about [joining the] Mexican American Chamber of Commerce . . . or whatever. Those types of clubs exist because those people have felt denied in the mainstream. I have never felt denied.

After retelling multiple experiences with racism throughout his life that are too numerous to include here (his interview lasted more than three hours, with a one-hour follow-up phone interview), Francisco concludes that he has "never felt denied." Francisco's perspective reinforces the abstract individualist belief that as long as he does his "own thing," racial inequality will not (and does not) impact his business significantly.

All entrepreneurs, regardless of their race or their experiences with racism, suggest that their individual efforts and ambition condition their entrepreneurial outcomes. Like Francisco, Doña Florencia, the owner of a profitable Honduran restaurant, stated that she "never experienced discrimination or racism" in the United States. This claim was made minutes after describing how she started her business after quitting a job in the medical services industry because her boss repeatedly refused to promote her, finally telling her that she "would not amount to anything, that my language barrier was too strong." Nevertheless, Doña Florencia easily dismisses instances of personal and institutional racism and discrimination, while favoring the themes of individual achievement and a strong belief in the American creed again and again.

> This is really the country of opportunities; this is really, really the land that allows you to do and perform if you just really, really want to make your dreams come true. You just have to work at it because nothing is handed to you "just because."

Latino/a entrepreneurs are more likely than Black entrepreneurs to both disregard racial and ethnic inequality and embrace the American creed. Keith Malone, a Black business owner, admits to experiencing racism and discrimination in the sandwich business. While he acknowledges that racial inequality negatively affected his ability to start and maintain a successful business, he ultimately concludes that individuals determine their fates.

Before opening his business, Mr. Malone operated a national sandwich chain franchise but left because of problems that he said developed from being the only Black franchise owner in the company. When he started his own business, he had a difficult time getting a bank loan for his new sandwich shop ("I got turned down by the best of them"), even though he had $48,000 in financial capital to invest from personal savings, family, and friends. He implied that the bank turned down his loan application because he was Black, even though the bank would not admit to it. Instead, "they give you a little sheet that says why you didn't qualify for this and that and its all in their own language. They have their own little lingo. . . . They don't specifically tell you exactly why you didn't get approved." Eventually, Mr. Malone received an SBA government-subsidized loan for small and minority-owned businesses (notably, one of only three minority business owners in this study to acquire one). Regardless of the difficulties in financing the restaurant and turning a profit (after almost ten years in business, he earns $12,500 a year), he concluded that being a business owner provides the best opportunity to "make it" in America. For Mr. Malone, being successful in business is not so much "a Black and White thing" because being "your own boss means you always control your own destiny. When its all said and done, it will be your fault whether you sink or swim; it's all on you."

Likewise, Joseph Robinson, one of the most successful Black restaurant owners in my sample in terms of longevity and economic progress (he inherited his soul food restaurant, now in its third generation, and earned $35,000 in 2008), succinctly stated this point.

> I'm a business owner who happens to be Black. Being Black or being White in business doesn't determine how successful you will be. It depends on what you put into your business that determines how successful you will be.

In the same way that Mr. Robinson connects success to what he puts into his business, regardless of being Black (or an heir), Sam Christensen, the fifty-eight-year-old White owner of Don Juan's Mexican Restaurante, claims that "a Black man can be very successful in business, and conversely a White man can fail." In their color-blind discourse, Francisco, Corina, Keith, Joseph, and Sam privilege individual ambition, drive, and skills over the presence or possibility of racial inequality in altering their entrepreneurial outcomes, in keeping with the American creed, rugged individualism, and abstract liberalism.

## Cultural Racism

In the second frame of color-blind racism, or cultural racism, Black and Latino/a entrepreneurs sometimes attribute unequal outcomes among their own groups or those of others to group-specific cultural deficiencies (or achievements). In contrast, White entrepreneurs do not generally refer to their racial group's cultural endowments to explain entrepreneurial outcomes, although they may justify the success or failure of other racial minority groups in this way. Ethnic-identified White entrepreneurs are the exception, however, as they may underscore the benefits of their specific ethnic group features or characteristics (for instance, "Greeks are hardworking") on their entrepreneurial activity.

As indicated earlier, Francisco does not believe that his experiences with racism have affected his ability to succeed in enterprise. Moreover, he contends that if Chicanos (second-generation Mexicans) have failed to participate in business ownership, it is due to their own cultural shortcomings.

> One thing that saddens me a little about the Hispanics . . . As they come here, the immigrants from Mexico and Honduras and El Salvador, they really haven't had to assimilate. . . . I just wish that they would try a little bit harder. Ah, here's my White side coming out. Try a little bit harder and maybe they could break them stereotypes. . . . The first generations of immigrants are here for a purpose. They know how tough it is somewhere else. They come over here to work, to have a good life for their children. . . . The first generation is so happy and blessed to be here. . . . I'm telling you as honestly and truthfully as I can. We used to criticize the Blacks: They're too lazy to work. And then the first group of Chicanos has fallen into the same trap: "Well, I'm the victim." You know, "I need food stamps and I can't work." They make every excuse in the world instead of fighting and bettering themselves.

Francisco is not the only one to characterize Latinos/as (or Blacks) as possessing a sense of entitlement that restricts their socioeconomic progress. By describing Blacks and Latinos/as in this way, minority entrepreneurs hold them accountable for the socioeconomic disadvantages they face regardless of their acknowledgment that racism or racial inequality exists. Ironically, Francisco's characterization of himself as White when criticizing Chicanos/as reveals his understanding that White racism or prejudice exists, and furthermore, that Latinos/as do not or perhaps should not express such prejudices against their own group.

Moreover, a common explanation offered by Black and Latino/a entrepreneurs for low rates of business ownership among their members is the lack of a cohesive community. In this study and others, Black business owners often lament the "haters" in their community and often conjure up a "crabs in a bucket" metaphor to illustrate how Blacks reinforce their subordinate racial group position within the hierarchy. That commonly used metaphor suggests that just like crabs in a bucket, Blacks tend to pull each other down rather than lifting or building each other up. Andre, the forty-six-year-old owner of Chicago Dogs, contends that Black racial group members are often in competition with one another, which leads to conflict:

> It's the crabs in a bucket mentality and especially because I'm not from here and I'm doing Chicago cuisine here in Houston. . . . I had a [Black] guy leaving once tell me, "You ain't from around here; we're gonna shut you down." This guy was supposed to be a friend. . . . Overall you just have to be smarter than them, so in the end it all makes me better.

Andre suggests that Blacks in Houston are "territorial," so it is possible that in his case the "crabs in a bucket" metaphor refers to Black southerners who do not want Black midwesterners to succeed. Nevertheless, for Andre, Black Houstonians' regional unity comes at the expense of racial unity. The "crabs in a bucket" metaphor was also used by Latino/a entrepreneurs. Señor Pineda, a very successful Honduran naturalized citizen who illegally crossed three borders to reach America, characterizes Hondurans and Latinos/as in this way:

> The Latino can't appreciate other cultures. I have a [Honduran] man come in and tell me, "Ah, this is not Honduran." And I tell him, "But, I'm Honduran; I never said this was Honduran food." I am the talented person and these people [Anglos] love it. The Latino is like a crab [in a bucket]. . . . There are a couple of Honduran men that come in and say to me, "What's the big fuss? You don't have shit." . . . Latinos are jealous; they can't have this. Hondurans . . . don't support because they can't do it.

Señor Pineda's claims of co-ethnic and co-racial conflict associated with "crabs in a bucket," are, from his perspective, rooted in Latinos/as cultural deficiencies, an inability to rise above their own limitations. In these examples, Black and Latino/a communities are characterized as reproducing their own stagnation or decline, serving to justify Black and Latino/a racial inequality in enterprise as the consequence of cultural deficiencies within the groups themselves.

Finally, Black and Latino/a entrepreneurs frequently make comments suggesting that "other groups" are more cohesive and supportive. Yet, the suggestion that specific groups are successful in enterprise *because* they are more cohesive is overly simplistic and debatable (Bates 1994; Sanders and Nee 1996; Valdez 2008a). Nonetheless, the classic and "common sense" approach to ethnic entrepreneurship maintains that for some groups, such as the Koreans, Chinese, and Cubans, "strong communities" generate social capital, including close-knit, co-ethnic ties that facilitate entrepreneurial success. This approach further implies that ethnic entrepreneurs could not achieve success without the support of their co-ethnic communities (Bates 1994; Valdez 2008a). The use of cultural stereotypes in positive or negative permutations, however, represents cultural racism, a second form of color-blind racism. That frame suggests that the cultural aptness or achievement of particular groups (such as Koreans) facilitates their entrepreneurial success through ethnic cohesion, whereas Black and Latino/a entrepreneurs suffer from cultural deficiencies that hinder their entrepreneurial outcomes.

Mrs. Tate indicates that the Chinese, in particular, demonstrate an ethnic cohesion that facilitates their entrepreneurial outcomes. Unlike Blacks, who she contends are less likely to patronize Black-owned businesses—especially those businesses in which the owner appears to be doing well—she states that if a "Chinese person opened up a restaurant, every Chinese person in the area would try to support it." Likewise, Doña Nadia, a forty-four-year-old Mexican immigrant business owner in Little Mexico states, "The Chinese, I think they are very united and the Mexicans aren't. . . . The Chinese help each other with anything. We [Mexicans] don't have much unity." Similarly, Martín contrasts Latinos'/as' lack of loyalty among members against the strong community cohesion of Middle Easterners or Chinese. It is clear from this common refrain that for Black and Latino/a entrepreneurs, a lack of group solidarity and support among group members is thought to limit their economic progress and business ownership overall.

### Naturalization of Racial Differences

A third form of color-blind racism is the naturalization of racial group differences. In this practice, the impact of race is explained away, often as the natural outcome of racial group inclinations. By naturalizing racial group differences, racialized outcomes such as racial residential segregation are understood as preferences that are "almost biologically driven and typical of all groups in a society" (Bonilla-Silva 2006:28). Black and Latino/a entrepreneurs often downplay their racially segregated customer base using this color-blind frame. For example, Ruben, a fifty-seven-year-old Cuban restaurateur whose restaurant is located at the border of Little Latin America and Houston Heights, explained his 95 percent Anglo customer base in this way.

> You see the Anglos coming in for lunch during the work week; they all work around here [points in the direction of Houston Heights]. But, you know, the weekend comes and it's all Hispanic. The Hispanics don't like to be around the Anglos, it makes them uncomfortable.

Ruben explains his predominately White clientele as an outgrowth of self-segregation on the part of Hispanics, who are more comfortable eating with other Hispanics than with Whites. Notably, he does not indicate that Whites are uncomfortable in the presence of Latinos/as; after all, they are perfectly willing to eat in a restaurant located in Little Latin America, which is 71 percent Latino. Yet, Whites were less likely to patronize Little Latin America's restaurants during nights or weekends and were also less likely to patronize other restaurants that were located in the interior of Little Latin America. Nevertheless, Ruben understood the distinct racial makeup of his restaurant as a natural phenomenon associated with a particular group's level of comfort or discomfort.

Similarly, Joseph Robinson, the forty-nine-year-old African American owner of a soul food restaurant in Greater Houston, concedes that racial segregation and discrimination "will always exist" and might even affect his customer base:

> People might choose not to eat here because its Black owned; they read the sign that says this is soul food and they know it's Black so they decide not to come, but they don't realize that it's just the food you eat on Sundays.

Nevertheless, he also felt that it was natural for an ethnic or racial group to patronize co-ethnic or co-racial-owned restaurants:

> All businesses attract all types of people. For instance, a Chinese or Italian restaurant owner would attract most of their own just the same way I would expect to attract most of my own, but I have a diverse group of [customers].

Notably, Mr. Robinson does not suggest that he caters to Blacks ("it's just the food you eat on Sundays"), nor does he suggest that Chinese or Italian entrepreneurs are necessarily preparing ethnic or racial group–specific cuisine, which would presumably increase co-ethnic or co-racial traffic. Rather, he expects that customers would be more likely to frequent co-ethnic or co-racial owned restaurants based on their shared racial or ethnic group membership.

Charity, the Black graduate research assistant who conducted this interview, reported that at the time the interview took place, during the lunch rush, all of the employees were Black but the customers were a diverse group of people. I visited this restaurant twice, once on the weekend and once midweek in the late afternoon. During my visits, the employees and customers appeared to be exclusively Black. Joseph's restaurant is located in Greater Houston rather than the predominately Black South Ward, so is likely to generate a more diverse clientele. It appears, however, that Whites are more likely to frequent the restaurant during the workday, as was the case for Latino/a-owned restaurants located at the border of Little Latin America and Houston Heights. In Mr. Robinson's account, it is clear that he acknowledges that racism affects the racial makeup of his customer base but also justifies it as an outcome of racial preferences—not only for Blacks, but for Chinese and Italians as well. Mr. Robinson's explanation for racial differences indicates some acknowledgment of racism, even as he underscores the importance of racial group preferences, in keeping with the naturalization component of color-blind racism.

### Minimizing Racism

Minimizing racism is the last form of color-blind racism. All entrepreneurs employ this form of color-blind racism, regardless of race. As reflected in the discussions above, many Black and Latino/a entrepreneurs either experience racism themselves or witness its occurrence among others. Moreover, many connect racial inequality to structural forces, such as segregation or institutional racism. Unlike White entrepreneurs, who are more likely to claim that racism is a thing of the past, most minority entrepreneurs believe that racism persists in the contemporary period. Nevertheless, minority entrepreneurs do not associate racism or unequal opportunity with their life chances in general or entrepreneurship in particular. Instead, they see themselves as rugged individualists who can overcome disadvantages through hard work and perseverance; this thinking requires them to minimize racism or its effects on enterprise by dismissing racism from consideration altogether, downplaying or neutralizing its effects.

More than one minority entrepreneur suggested that discrimination based on race prevented them from receiving a bank loan. For example, Joseph Robinson, the owner of a soul food restaurant in business for three generations, went to several national banks to acquire start-up capital. He obtained a small business loan from a local bank after being turned down several times by bigger, national banks. When asked why he got turned down before the SBA loan came through, he replied:

> Their excuse is that they don't have a lot of faith in mom-and-pop operations and that restaurants come and go.
>
> *You said "excuse." Why do you call it that?*
> Because I think the real reason is that they didn't want to give money to a minority restaurant. They had no confidence or faith in it. Even with the history of successful years [thirty-five years], they still denied me. . . . Opportunities to acquire loans and things like that are not as easy for minority business owners as [for] other restaurants [owned by] people in the majority. They go into a bank for a loan and they get it; I go in there and I got turned down eight times before I got this loan.

Rob, in contrast, dismisses racism from playing a role in acquiring a business loan (recall that Rob's financial situation was strong enough that he "did not need to borrow from a bank"). Rob suggested an alternative explanation for being turned down:

> I don't think that [being turned down] is racist. It's just a matter of not being knowledgeable enough, not having . . . really the knowledge of what they want to get themselves into it. . . . Well, say you want to try to open up a candy store; you've never sold any candies before, so what is your background? I mean, how much do you know about this business? They [would-be minority entrepreneurs] feel like they've been thrown out [of a bank], but it's not necessarily because you are from a different culture. It's just asking somebody to trust you on a dream. . . . It just doesn't work that way in business.

Rob dismisses the possibility of institutional racism, "an organized network [such as the financial system] that enacts normative practices that disadvantage others based on their ethnic or racial group membership" (Constantine and Sue 2006:34; Thompson and Neville 1999), in blocking minority loan acquisition. Instead, he suggests that would-be minority business owners are not qualified, as they lack the experience necessary to run a business. In Joseph's case, however, a not insignificant amount of financial collateral and a third-generation, family-owned business would seem to meet the financial and experience threshold to satisfy Rob and arguably one or more national banks. Additionally, while research that has shown that minority businesses are likely to be located in poverty-stricken areas, where higher levels of violent crime and burglary may prevent loans from being granted (Kaplan and House-Soremekun 2009), Joseph's business was located in Greater Houston, a more ethnically and racially diverse area than the predominately Black and impoverished South Ward.

Señor Pineda, the Honduran naturalized citizen owner of Green Peppers in Greater Houston, dismisses discrimination or racism targeting Latinos/as because they did not experience slavery. He then suggests that Latinos/as, and immigrants in particular, are culturally deficient, preferring to work for wages rather than "compete."

> Of course there are marginalized people, but to be marginalized you have to be marginalized by *slavery*. If [Latinos] are marginalized with problems that don't exist, for me they don't exist. . . . I say that the Latino definitely comes [to the United States], but he doesn't come to compete. He comes to work, just for a check that he will spend. If you compete and see what others have, you will learn. But not only learn—you will also be able to enjoy and compensate yourself.

Accordingly, if Latinos/as were oriented toward learning and ambition, they would improve their life chances. For Señor Pineda, racism does not affect Latinos'/as' life chances, but their cultural deficiencies do. In this passage, two frames of color-blind racism are observed: the minimization of racism and cultural racism.

Finally, minority entrepreneurs sometimes neutralize the effects of racism on their life chances by suggesting that everyone has an equal opportunity to experience oppression. Francisco, who expressed his belief in abstract liberalism and cultural racism, minimized the effects of racism by equating racial oppression among Latinos/as and Blacks with nonracial oppression, more generally:

> I used to have a White friend. We'd always joke, and a Black friend; all three of us would get together and drink beer, and me and my Black friend would tell

the White guy, we'd say, "You know the difference between us minorities and you White guys? We're being screwed by society and we know it! You're a White guy, you're being screwed by society and you don't know it, because you think that you're White and that makes you privileged. Nah, you're getting screwed too!"

The idea that non-Whites experience racism in the same way as Whites is expressed by a number of entrepreneurs, particularly Whites. Sam Christensen also suggested that any discussion of racial inequality on the part of Blacks or Whites (specifically, reverse discrimination) is a "crutch . . . a crutch for the White man, a crutch for the Black man." By minimizing racism or equating it with White oppression, the playing field is leveled, racism benign, and racial inequality, if it does exist, is not attributed to race anyway.

## Conclusion

Consistently, White, Latino/a, and Black entrepreneurs characterize themselves as hardworking rugged individualists who are striving for the American dream. Regardless of class, gender, race, or ethnicity, the American creed ideology is fully adopted by American entrepreneurs. Even among those who recognize that structural inequality privileges some and oppresses others, entrepreneurs do not link their socioeconomic fate to systemic inequality. These findings underscore the reproduction of the American social structure, which celebrates individualism and downplays classism, racism, and sexism. Within the American society, Black and Latino/a entrepreneurs reproduce the ideology of individualism and meritocracy, even as they experience structural inequality. Color-blind racism is the dominant ideological lens from which Latino/a, Black, and White entrepreneurs understand race relations, specifically, racial inequality and racism. Their use of the color-blind frames of abstract individualism, cultural racism, the naturalization of racial phenomena, and minimizing racism, singly or in combination, contributes to the reproduction of racial inequality in America.

Ethnic and racial minorities' role or agency in shaping racial inequality does not have the same impact as Whites' racial reproduction, as this latter group maintains the dominant, privileged, and more powerful position along the American racial hierarchy (as well as other systems of oppression, such as class). As embedded members within a society that is stratified by race, however, minority group members are socialized to perpetuate the dominant color-blind ideology. The cost of doing so limits their role in recognizing the effects of structural inequality on their economic and social lives, facilitating change, or altering this hegemonic discourse. While fostering a reproduction of the status quo, it limits an alternative understanding of race relations that may ultimately forge a new discourse on the role of race in shaping their life chances.

# 8 Conclusion
## Embedded Entrepreneurs in Brown, Black, and White

A COMMON ASSUMPTION is that with hard work and perseverance, anyone can achieve the American dream of owning and operating a successful business. The experience of ethnic entrepreneurs would seem to lend credibility to this claim, as Korean grocers, Chinese launderers, and Cuban restaurateurs often achieve phenomenal rates of business ownership and economic mobility in the United States. The classic theory of ethnic enterprise attributes entrepreneurial success among these groups, in part, to essential ethnic group characteristics and features (Lee 2002; Light 1972; Portes and Rumbaut 2001). With strong ethnic networks to generate social capital resources, co-ethnic group members have the support that they need to start, maintain, and thrive in a business. A closer look at those quintessential ethnic entrepreneurs, however, reveals that they are disproportionately middle-class and male. Nevertheless, ethnicity, the classic argument goes, is essential, whereas class is generally reduced to individual characteristics or conflated with ethnicity, and gender is overlooked. Yet, the attributes of group affiliation associated with class, gender, and race combine to affect the entrepreneurial outcomes of ethnic groups in complex ways, just as the attributes of ethnic group affiliation combine to affect the entrepreneurial outcomes of class, gender, and racial groups.

In emphasizing the role of ethnic group membership, the ethnic entrepreneurship approach redirects its focus away from business ownership that is observed among nonethnic groups, such as women, the lower classes, and racial groups. Ethnic affiliation, however, does not explain entrepreneurial differences within or across these different groups, nor is it in and of itself a necessary precondition for entrepreneurship. For example, Korean women, lower-class Cuban Marielitos, and racialized groups, such as Mexicans and Blacks, also engage in entrepreneurialism, although they report markedly lower rates of business ownership, which are often associated with economic stagnation or decline. Diminished outcomes among these "survival entrepreneurs" suggest a dream denied—or at least severely dampened. By neglecting the entrepreneurial experiences of these groups, the common assumption that entrepreneurial activity is disproportionately ethnic and associated with socioeconomic progress—a way of "making it" in America—is at best premature and likely overstated.

Moving beyond the traditional approach, this book introduces a new perspective that connects two separate threads of sociological knowledge: a macrolevel theory of intersectionality advanced by ethnic and racial minority feminist scholars, which explains structural oppression and privilege as stemming from the intersection of race, class, and gender, and the traditional ethnic entrepreneurship paradigm, which emerged in concert with theories of immigrant incorporation and assimilation. The embedded market approach examines how systems of oppression and privilege that comprise the highly stratified American social structure condition the life chances of entrepreneurs from different social locations, even within the same ethnic group. This approach challenges proponents of the ethnic entrepreneurship paradigm to consider how race, class, gender, and *not only* ethnicity intersect to affect the entrepreneurial outcomes of a diverse group of entrepreneurs. In so doing, it pushes our knowledge of entrepreneurship beyond an ethnicity-centered, group-level analysis to reveal a more complete picture of how entrepreneurial activity is shaped by structural inequality.

At the same time, this study takes seriously the concern raised by ethnic and racial minority feminist scholars that although an intersectional approach has been used quite effectively to explain the experiences of women of color in certain segments of the labor market, for example, low-skilled, immigrant women domésticas in cities across the developed world (see the remarkable work of Pierrette Hondagneu-Sotelo 1994, 2001; Mary Romero 1992; Rhacel Salazar Parreñas 2001; and Patricia Zavella 1987), there is a dearth of comparative studies of intersectionality that examine "multiple comparisons and multi-dimensional conceptualizations" or that theorize about how such complex relations might work in specific institutions (Browne and Misra 2003:506). When an intersectional approach is advanced to study ethnic entrepreneurship, scholars employ a similar methodological strategy: they investigate one location along the "matrix of domination," such as self-employed, low-skilled, unauthorized Mexican immigrant male gardeners (Ramirez and Hondagneu-Sotelo 2009), Central American male day laborers or street vendors (Valenzuela 2003; Zlolniski 2006), or working-class, Black women hair salon owners (Harvey 2005). This strategy allows for a closer look at the socioeconomic experiences of a specific segment of the matrix, and in particular, the most vulnerable and understudied populations. A comparative aspect is still needed, however, to fully understand how privilege and oppression play out—what a given social location means for the life chances of those who are differently positioned within the matrix but are engaged in similar economic activities. This study attempts to fill that empirical and theoretical void to offer a comprehensive and systematic explanation of intersectionality across multiple social locations, by focusing on a diverse group of restaurateurs in Houston.

The embedded market approach starts with the premise that the American social structure is comprised of three systems of oppression and privilege: capitalism, patriarchy, and White supremacy. These interdependent systems give rise to class, gender, racial, and ethnic group hierarchies that intersect to shape the social location of groups of individuals. Social location, in turn, specifies group members' embedded position within the larger, unequal social structure. It also informs the degree of agency that they can generate to compensate for structural inequality. For Latinos/as from different social locations, the integration of structure and agency conditions their differential market capacity, which shapes their entrepreneurial life chances.

Market capacity is comprised of market, social, and government capital resources that Latinos/as bring to the market. The importance of market capital, which stems from resources rooted in class background, is especially apparent in the case of ethnic and racial minorities and women. Those with greater access to market capital resources outperform those with fewer market capital resources and, furthermore, enjoy greater social capital and government capital resources overall. In contrast, social capital, which is rooted in agentic processes stemming from long-term symmetrical relationships of reciprocity (Polanyi 1944, 1957), may generate resources that provide economic and social support, but this support is often compensatory, contingent, and ultimately inadequate in the face of market uncertainty or disadvantage. Whether it is sufficient to overcome structural inequality, however, is circumscribed by Latinos'/as' social location.

The limited, compensatory quality of social capital is not unexpected or surprising, given that reciprocal relationships are, after all, "embedded in the economic system" in a market economy (Polanyi 1944). As even Portes and Sensenbrenner (1993:1338) concede, reciprocal relationships may facilitate economic action through social capital, but they can also "constrain actors or even derail [social capital] from its original goals." On this point, Nee and Ingram (1988) conclude that social relationships are fragile and unpredictable; thus, economic activity that emerges from reciprocal ties may be limited in scope. Moreover, although government capital provides an additional, secondary resource that may facilitate entrepreneurialism, for example, by providing government-backed loans and tax breaks for small businesses, in practice such resources are rarely used by entrepreneurs, least of all Latino/a immigrants. The disproportionate lack of access to or use of government capital by Latino/a immigrants reflects their lower rates of polity membership (that is, they are more likely to be unauthorized or noncitizens). Among Latino/a members of the polity, it also reflects a lack of information regarding the opportunities for government aid that are available to minority entrepreneurs and small business owners, a lack of the skills needed to finesse the arduous application process, and a lack of creditworthiness.

Thus, it is largely through the accumulation and strength of market capacity that the integration of structure and agency influences every aspect of embedded entrepreneurs' life chances, even as it reflects their social location within the unequal American social structure. A consideration of this process of integration thus helps to explain Latinos'/as' social and economic lives. In this study, it helps to inform the ethnic and racial formation process, including Latinos'/as' contingent ethnic or racial self-identity, whether they externally impose a racial group identity upon others, and the degree to which they may confront or resist an ethnic or racial label. These social group formations are nontrivial in the American economy, insofar as they provide the basis for social capital accumulation or attenuation, which affects their subsequent economic action. The integration of structure and agency also influences embedded entrepreneurs' self-perception as rugged individualists, even in the face of extreme structural inequality, or perhaps in spite of it. Finally, it affects their motivations for and expectations of entrepreneurship, their ability to start and maintain businesses, their perception of what entrepreneurial success really means, and the extent to which they believe they have achieved it.

Most Latinos/as become entrepreneurs to make money and be their own bosses, and this finding is in keeping with previous survey research. My interviews with fifty-four Latino/a, White, and Black restaurateurs, however, reveal additional motivations that are directly related to their embedded social locations: specifically, in the job satisfaction that more privileged entrepreneurs expect to find in their pursuit of entrepreneurship and the dissatisfaction with previous employment that exploited or disadvantaged entrepreneurs hope to escape. Specifically, lower class Latinos/as who are of predominately Mexican descent seek an escape from dirty, dangerous, and difficult jobs; middle-class Latinos/as pursue opportunities to employ new skills or combat "blocked mobility" (discrimination in employment that prevents promotions or advancement); and women express the desire to help or bring joy to themselves, their customers, or their community.

Although Black and White entrepreneurs share some of these same motivations and expectations, racial dynamics create additional factors that vary across race. In particular, White entrepreneurs, who are disproportionately middle-class and male, are not motivated by blocked mobility, dirty, dangerous, or difficult work, or social justice issues. They are, however, more likely to "fall into" business ownership by electing to take over the family business. White, middle-class men are especially likely to inherit a family business. As heirs to financially successful, established businesses, these accidental entrepreneurs reap the rewards of entrepreneurial capital that is reproduced and transmitted intergenerationally (Aldrich, Renzulli, and Langton 1998). In contrast, Black entrepreneurs are least likely to engage in enterprise for purely economic concerns. Given their disadvantaged social location, the ease with which they disregard financial remuneration through enterprise is quite remarkable; yet, they simply expect that their entrepreneurial pursuits will not provide them with a monetary reward. Instead, many Black entrepreneurs engage in business ownership for largely noneconomic reasons, such as achieving autonomy over their labor or giving back to the community.

Taken together, these findings expose how the social location of embedded entrepreneurs creates and shapes distinctly different entrepreneurial motivations within and across different ethnic and racial groups: middle-class White and Latino/a men have advantages that encourage profit seeking and enjoyment, while Black men and women are disenfranchised to such an extent that they often divorce their economic action from economic considerations. Beyond motivations, the social location of embedded entrepreneurs also sets the stage for the ways in which Latinos/as, Blacks, and Whites from diverse backgrounds get started in and maintain their businesses.

Entrepreneurs from different social locations perform differently in enterprise. This is due, in large part, to differences in accumulated market capacity. In particular, the more market capacity an entrepreneur has, the greater his or her economic returns. Social locations at the top of the class, gender, racial, and ethnic hierarchies generate greater market capacity; social locations at the bottom produce less overall market capacity. Hence, White middle-class and male entrepreneurs garner the greatest economic rewards in enterprise. Middle-class Latino/a men lag far behind their White counterparts in earnings; however, they earn significantly more than lower-class Latino/a men and women, the latter group regardless of class. The lower earnings among Latina entrepreneurs are associated with their lack of market and social capital resources relative to Latino/a men, and highlight the significant role that gender plays in shaping Latino/a inequality. Moreover, income disparities are more pronounced for the Mexican-origin population—the most disadvantaged of the Latin American–origin ethnic groups (with respect to their ability to secure market capital resources). Lastly, Black entrepreneurs' earnings closely resemble those of Latina entrepreneurs, due to their disproportionately disadvantaged status, which limits considerably their overall market capacity. To compensate for their lower earnings returns, Black entrepreneurs may take on an additional job or rely on a spouse or partner to make ends meet. Nevertheless, they do not seek a voluntary exit from enterprise, because of the noneconomic benefits they enjoy.

In sum, findings suggest that the intersection of class, gender, race, and ethnicity significantly influences embedded entrepreneurs' economic returns. Furthermore, disparities between expectations and economic outcomes appear to shape a dynamic, contingent, and oftentimes noneconomic meaning of success, especially among those entrepreneurs who do not generate a profit. For example, a lower-class Latina may laud her "flexible" schedule but work on average seventy or more hours per week; a struggling unauthorized Mexican immigrant man may call himself a success but equates success with economic survival ("I'm still alive") rather than socioeconomic mobility. Ultimately, Latino/a, Black, and White entrepreneurs' discourse of success belies their unequal position, as structural inequality mediates the meaning not only of success, but of the American dream itself.

It is telling that several Mexican immigrant entrepreneurs in Little Mexico shared the same story of a Salvadoran immigrant man who, with his family, showed up in Little Mexico one day. He introduced himself to strangers and begged for food and water for his children and a place to stay for a few days. They told of how he borrowed some money from a Mexican couple, promising to pay it back with interest. They went on to describe his entrepreneurial activity—how he bought and sold watermelons at a Houston flea market—and went on to become "a millionaire." The idea that through hard work, ingenuity, and a bit of luck, a "nobody" can become a "somebody" is the cornerstone of the American creed ideology. Latino/a entrepreneurs express a deep-seated belief in this creed, for it is largely what keeps them going.

Consistently, Latino/a, White, and Black entrepreneurs characterize themselves as hardworking, rugged individualists who are striving to attain the American dream. Regardless of class, gender, race, or ethnicity, the American creed ideology that hard work, dedication, a positive outlook, and courage are all one needs to succeed is fully adopted by American entrepreneurs. Even among those who recognize that structural inequality privileges some and oppresses others, entrepreneurs do not link their fate to the unequal American social structure. Instead, embedded entrepreneurs reproduce the ideology of individualism and meritocracy, even as they experience structural inequality. The reality for most Latino/a and Black entrepreneurs is that the American dream remains, at best, only partially fulfilled. Although entrepreneurialism holds the promise of "making it" in America, differences persist among Whites, Latinos/as, and Blacks, between men and women, between the middle and lower classes, and among all other intersections along the "matrix of domination." It appears that these unequal outcomes substantiate the constraints of individual agency within the American social structure, which explains ethnic and nonethnic differences in American enterprise.

Ultimately, this book offers a new approach to American enterprise that challenges the existing literature on ethnic entrepreneurship and socioeconomic incorporation. By considering the effects of class, gender, race, *and* ethnicity, my analysis provides a more comprehensive and systematic explanation of the role of group membership in fostering entrepreneurship within a highly stratified society. The embedded market approach reveals how the integration of structure and agency shapes, transforms, and reproduces the divergent life chances of embedded entrepreneurs in America. By exposing the unequal structure in which differently positioned Latinos/as engage and succeed in enterprise, the book challenges the notion that the American creed guarantees prosperity for rugged individualist entrepreneurs. It complicates the accepted "common sense" notion that success is equated with American business ownership by revealing how the integration of structure and agency circumscribe embedded entrepreneurs' success in American enterprise.

# Notes

## Chapter 1

1. To protect the privacy of my study participants and their families, I use pseudonyms for respondents' names and communities.

2. Previous research demonstrates that the term *American* is used by immigrant minorities (and Whites) to refer almost exclusively to U.S.-born, non-Hispanic Whites (Espiritu 2001:419–20; Gallagher 2003; Morrison 1992:47). This is also the case with my respondents.

3. For most of the interviews the formal designations of Mr./Ms./Mrs., Don/ Doña, and Señor/Señora—depending on whether the interviews were conducted in English or Spanish—were used throughout. Some respondents, however, introduced themselves by their first name or requested its use at some point during the interview. In those instances I am likely to switch between the use of formal and informal designations.

4. Because this study focuses on Latino/a immigrants only, nativity is always presumed to be included alongside ethnicity.

5. Another dimension of intersectionality is sexuality. Although sexuality also affects the position of individuals and collectivities within the American social structure, a social structure that privileges heterosexuality, this study does not investigate the effects of sexuality on enterprise. I made this decision in part because of the culturally sensitive nature of the topic to the African American and Latino/a immigrant populations, and in part because of the large number of respondents who were married to members of the opposite sex (leading to the reasonable presumption that the majority of those respondents are likely to classify themselves as heterosexual). Furthermore, respondents did not refer (nor were they prompted to refer) explicitly to the role of nonheterosexual relationships, ties, or networks in facilitating or hindering enterprise, though they were not precluded from such discussions.

6. In claiming that the integration of structure and agency shapes, maintains, and reproduces Latino/a entrepreneurs' life chances, I draw on a central tenet of Giddens's (1992) theory of *structuration*, specifically that of the duality of structure. The proposition maintains that "the rules and resources drawn upon in the production and reproduction of social action are at the same time the means of system reproduction" (Giddens 1992:19).

7. Fred Block (2003) was the first to use this terminology to capture the structure and functioning of the modern market economy as an instituted process, following from the work of Karl Polanyi (1944, 1957). I adapt this term and develop it to apply specifically to the relationship between group affiliation and American entrepreneurship, which I acknowledge differs substantially from Block's and Polanyi's original use.

8. I use the racial categories Latino/a, White, and Black instead of compound ethnic labels (e.g., Hispanic American) to underscore the distinct role of race and its impact on economic action. I capitalize racial group labels and ethnic group labels (e.g., Latino/a, Mexican) throughout, as these distinct dimensions of intersectionality are socially constructed groupings that equally shape members' social location.

9. Although self-employment encompasses a wide range of activities, the majority of the self-employed (approximately 80 percent) are small-business owners who work on their own account, hire one or no employees, or rely on unpaid family labor (Hakim 1988; Rath 2002). Thus I use the terms *self-employment* and *self-employed* interchangeably with *entrepreneurship* and *entrepreneur*, which is in keeping with the literature on ethnic enterprise.

10. Because the number of South and Central American immigrants in the United States is relatively small, and the proportion that is self-employed is smaller still, I collapse these groups into one category, "Other Latino/a," when reporting these statistics.

11. B4-u-eat.com: Houston Restaurant Guide, www.b4-u-eat.com.

12. *Texas Monthly*, quoted in Texas State Historical Association, Handbook of Texas Online, http://tshaonline.org/handbook/online/articles/FF/hpfhk.html (accessed June 3, 2009).

## Chapter 2

1. The term *White supremacy* is used here to represent a "racialized social system," or a central system of racial oppression in the American social structure that is constituted by the racial hierarchy (Bonilla-Silva 1994; Feagin 2006). The White racial hierarchy "runs from the privileged White position and status at the top to an oppressed Black position and status at the bottom, with different groups of color variously positioned *by Whites* between the two ends of this central racial-status continuum" (Feagin 2006:21; Feagin's emphasis).

2. From this point on, I do not distinguish between middle-class and upper-class entrepreneurs, as only one Latino/a entrepreneur in the sample qualifies for affiliation in the latter class position. In this study of Latino/a entrepreneurs, the important class distinction is between the middle and lower classes.

3. Similarly, Schumpeter ([1951] 2009) acknowledges that some measure of economic integration is necessary for a would-be entrepreneur to engage in market exchange relationships when he states, "If the entrepreneur borrows at a fixed rate of interest and undertakes to guarantee the capitalist against loss whatever the results of the enterprise, he can do so only if he owns other assets with which to satisfy the creditor capitalist when things go wrong" (Schumpeter [1951] 2009:256). Here he notes that an entrepreneur is not the only one engaging in risk-taking activity when entering a business—the lending source takes on risk as well.

## Chapter 3

1. Self-employment in the informal sector generates income that is off the books, "unregulated by the institutions of society" (Castells and Portes 1989:12). Informal self-employment is especially likely among low-income-earning groups, immigrant minority women, and quasi-employed groups, such as housewives and retired persons (Raijman 2001:48). Although self-employment is difficult to measure, an accounting of informal self-employment among disadvantaged immigrant, ethnic, and racial minority groups such as Mexicans and Blacks would narrow but not close the self-employment gap between entrepreneurial and nonentrepreneurial groups (Raijman 2001).

2. Unlike earlier waves of Cuban immigrants that arrived to the U.S. in the mid-1960s, the more recent, 1980s wave of Mariel Cuban exiles was not granted political asylum by the United States government and thus faced a harsher context of reception than the earlier waves (Portes and Jensen 1989:932).

3. The "1.5 generation" refers to immigrant children that were brought to the host country by families at the age of five years or younger. These children are classified as immigrants; however, they are socialized in the United States from a young age so are thought to assimilate to a greater extent than those immigrants who arrived as adults (Portes and Rumbaut 2001).

4. I use the term *Black* throughout the book to underscore the role of race, racial identity, and racial group status as it relates to the American social structure, in keeping with my theoretical framework. In the descriptions or accounts provided by Black business owners, I refer to "African American" or other ethnic identities among Blacks (and Whites, e.g., Greek) if they self-identify primarily as such.

## Chapter 4

1. The second generation is defined as the U.S.-born children of immigrant (first-generation) parents (see Portes and Rumbaut 2001, 2006).

2. This assumption is presumably supported by an analysis that demonstrates no significant differences across these groups in lending after controlling for influential background characteristics, although no such analysis or results are reported.

## Chapter 5

1. Exposing the earnings of the self-employed is difficult, as they often skip or refuse to answer questions or underreport their earnings in surveys (Fairlie 2004). This survey is at least as accurate as existing surveys, and probably more so, as the non-response rate to the income questions in this sample was only 6 percent, which compares favorably to other surveys of this kind.

2. The federal and state governments do not offer guidelines to determine lower-, middle-, and upper-class income, nor does income alone sufficiently capture the distinct characteristics of different classes. For a rough approximation of lower, middle, and upper classes, I use median income. The Census Bureau separates income distribution into quintiles. A broad definition of middle class income may encompass three middle quintiles (Cashell 2007). A similarly generous definition of middle class income based on survey data, suggests a range of 50 to 200 percent of median household income (Burtless 1990:84). Accordingly, the median income in 2007 was $48,200, which corresponds roughly to a middle income range of $24,000 to $96,000, close to the range included here.

3. The pre-2009 minimum wage was $6.55; the minimum wage post-2009 is $7.25; see United States Department of Labor, Wage and Hour Division (WHD) Minimum Wage Laws in the States, July 1, 2010, www.dol.gov/esa/minwage/america.htm#Texas, accessed July 27, 2010.

4. The rest of the passage includes the following: "I couldn't make much sometimes. . . . God gave me the lottery and that's how I got through." Remarkably, Don José played the lottery and won in 1987, which allowed him to pay off his medical bills for diabetes and heart disease (it goes without saying that he does not have health insurance) and some of his other debts, including the loan he received from co-ethnics (see Chapter 3). If not for the lottery winnings, Don José is convinced that his restaurant would have closed, as it was not (and is not) generating enough income to facilitate economic mobility or even, at times, survivability.

## Chapter 6

1. Unlike traditional racial groups (i.e., Whites or Blacks), Latinos/as are not recognized as a distinct racial group by America's mainstream institutions, such as the U.S. federal government. Instead, Latinos/as are defined as a panethnic group—a social group identity that combines multiple ethnic subgroups whose ethnic identities are circumscribed by distinct national-origin boundaries (Padilla 1985), and that collectively are perceived to share certain homogeneous characteristics and features

(Lopez and Espiritu 1990). The Latino/a panethnic category includes persons of "Mexican, Puerto Rican, Cuban, Central or South American or other Spanish culture or origin, *regardless of race*" (Katzen 1997:1); emphasis added). In practice, the panethnic label *Latino/a* or *Hispanic* is often used by affiliated members and other groups as a socially constructed racial classification (Valdez 2009). Because this term ultimately reflects the process of racialization, and best represents a socially constructed and emergent racial identity, I use the term *Latino/a* to refer to a racial classification rather than a panethnic one.

2. In the American context, whether that racial identity is constructed as White, Black, biracial, multiracial, or, as argued here, Latino/a, may be somewhat negotiable; *that one possesses a racial identity is not.*

3. In some cases, ethnic identity may serve this purpose without the emergence of panethnic identity. In geographically concentrated areas of immigrant settlement where one Latin American or Asian national-origin group dominates, ethnic identity may serve the same function as racial identity. For example, although a small but growing Salvadoran community resides in Los Angeles, the majority of Los Angelinos refer to *all Latinos/as* as Mexican, regardless of national origin. In this context, the ethnic identity *Mexican* is racialized to include all Latino-origin group members.

4. In their respective home countries, would-be migrants might identify with reference to their city, region, state, or other markers of common history or customs. Upon arrival in the United States, however, national origin often becomes a primary, "anchoring" identity among immigrant co-nationals in the United States (Itzigsohn and Dore-Cabral, 2000; Moore 1990). For immigrants in America, the use of national identity over other home-country identities facilitates a sense of belonging and homogeneity among co-nationals in America, whose origins lie within a common circumscribed territory. National identity is distinguished as a primary identity and is generally self-defined (Connor 1978). Moreover, research reveals that one's national identity often takes precedence over other socially constructed secondary identities, such as panethnicity or race (Itzigsohn and Dore-Cabral 2000; Moore 1990). My respondents use national origin and ethnicity interchangeably, as conceptually these identities represent a self-defined and often primary identity that connotes a similar and shared history, culture, and kinship, in keeping with previous research (Itzigsohn and Dore-Cabral 2000; Jones-Correa and Leal 1996).

5. See Bonilla-Silva 1997; Feagin 2006; Nagel 1994; Omi and Winant 1994; Padilla 1985; Waters 1990; Yancy, Erikson, and Juliani 1976.

6. The term *American* is often used interchangeably with or in place of the racial classification *White* by immigrants in the United States; see Espiritu 2001; Espiritu and Wolf 2001; Gallagher 2004.

# References

Aaltio, Iiris, Paula Kyro, and Elisabeth Sundin. 2008. *Women Entrepreneurship and Social Capital: A Dialogue and Construction*. Copenhagen: Copenhagen Business School Press.

Alba, Richard and Victor Nee. 2003. *Remaking the American Mainstream: Assimilation and Contemporary Immigration*. Cambridge, MA: Harvard University Press.

Aldrich, Howard E., and Jennifer E. Cliff. 2003. The Pervasive Effects of Family on Entrepreneurship: Toward a Family Embeddedness Perspective. *Journal of Business Venturing* 18 (5): 573–96.

Aldrich, Howard E., L. A. Renzulli, and N. Langton. 1998. Passing on Privilege: Resources Provided by Self-Employed Parents to Their Self-Employed Children. *Research in Social Stratification and Mobility* 16:291–318.

Bashi, Vilna. 1998. Racial Categories Matter Because Racial Hierarchies Matter: A Commentary. *Ethnic and Racial Studies* 21 (5): 959–69.

Bates, Timothy. 1990. Entrepreneur Human Capital Inputs and Small Business Longevity. *Review of Economics and Statistics* 72:551–59.

———. 1994. Social Resources Generated by Group Support Networks May Not Be Beneficial to Asian Immigrant-Owned Small Businesses. *Social Forces* 72 (3): 671–90.

———. 1997. *Race, Self-Employment and Upward Mobility: An Illusive American Dream*. Baltimore, MD: Johns Hopkins University Press.

Benz, Matthias. 2009. Entrepreneurship as a Non-Profit-Seeking Activity. *International Entrepreneurship and Management Journal* 5 (1): 23–44.

Bernard, Russell H. 1988. *Research Methods in Cultural Anthropology*. Newbury Park, CA: Sage Publications.

Blanchard, Lloyd, John Yinger, and Bo Zhao. 2004. Do Credit Market Barriers Exist for Minority and Women Entrepreneurs? Syracuse University Working Paper Series, Syracuse, NY.

Blanchflower, David G. 2004. Self-Employment: More May Not Be Better. National Bureau of Economic Research (NBER) Working Paper w10286, Department of Economics, Dartmouth College, Hanover, NH.

Blanchflower, David G., P. Levine, and D. Zimmerman. 2003. Discrimination in the Small Business Credit Market. *Review of Economics and Statistics* 85 (4): 930–43.

Block, Fred. 2003. Karl Polanyi and the Writing of the Great Transformation. *Theory and Society* 32 (3): 275–306.

Boden, R., Jr., and Alfred Nucci. 2000. On the Survival Prospects of Men's and Women's New Business Ventures. *Journal of Business Venturing* 15 (4): 347–62.

Bonacich, Edna. 1973. A Theory of Middleman Minorities. *American Sociological Review* 38 (5): 583–94.

———. 1975. Small Business and Japanese American Ethnic Solidarity. *Amerasia Journal* 3 (1): 96–112.

Bonacich, Edna, and John Modell. 1981. *The Economic Basis of Ethnic Solidarity: A Study of Japanese Americans.* Berkeley: University of California Press.

Bonilla-Silva, Eduardo. 1994. Rethinking Racism: Toward a Structural Interpretation. Working Paper Series 526, Center for Research on Social Organization, University of Michigan, Ann Arbor.

———. 1997. Rethinking Racism: Toward a Structural Interpretation. *American Sociological Review* 62:465–80.

———. 2006. *Racism Without Racists: Color-Blind Racism and the Persistence of Racial Inequality in the United States.* 3rd ed. New York: Rowman and Littlefield.

Bonilla-Silva, Eduardo, and Gianpaolo Baiocchi. 2001. Anything But Racism: How Sociologists Limit the Significance of Racism. *Race and Society* 4 (1): 117–31.

Bonilla-Silva, Eduardo, and David G. Embrick. 2001. Are Blacks Color-Blind Too? An Interview-Based Analysis of Black Detroiters Racial Views. *Race and Society* 4 (1): 47–67.

Borjas, George J. 1985. Assimilation, Changes in Cohort Quality, and the Earnings of Immigrants. *Journal of Labor Economics* 3 (4): 463–89.

———. 1986. The Self-Employment Experience of Immigrants. *Journal of Human Resources* 21 (4): 485–506.

———. 1988. Self-Selection and the Earnings of Immigrants. *The American Economic Review* 77 (4): 531–53.

———. 1990. *Friends or Strangers: The Impact of Immigrants on the American Economy.* New York: Basic Books.

Borjas, George J., and Stephen G. Bronars. 1989. Consumer Discrimination and Self-Employment. *Journal of Political Economy* 97 (3): 581–605.

Boyd, Robert L. 1998. Residential Segregation by Race and the Black Merchants of Northern Cities During the Early Twentieth Century. *Sociological Forum* 13 (4): 595–609.

Brewer, Rose M. 1993. Theorizing Race, Class and Gender: The New Scholarship of Black Feminist Intellectuals and Black Women's Labor. In *Theorizing Black Feminisms: The Visionary Pragmatism of Black Women*, ed. Stanlie M. James and Abena P. A. Busia, 13–30. New York: Routledge.

Browne, Irene, and Joya Misra. 2003. The Intersection of Gender and Race in Labor Markets. *Annual Review of Sociology* 29:487–513.

Butler, John Sibley. 2005. *Entrepreneurship and Self-Help Among Black Americans: A Reconsideration of Race and Economics*. New York: State University of New York Press.

Butler, John S., and Patricia G. Greene. 1997. Ethnic Entrepreneurship: The Continuous Rebirth of American Enterprise. In *Entrepreneurship 2000*, ed. Donald L. Sexton and Raymond W. Smilor, 267–89. Chicago: Upstart Publishing Company.

Carroll, Glenn R., and Elaine Mosakowski. 1987. The Career Dynamics of Self-Employment. *Administrative Science Quarterly* 32:570–589.

Cashell, Brian W. 2007. Who Are the "Middle Class"? CRS Report for Congress, Washington, DC, March 20. Available at http://assets.opencrs.com/rpts/RS22627_20070320.pdf, accessed on July 31, 2010.

Castells, Manuel, and Alejandro Portes. 1989. World Underneath: The Origins, Dynamics, and Effects of the Informal Economy. In *The Informal Economy: Studies in Advanced and Less Developed Countries*, ed. Alejandro Portes, Manuel Castells, and Lauren A. Benton, 11–37. Baltimore, MD: Johns Hopkins University Press.

Cavalluzzo, Ken, Linda Cavalluzzo, and John Wolken. 2002. Competition, Small Business Financing, and Discrimination: Evidence from a New Survey. *Journal of Business* 75 (4): 641–79.

Cavalluzzo, Ken, and John Wolken. 2005. Small Business Loan Turndowns, Personal Wealth and Discrimination. *Journal of Business* 78 (6): 2153–77.

Clark, William A. V., and Sarah A. Blue. 2004. Race, Class, and Segregation Patterns in U.S. Immigrant Gateway Cities. *Urban Affairs Review* 39 (6): 667–88.

Coleman, James. 1988. Social Capital in the Creation of Human Capital. *American Journal of Sociology* 94:S95–S120.

Coleman, Susan. 2002. The Borrowing Experience of Black and Hispanic-Owned Small Firms: Evidence from the 1998 Survey of Small Business Finances. *Academy of Entrepreneurship Journal* 8 (1): 1–20.

———. 2003. Borrowing Patterns for Small Firms: A Comparison by Race and Ethnicity. *Journal of Entrepreneurial Finance and Business Ventures* 7 (3): 87–108.

Collins, Patricia Hill. 1997. How Much Difference Is Too Much? Black Feminist Thought and the Politics of Postmodern Social Theory. *Current Perspectives in Social Theory* 17:3–37.

———. 2000. *Black Feminist Thought: Knowledge, Consciousness, and the Politics of Empowerment*. Rev. 10th ed. New York: Routledge.

Conley, Dalton. 1999. *Being Black, Living in the Red: Race, Wealth, and Social Policy in America*. 2nd ed. Berkeley: University of California Press.

Conley, Dalton, and Miriam Ryvicker. 2005. The Price of Female Headship: Gender, Inheritance, and Wealth Accumulation in the United States. *Journal of Income Distribution* 13 (3/4): 41–56.

Connor, Walker. 1978. A Nation Is a Nation, Is a State, Is an Ethnic Group Is a. . . . *Ethnic and Racial Studies* 1 (4): 379–88.

Constantine, Madonna G., and Derald Wing Sue. 2006. *Addressing Racism: Facilitating Cultural Competence in Metal Health and Educational Settings*. Hoboken, NJ: Wiley.

Cornell, Stephen, and Douglas Hartmann. 1998. *Ethnicity and Race: Identities in a Changing World*. Thousand Oaks, CA: Pine Forge Press.

Crenshaw, Kimberle Williams. 1988. Race, Reform and Retrenchment: Transformation and Legitimation in Anti-Discrimination Law. *Harvard Law Review* 101:1331–87.

———. 1991. Mapping the Margins: Intersectionality, Identity Politics, and Violence Against Women of Color. *Stanford Law Review* 43 (6): 1241–99.

Curry, Sarah. 2008. Bureaucracy, Banking, and Business: The Effects of Nativism and Politico-Institutional Environment on Immigrant Entrepreneurs and Gatekeepers in Northern Virginia. Master's thesis, George Mason University, Washington, DC.

Daniels, Roger. [1988] 1995. *Asian America: Chinese and Japanese in the United States Since 1850*. 3rd ed. Seattle: University of Washington Press.

De León, Arnoldo. 2001. *Ethnicity in the Sunbelt: Mexican Americans in Houston*. College Station: Texas A&M University.

Douglas, Evan, and Dean Shepherd. 2000. Entrepreneurship as a Utility-Maximizing Response. *Journal of Business Venturing* 15 (3): 231–52.

———. 2002. Self-Employment as a Career Choice: Attitudes, Entrepreneurial Intentions, and Utility Maximization. *Entrepreneurial Theory and Practice* 26 (3): 81–90.

Douglas, Karen M., and Rogelio Saenz. 2008. No Vehicle, No English, and No Citizenship: The Vulnerability of Mexican Immigrants in the United States. In *Globalization and America: Race, Human Rights, and Inequality*, ed. Angela J. Hattery, Earl Smith, and David G. Embrick, 161–80. New York: Rowman and Littlefield.

Drake, St. Clair, and Horace R. Cayton. 1962. *Black Metropolis: A Study of Negro Life in a Northern City*. 2nd ed. New York: Harper Torchbooks.

Dunn, Thomas, and Douglas Holtz-Eakin. 1996. Financial Capital, Human Capital, and the Transition to Self-Employment: Evidence from Intergenerational Links. NBER Working Papers 5622, National Bureau of Economic Research, Syracuse University, Syracuse, NY.

Eagly, Alice, and Wendy Wood. 1991. Explaining Sex Differences in Social Behavior: A Meta-Analytic Perspective. *Personality and Social Psychology Bulletin* 17 (3): 306–15.

Espiritu, Yen Le. 2001. We Don't Sleep Around Like White Girls Do: Family, Culture, and Gender in Filipina American Lives. *Signs: Journal of Women in Culture and Society* 26 (2): 415–40.

———. 2008. *Asian American Women and Men: Labor, Laws, and Love.* New York: Rowman and Littlefield.

Espiritu, Yen Le, and Diane L. Wolf. 2001. The Paradox of Assimilation: Children of Filipino Immigrants in San Diego. In *Ethnicities: Children of Immigrants in America*, ed. Ruben Rumbaut and Alejandro Portes, 157–86. Berkeley: University of California Press.

Fairlie, Robert. 2004. Earnings Growth Among Young Less-Educated Business Owners. *Industrial Relations* 43 (3): 634–59.

Fairlie, Robert, and Alicia Robb. 2004. Families, Human Capital, and Small Business: Evidence from the Characteristics of Business Owners Survey. Yale University Economic Growth Center Working Paper/IZA Discussion Paper 1296 (871), New Haven, CT.

———. 2008. *Race and Entrepreneurial Success: Black-, Asian-, and White-Owned Businesses in the United States.* Cambridge, MA: MIT Press.

Fairlie, Robert W., and Christopher Woodruff. April 2006. Mexican-American Entrepreneurship. Entrepreneurship Seminar Series, 06-03, Hudson Institute Center for Employment Policy, Washington, DC.

Feagin, Joe R. 1988. *Free Enterprise City: Houston in Political and Economic Perspective.* New Brunswick, NJ: Rutgers University Press.

———. 1999. Excluding Blacks and Others from Housing: The Foundation of White Racism. *Cityscape: A Journal of Policy Development and Research* 4 (3): 79–91.

———. 2006. *Systemic Racism: A Theory of Oppression.* New York: Routledge.

Feagin, Joe, Hernan Vera, and Pinar Batur. 2000. *White Racism.* New York: Routledge.

Foley, Neil. 1999. *The White Scourge: Mexicans, Blacks, and Poor Whites in Texas Cotton Culture.* Berkeley: University of California Press.

Fratoe, Frank A. 1988. Social Capital and Small Business Owners. *Review of Black Political Economy* 16 (4): 33–50.

Gallagher, Charles. 2003. White Reconstruction in the University. In *Privilege: A Reader*, ed. Abbey Ferber and Michael Kimmel, 299–318. Boulder, CO: Westview Press.

———. 2004. Transforming Racial Identity Through Affirmative Action. In *Race and Ethnicity: Across Time, Space, and Discipline*, ed. Rodney D. Coates, 153–70. Leiden, Netherlands: Brill.

Georgellis, Yannis, John Sessions, and Nikolaos Tsitsianis. 2007. Pecuniary and Non-Pecuniary Aspects of Self-Employment Survival. *Quarterly Review of Economics and Finance* 47:94–112.

Giddens, Anthony. 1973. *The Class Structure of the Advanced Societies*. London: Hutchinson.

———. 1992. *The Constitution of Society: Outline of the Theory of Structuration*. Berkeley: University of California Press.

Gimenez, Martha. 2007. Back to Class: Reflections on the Dialectics of Class and Identity. In *More Unequal: Aspects of Class in the United States*, ed. Michael D. Yates, 107–18. New York: Monthly Review Press.

Glenn, Evelyn Nakano. 1999. *Unequal Freedom: How Race and Gender Shaped American Citizenship and Labor*. Cambridge, MA: Harvard University Press.

Goldthorpe, J. H., David Lockwood, Frank Bechhofer, and Jennifer Platt. 1969. *The Affluent Worker in the Class Structure*. Cambridge, MA: Harvard University Press.

Granovetter, Mark. 1985. Economic Action and Social Structure: The Problem of Embeddedness. *American Journal of Sociology* 91 (3): 481–510.

Hakim, Catherine. 1988. Self-Employment in Britain: Recent Trends and Current Issues. *Work, Employment & Society* 2 (4): 421–50.

Hamilton, Barton H. 2000. Does Entrepreneurship Pay? An Empirical Analysis of the Returns to Self-Employment. *Journal of Political Economy* 108 (3): 604–31.

Harris, Abram L. 1936. *The Negro as Capitalist: A Study of Banking and Business Among American Negroes*. College Park, MD: McGrath Publishing.

Harrison, Bennett, and Barry Bluestone. 1988. *The Great U-Turn: Corporate Restructuring and the Polarizing of America*. New York: Basic Books.

Hartmann, Heidi. 1976. Capitalism, Patriarchy, and Job Segregation by Sex. *Signs* 1 (3): 137–69.

Harvey, Aida M. 2005. Becoming Entrepreneurs: Intersections of Race, Class, and Gender at the Black Beauty Salon. *Gender and Society* 19 (6): 789–808.

Healy, Karen, Michele Haynes, and Anne Hampshire. 2007. Gender, Social Capital and Location: Understanding the Interactions. *International Journal of Social Welfare* 16 (2): 110–18.

Hondagneu-Sotelo, Pierrette. 1994. *Gendered Transitions: Mexican Experiences of Immigration*. Berkeley: University of California Press.

———. 2001. *Doméstica: Immigrant Workers Cleaning and Caring in the Shadows of Affluence*. Berkeley: University of California Press.

Itzigsohn, José, and Carlos Dore-Cabral. 2000. Competing Identities? Race, Ethnicity and Panethnicity Among Dominicans in the United States. *Sociological Forum* 15 (2): 225–47.

Johnson, Steve A., David A. Schauer, and Dennis L. Soden. 2002. Analysis of Small Business Lending in Texas. Institute for Policy and Economic Development Technical Report, University of Texas at El Paso. Available at http://digitalcommons

.utep.edu/cgi/viewcontent.cgi?article=1017&context=iped_techrep, accessed on July 1, 2010.

Jones-Correa, Michael, and David L. Leal. 1996. Becoming "Hispanic": Secondary Panethnic Identification Among Latin American–Origin Populations in the United States. *Hispanic Journal of Behavioral Sciences* 18 (2): 214–54.

Kaplan, David H., and Bessie House-Soremekun. 2009. Entrepreneurship and Neighborhood Among African Americans in Cleveland, Ohio. *International Journal of Business and Globalization* 3 (3): 256–70.

Katzen, Sally. 1997. Revisions to the Standards for the Classification of Data on Race and Ethnicity. *Federal Register Notice,* October 30. Office of Management and Budget, Washington, DC.

Kim, Kwang Chung, and Won Moo Hurh. 1985. Ethnic Resources Utilization of Korean Immigrant Entrepreneurs in the Chicago Minority Area. *International Migration Review* 19 (1): 82–111.

Kirschenman, Joleen and Kathryn M. Neckerman. 1991. We'd Love to Hire Them But . . . The Meaning of Race for Employers. In *The Urban Underclass,* ed. Christopher Jencks and Paul E. Peterson, 203–32. Washington, DC: The Urban Institute.

Klineberg, Stephen L. 2002. *Houston's Economic and Demographic Transformations: Findings from the Expanded 2002 Survey of Houston's Ethnic Communities.* Houston, TX: Rice University.

Lamont, Michele, and Virag Molnar. 2002. The Study of Boundaries in the Social Sciences. *Annual Review of Sociology* 28:167–95.

Lee, Jennifer. 2000. Striving for the American Dream: Struggle, Success, and Intergroup Conflict Among Korean Immigrant Entrepreneurs. In *Contemporary Asian America,* ed. Min Zhou and James V. Gatewood, 278–94. New York: New York University Press.

———. 2002. *Civility in the City: Blacks, Jews, and Koreans in Urban America.* Cambridge, MA: Harvard University Press.

Lentz, Bernard F., and David Laband. 1990. Entrepreneurial Success and Occupational Inheritance Among Proprietors. *Canadian Journal of Economics* 23 (3): 563–80.

———. 1993. Is There Sex Discrimination in the Legal Profession? Further Evidence on Tangible and Intangible Margins. *Journal of Human Resources* 28 (2): 230–58.

Levenstein, Margaret. 2004. African American Entrepreneurship: The View from the 1910 Census. In *Immigrant and Minority Entrepreneurship: The Continuous Rebirth of American Communities,* ed. John S. Butler and George Kozmetsky, 1–18. Westport, CT: Praeger Publishers.

Light, Ivan Hubert. 1972. *Ethnic Enterprise in America: Business and Welfare Among Chinese, Japanese and Blacks.* Berkeley: University of California Press.

———. 2002. Immigrant Place Entrepreneurs in Los Angeles, 1970–1999. *International Journal of Urban and Regional Research* 26 (2): 215–28.

Light, Ivan Hubert, and Edna Bonacich. 1988. *Immigrant Entrepreneurs: Koreans in Los Angeles*. Los Angeles: University of California Press.

Light, Ivan Hubert, and Edna Roach. 1996. Self-Employment: Mobility Ladder or Economic Lifeboat? In *Ethnic Los Angeles*, ed. Roger Waldinger and Mehdi Bozorgmehr, 193–214. New York: Russell Sage.

Light, Ivan Hubert, George Sabagh, Mehdi Bozorgmehr, and Claudia Der-Martirosian. 1994. Beyond the Ethnic Enclave Economy. *Social Problems* 41 (1): 65–80.

Logan, John, Richard Alba, and Timothy McNulty. 1994. Ethnic Economies in Metropolitan Regions: Miami and Beyond. *Social Forces* 72 (3): 691–724.

Lopez, David, and Yen Le Espiritu. 1990. Panethnicity in the United States: A Theoretical Framework. *Ethnic and Racial Studies* 13 (2): 198–224.

Lovell-Troy, A. 1980. Clan Structure and Economic Activity: The Case of the Greeks in Small Business in Enterprise. In *Urban America: Patterns of Minority Business Enterprise*, ed. Scott Cummings, 58–85. National University Publications. New York: Kennikat Press.

Loveman, Mara. 1999. Is "Race" Essential? Comment on Bonilla-Silva. *American Sociological Review* 64:891–98.

Mahler, Sarah J. 1995. *American Dreaming: Immigrant Life on the Margins*. Princeton, NJ: Princeton University Press.

Marger, Martin N. 1990. East Indians in Small Business: Middleman Minority or Ethnic Enclave? *New Community* 16 (4): 551–59.

Massey, Douglas, and Nancy Denton. [1993] 1998. *American Apartheid: Segregation and the Making of the Underclass*. Cambridge, MA: Harvard University Press.

McKinney, Karyn D. 2004. *Being White: Stories of Race and Racism*. New York: Routledge.

Mills, Charles W. 2003. White Supremacy as Sociopolitical System: A Philosophical Perspective. In *White Out: The Continuing Significance of Race*, ed. Ashley W. Doane and Eduardo Bonilla-Silva, 35–48. New York: Routledge.

Minniti, Maria, and Carlo Nardone. 2007. Being in Someone Else's Shoes: The Role of Gender in Nascent Entrepreneurship. *Small Business Economics* 28 (2–3): 223–38.

Minton, Harry M. 1901. *Early History of Negroes in Business in Philadelphia*. New York: American History Society.

Moore, Joan. 1990. Hispanic/Latino: Imposed Label or Real Identity? *Latino Studies Journal* 1:33–47.

Moore, Wendy Leo. 2007. *Reproducing Racism: White Space, Elite Law Schools, and Racial Inequality*. New York: Rowman and Littlefield.

Morrison, Toni. 1992. *Playing in the Dark: Whiteness and the Literary Imagination.* Cambridge, MA: Harvard University Press.

Myrdal, Gunnar. 1944. *An American Dilemma: The Negro Problem and Modern Democracy.* New York: Harper and Brothers.

Nagel, Joanne. 1994. Constructing Ethnicity: Creating and Recreating Ethnic Identity and Culture. *Social Problems* 41:152–76.

Nee, Victor, and Paul Ingram. 1988. Embeddedness and Beyond: Institutions, Exchange, and Social Structure. In *The New Institutionalism in Sociology,* ed. Mary C. Brinton and Victor Nee, 19–45. Stanford, CA: Stanford University Press.

Nee, Victor, and Brett de Bary Nee. 1973. *Longtime Californ': A Study of an American Chinatown.* New York: Pantheon Books.

Nee, Victor, Jimy M. Sanders, and Scott Sernau. 1994. Job Transitions in an Immigrant Metropolis: Ethnic Boundaries and the Mixed Economy. *American Sociological Review* 8:75–93.

Nowikowski, Susan. 1984. Snakes and Ladders: Asian Business in Britain. In *Ethnic Communities in Business: Strategies for Economic Survival,* ed. Robin Ward and Richard Jenkins, 149–65. Cambridge: Cambridge University Press.

Okihiro, Gary Y. 1994. *Margins and Mainstreams: Asians in American History and Culture.* Seattle: University of Washington Press.

Oliver, Melvin, and Thomas Shapiro. 2006. *Black Wealth/White Wealth: A New Perspective on Racial Inequality.* 2nd ed. New York: Routledge.

Omi, Michael, and Howard Winant. 1994. *Racial Formation in the United States: From the 1960s to the 1990s.* New York: Routledge.

Padilla, Felix. 1985. *Latino Ethnic Consciousness.* Notre Dame, IN: University of Notre Dame Press.

Parreñas, Rhacel Salazar. 2001. *Servants of Globalization: Women, Migration, and Domestic Work.* Palo Alto, CA: Stanford University Press.

Pearce, Susan C. 2005. Today's Immigrant Woman Entrepreneur. *Immigration Policy In Focus* 4:1.

Perea, Juan F. 1997. The Black/White Paradigm of Race: The Normal Science of American Racial Thought. *California Law Review* 85:1213–50.

Polanyi, Karl. 1944. *The Great Transformation: The Political and Economic Origins of Our Time.* Boston: Beacon Press.

———. 1957. The Economy as Instituted Process. In *Primitive, Archaic and Modern Economies: Essays of Karl Polanyi,* ed. G. Dalton, 139–74. New York: Doubleday.

Portes, Alejandro. 1987. The Social Origins of the Cuban Enclave Economy of Miami. *Sociological Perspectives* 30 (4): 340–72.

Portes, Alejandro, and Richard Bach. 1985. *Latin Journey: Cuban and Mexican Immigrants in the United States.* Berkeley: University of California Press.

Portes, Alejandro, and Lief Jensen. 1989. The Enclave and the Entrants: Patterns of Ethnic Enterprise in Miami Before and After Mariel. *American Sociological Review* 54 (6): 929–49.

Portes, Alejandro, and Ruben Rumbaut. 2001. *Legacies: The Story of the Immigrant Second Generation*. Berkeley: University of California Press.

———. 2006. *Immigrant America: A Portrait*. Berkeley: University of California Press.

Portes, Alejandro, and Julia Sensenbrenner. 1993. Embeddedness and Immigration: Notes on the Social Determinants of Economic Action. *American Journal of Sociology* 93 (6): 1320–50.

Portes, Alejandro, and Alex Stepick. 1993. *City on the Edge: The Transformation of Miami*. Berkeley: University of California Press.

Portes, Alejandro, and Min Zhou. 1993. The New Second Generation: Segmented Assimilation and Its Variants. *Annals of the American Academy of Political and Social Science* 530:74–96.

———. 1996. Self-Employment and the Earnings of Immigrants. *American Sociological Review* 61 (2): 219–30.

Quillian, Lincoln. 2003. The Decline of Male Employment in Low-Income Black Neighborhoods, 1950–1990. *Social Science Research* 32 (2): 220–50.

Raijman, Rebecca. 2001. Mexican Immigrants and Informal Self-Employment in Chicago. *Human Organization* 60 (1): 47–55.

Ramirez, Hernan, and Pierrette Hondagneu-Sotelo. 2009. Mexican Immigrant Gardeners: Entrepreneurs or Exploited Workers? *Social Problems* 56 (1): 70–88.

Rath, Jan. 2002. *Unravelling the Rag Trade: Immigrant Entrepreneurship in Seven World Cities*. Oxford: Berg Publishers.

Rhode, Deborah L. 1999. *Speaking of Sex: The Denial of Gender Inequality*. Cambridge, MA: Harvard University Press.

Richtermeyer, Gwen. October 2002. Minority Entrepreneurs: A Review of Current Literature. Business Research and Information Development Group, University of Missouri, Columbia.

Robb, Alicia M., and Robert W. Fairlie. 2006. Tracing Access to Financial Capital Among African Americans from the Entrepreneurial Venture to the Established Business. Working paper, University of California, Santa Cruz.

Rodriguez, Clara E., and Hector Cordero-Guzman. 1992. Placing Race in Context. *Ethnic and Racial Studies* 15 (4): 523–42.

Rodriguez, Nestor P. 1993. Economic Restructuring and Latino Growth in Houston. In *In the Barrios: Latinos and the Underclass Debate*, ed. Joan Moore and Raquel Pinderhughes, 101–28. New York: Russell Sage Foundation.

Roediger, David R. 2007. *The Wages of Whiteness: Race and the Making of the American Working Class*. London: Verso.

Romero, Mary. 1992. *Maid in the U.S.A.* New York: Routledge.

Ruggles, Steven, Matthew Sobek, Trent Alexander, Catherine A. Fitch, Ronald Goeken, Patricia Kelly Hall, Miriam King, and Chad Ronnander. 2009. *Integrated Public Use Microdata Series: Version 4.0* (machine-readable database). Minneapolis: Minnesota Population Center (producer and distributor).

Saenz, Rogelio. 2004. Latinos and the Changing Face of America. Report published by Russell Sage Foundation, New York, and the Population Reference Bureau, Washington DC, Census Brief Series.

Sanders, Jimy and Victor Nee. 1996. Social Capital, Human Capital, and Immigrant Self-Employment: The Family as Social Capital and the Value of Human Capital. *American Sociological Review* 61 (2): 231–49.

Schumpter, Joseph A. [1951] 2009. *Essays: On Entrepreneurs, Innovations, Business Cycles, and the Evolution of Capitalism,* ed. Richard V. Clemence. Piscataway, NJ: Transaction Publishers.

Shah, Yaksha. 2005. History of Gulfton. Unpublished manuscript.

Silverman, Robert M. 2000. *Doing Business in Minority Markets: Black and Korean Entrepreneurs in Chicago's Ethnic Beauty Aids Industry.* New York: Garland.

Smith, Barbara Ellen, and Jamie Winders. 2008. "We're Here to Stay": Economic Restructuring, Latino Migration and Place-Making in the U.S. South. *Transactions of the Institute of British Geographers* 33 (1): 60–72.

Stavrou, Eleni T. 1999. Succession in Family Business: Exploring the Effects of Demographic Factors on Offspring Intentions to Join and Take Over the Business. *Journal of Small Business Management* 37:43–61.

Sui, D. Z., and Wu, X. B. 2006. Changing Patterns of Residential Segregation in a Prismatic Metropolis: A Lacunarity-Based Study in Houston, 1980–2000. *Environment and Planning B: Planning and Design* 33 (4): 559–80.

Swarns, Rachel L. 2004. Hispanics Resist Racial Grouping by Census. *New York Times,* October 24.

Swedberg, Richard, and Mark Granovetter. 1992. *The Sociology of Economic Life.* Boulder, CO: Westview.

Tatum, Beverly. 1997. *Why Are All the Black Kids Sitting Together in the Cafeteria? And Other Conversations About Race.* New York: Basic Books.

Thompson, Chalmer E., and Helen A. Neville. 1999. Racism, Mental Health, and Mental Health Practice. *Counseling Psychologist* 27 (2): 155–223.

Travis, C., B. McKenzie, D. Wiley, and A. Kahn. 1988. Sex and Achievement Domain: Cognitive Patterns of Success and Failure. *Sex Roles* 19 (7/8): 509–25.

Unger, R., and M. Crawford. 1992. *Women and Gender: A Feminist Psychology.* New York: McGraw-Hill.

U.S. Bureau of the Census. 2000. *American FactFinder Fact Sheet.* Allegany County, NY. Available at www.census.gov/, accessed July 31, 2010.

Valdez, Alverado. 1993. Persistent Poverty, Crime, and Drugs: U.S.-Mexican Border Region. In *In the Barrios: Latinos and the Underclass Debate*, ed. Joan Moore and Raquel Pinderhughes, 173–94. New York: Russell Sage Foundation.

Valdez, Zulema. 2003. Beyond Ethnic Entrepreneurship: Ethnicity and the Economy in Enterprise. Working Paper 7/2002, Center for U.S.-Mexican Studies, University of California, San Diego.

———. 2006. Segmented Assimilation Among Mexicans in the Southwest. *Sociological Quarterly* 47:397–424.

———. 2008a. Beyond Ethnic Entrepreneurship: An Embedded Market Approach to Group Affiliation in American Enterprise. In Race, Gender, Class and Capitalism, ed. Fred L. Pincus and Natalie J. Sokoloff, special issue, *Race, Gender and Class: An Interdisciplinary Journal* 15 (1–2): 156–69.

———. 2008b. The Effect of Social Capital on White, Korean, Mexican and Black Business Owners' Earnings in the U.S. *Journal of Ethnic and Migration Studies* 34 (6): 955–73.

———. 2009. Agency and Structure in Panethnic Identity Formation: The Case of Latino/a Entrepreneurs. In *How the United States Racializes Latinos: White Hegemony and Its Consequences*, ed. Jose Cobas, Jorge Duany, and Joe R. Feagin, 200–213. Boulder, CO: Paradigm Publishers.

Valenzuela, Abel. 2003. Day Labor Work. *Annual Review of Sociology* 29:307–33.

van Praag, C. Mirjam. 2003. Business Survival and Success of Young Small Business Owners: An Emprical Analysis. TI 2003-050/3, Tinbergen Institute Discussion Paper, Tinbergen Institute, Amsterdam.

Verdaguer, Maria Eugenia. 2009. *Class, Ethnicity, Gender and Latino Entrepreneurship*. New York: Routledge.

Wainright, Jon S. 2006. Race, Sex, and Business Enterprise: Evidence from the State of Maryland. Executive Summary. Available at www.mdot.state.md.us/MBE_Program/Documents/FinalReportNERAMaryland_ESonly.pdf, accessed August 15, 2009.

Walby, Sylvia. 1989. Theorizing Patriarchy. *Sociology* 23 (2): 213–34.

———. 1997. *Gender Transformations*. New York: Routledge.

Waldinger, Roger, Howard Aldrich, Robin Ward, et al. 1990. *Ethnic Entrepreneurs: Immigrant Business in Industrial Societies*. Newbury Park, CA: Sage Publications.

Waldinger, Roger, and Cynthia Feliciano. 2004. Will the New Second Generation Experience "Downward Assimilation"? Segmented Assimilation Re-Assessed. *Ethnic and Racial Studies* 27 (3): 376–402.

Warren, Tracey, Karen Rowlingson, and Claire Whyley. 2001. Female Finances: Gender, Wage Gaps, and Gender Asset Gaps. *Work, Employment and Society* 15 (3): 465–88.

Washington, Booker T. 1907. *The Negro in Business*. Coshocton, OH: Hertel, Jenkins & Company.

Waters, Mary C. 1990. *Ethnic Options: Choosing Identities in America*. Berkeley: University of California Press.

———. 1991. The Role of Lineage in Identity Formation Among Black Americans. *Qualitative Sociology* 14 (2): 57–76.

Weber, Lynn. 2001. *Understanding Race, Class, Gender and Sexuality: A Conceptual Framework*. Boston: McGraw-Hill.

Weber, Max. 1930. *The Protestant Ethnic and the Spirit of Capitalism*. New York: Scribners.

Wells, Amy Stuart, and Robert L. Crain. 1997. *Stepping Over the Color Line: African-American Students in White Suburban Neighborhoods*. New Haven, CT: Yale University Press.

Western, Mark, and Erik Olin Wright. 1994. The Permeability of Class Boundaries to Intergenerational Mobility Among Men in the United States, Canada, Norway and Sweden. *American Sociological Review* 59 (4): 606–29.

Wilson, Kenneth, and Allen W. Martin. 1982. Ethnic Enclaves: A Comparison of Cuban and Black Economies in Miami. *American Journal of Sociology* 88 (1): 135–60.

Wilson, Kenneth L., and Alejandro Portes. 1980. Immigrant Enclaves: An Analysis of the Labor Market Experiences of Cubans in Miami. *American Journal of Sociology* 86 (2): 295–319.

Wilson, William J. 1978. *The Declining Significance of Race: Blacks and Changing American Institutions*. Chicago: University of Chicago Press.

———. 1987. *The Truly Disadvantaged: The Inner City, the Underclass, and Public Policy*. Chicago: University of Chicago Press.

———. 1997. *When Work Disappears: The World of the New Urban Poor*. New York: Vintage.

Woodward, Michael. 1997. *Black Entrepreneurs in America: Stories of Struggle and Success*. New Brunswick, NJ: Rutgers University Press.

Yancey, William, Eugene Erikson, and Richard Juliani. 1976. Emergent Ethnicity: A Review and Reformulation. *American Sociological Review* 41:391–403.

Yoon, In-Jin. 1991. The Changing Significance of Ethnic and Class Resources in Immigrant Businesses: The Case of Korean Immigrant Businesses in Chicago. *International Migration Review* 25 (2):303–31.

Yuengert, Andrew M. 1995. Testing Hypotheses of Immigrant Self-Employment. *Journal of Human Resources* 30:194–204.

Zavella, Patricia. 1987. *Women's Work and Chicano Families: Cannery Workers of the Santa Clara Valley*. New York: Cornell University Press.

————. 1991. Reflections on Diversity Among Chicanas. *Frontiers: A Journal of Women Studies* 12 (2): 73–85.

Zhou, Min. 1992. *New York's Chinatown: The Socioeconomic Potential of an Urban Enclave*. Philadelphia: Temple University Press.

————. 1997. Segmented Assimilation: Issues, Controversies, and Recent Research on the New Second Generation. *International Migration Review* 31:975–1019.

Zlolniski, Christian. 2006. *Janitors, Street Vendors, and Activists: The Lives of Mexican Immigrants in Silicon Valley*. Berkeley: University of California Press.

# Index